WALL
STREET
JOURNAL
BOOKS

to Sarah, with love – Dad

Floating Off The Page

The Best Stories from

The Wall Street Journal's

"Middle Column"

EDITED BY

KEN WELLS

Foreword by Michael Lewis

A WALL STREET JOURNAL BOOK

Published by Simon & Schuster

New York London Toronto Sydney Singapore

A WALL STREET JOURNAL BOOK
Published by Simon & Schuster, Inc.
Rockefeller Center
1230 Avenue of the Americas
New York, NY 10020

This Wall Street Journal Book edition 2003

For information about special discounts for bulk purchases,
please contact Simon & Schuster Special Sales:
1-800-456-6798 or business@simonandschuster.com

Designed by Leslie Phillips

Manufactured in the United States of America

1   3   5   7   9   10   8   6   4   2

Library of Congress Cataloging-in-Publication Data
Floating off the page : the best stories from the Wall Street
journal's "Middle column" / edited by Ken Wells.
    p.   cm.—(A Wall Street Journal book)
    I. Wells, Ken.   II. Wall Street journal.   III. Series.
AC5 .F56 2002
081—dc21   2002016747
                ISBN: 0-7432-2663-1
                0-7432-2664-X (Pbk)

To the talented writers and editors
of The Wall Street Journal, *past and present,*
who have written and nurtured the
A-hed over its six decades

Contents

Foreword *xiii*
Introduction *1*

CHAPTER ONE
THE WAY WE ARE NOW

CHAPTER FIVE
OBSESSIONS

CHAPTER SIX
WHAT WE WROTE HOME ABOUT

CHAPTER SEVEN
PLAY'S THE THING

Foreword: Ruminations on the A-Hed

BY MICHAEL LEWIS

It isn't often that a bunch of old newspaper articles get thrown together to make a book. It's almost never that old newspaper articles deserve to be thrown together to make a book. These here do—but only because they aren't typical newspaper articles. They are quixotic reportage, with a whiff of the literary about them. The only reason they are considered newspaper journalism at all is that they come camouflaged—bundled in amongst the highly serious stuff on Page One of *The Wall Street Journal.* They gained respectability through association. They are the king's jester.

Most front-page newspaper journalism begins with the presumption of its subject's importance and timeliness. The subject is a politician on the make, or a businessman on the rise, or a new scandal, or a hot issue. In any case, the writer doesn't have to explain to his audience why he has chosen to write about what he's writing about. It's obvious! The trick for the writer is to make this subject, which everyone agrees is deeply important, interesting for everyone to read. Once he's accomplished this feat he isn't required to do much more to engage his audience. This is a big problem—the problem central to so much serious news written by serious journalists. It can be—often is—boring.

For more than five decades, the middle column of *The Wall Street Journal* has been the antidote to boredom, written by people who, at least while on this peculiar assignment, take delight in standing the usual front-page journalistic convention on its head. They find a subject that is merely delightful to read about—a man who has built a medieval catapult to throw grand pianos across his sheep pasture, for example—and try to persuade you of its significance. Or not. The very fact that it appears on the front page of *The Wall Street Journal*, surrounded by all that other serious gray matter, confers a certain importance on the piece. A goodly portion of the 1.8 million serious businesspeople who subscribe to the *Journal* will read it. Hundreds of thousands of business conversationalists will break the ice with some mention of the thing. (Q: "Did you know, Penelope, that armies in the Middle Ages routinely flung dead, plague-filled cows at one another?" A: "No? *Really?*")

Still, the pieces collected in this book raise an obvious question: How did they, as a group, come to exist in the first place? How is it that the newspaper of record for the world's busiest readers has become a feature-writing showcase for pieces about catfish grabbing, or the absence of bananas in Greece, or a first-person account of learning to be a belly dancer? I do not know; but I can guess. Even the sort of businesspeople who digest their news in tiny paragraph summaries have a need in their lives for stories. And so a deal has been struck, between business writers and business readers. The readers agree to relax for a minute and read something that will not lead immediately to profits or professional advancement. In exchange they receive the little jolt of human interest we all require to get through our days—to chuckle knowingly, to make chitchat unrelated to work with our colleagues and spouses, to revive the usually dormant regions of our brains.

But as much as the readers get out of the deal, the writers get more. Freed from the most oppressive constraint of journalism—the need to explain why what captures one's fancy is important enough to be printed in a newspaper—they can write about what genuinely engages their interest. The quality of the *Journal*'s prose is always highest in its middle column because the people making it are having fun. They are practicing their craft in its highest form. They are allowed to keep what made them smile or laugh or wince or even cry as they wrote it. (Consider this droll aside in the story about a shortage of bananas in Greece: "The Greek word for banana is pronounced banana.")

It may seem like a small thing for a writer to take pleasure in his work. It's not. It makes all the difference in the world to a reader—especially a reader who brings with him no complicated agenda. I can remember, as a college student preparing to enter the job market, feeling compelled to pick up *The Wall Street Journal*. But the only pieces I can remember having read were the ones that ran down the middle of the front page.

Michael Lewis is the author of *Liar's Poker* and *The New New Thing* and is a regular contributor to *The New York Times Magazine*.

Floating
Off
The Page

Introduction

> *"A-hed"—Named because it is shaped roughly like a*
> *capital A, it is* The Wall Street Journal's *internal desig-*
> *nation for a one-column, three-line, 18-point Caslon*
> *Italic headline, with an indented one-column, three-*
> *line, 12-point Scotch Roman deck, framed in a box*
> *formed by a quarter-point rule, and anchored on each*
> *side by dingbats. Alternatively, the feature story that*
> *sits under that headline in the "middle column" of the*
> Journal's *front page. When executed properly, with*
> *solid reporting, wit and fine writing, it is so light and*
> *engaging that it seems to float off the page.**

What, you may ask, are feuding nudists, dueling translators of the
Bible into Klingon, and the makers of high-quality prison underwear
doing on the front page of *The Wall Street Journal*?

They have shared the umbrella of the "A-hed" and become part of
its lore.

When the first A-hed appeared on Page One of this newspaper on
Dec. 17, 1941, the kernel of a great idea had clearly been planted.
World War II had been under way for ten days and the nation, according to the short piece that didn't carry a byline, was caught with
a peculiar shortage for those suddenly patriotic times—American
flags.

For its time, that story amounted to a flight of sheer whimsy. The
Journal back then was known exclusively for its single-minded cov-

---

* See page 3.

1

erage of business. That valuable piece of journalistic real estate known as the "middle column" was not yet fixed in its offerings; it had taken various styles of headlines and was given over to numerous matters core to the paper's purpose—commodities charts, stock trends, business briefs. But the paper, already more than a half-century old, was in the throes of major change, and that first A-hed was a glimpse of its broader future.

Of course, the *Journal* is still predominantly and preeminently a business publication, but regular readers of our pages know that the modern paper, here and globally, energetically covers politics, social issues, societal trends and, in its Friday Weekend section, travel, leisure, arts and even sports. And five days a week, on its front page, the *Journal* delivers up an A-hed whose chief purpose is analogous to an aperitif or fine dessert—it sweetens and pleases the palate of readers ready to tackle (or take a break from) stories about bonds, microchips and commodities futures. Not that an A-hed can't be serious; in its early days it usually was, and it still sparingly is—witness, herein, former *Journal* staffer Charlie McCoy's moving tale about the efforts to save an oil-smeared sea otter during the 1989 *Exxon Valdez* oil spill, or Joshua Harris Prager's story on the personal trials of former major-league baseball player Bill Buckner long after his game-turning error in the 1986 World Series.

The credit for inventing the A-hed concept surely goes to Bernard "Barney" Kilgore, father of the modern *Wall Street Journal*, and Bill Kerby, the *Journal*'s first Page One editor. Mr. Kilgore, a mild-mannered Midwesterner, joined the paper right out of DePauw University and became its managing editor in 1941 at the age of 30. More clearly than anyone before, he saw the *Journal*'s future as a truly national newspaper, one that would keep itself rooted in Wall Street but, on its front page, deliver the wider world in a voice that tempered the urgency of a metropolitan newspaper with the analysis and stylish writing of a good magazine. His famous declaration— "Don't write banking stories for bankers. Write for the banks' customers"—cut the *Journal* loose from its stiff, almost technical writing style. He created a rewrite and editing staff for Page One and put Mr. Kerby in charge of it. Whole new forms were invented—What's News, which delivered world, national and business news in punchy capsules; the Column 1 "leder," whose aim was and is to illuminate matters of social, cultural or political importance, or to demystify events in the news; and, not least, the A-hed.

Year after year, the middle column, according to *Wall Street Journal* readership surveys, continues to be among the paper's best-read features. It has been emulated by countless U.S. newspapers and some magazines; journalism professors across the nation routinely clip it and give it to students with the admonition: "If you wish to write well, learn to write like this." In 1971, a *Fortune* magazine feature on the *Journal* helped to cement the A-hed's place as an icon of contemporary journalism by describing it as a story often so engaging and light "as almost to float off the page" (hence the title of this book).

If Mr. Kilgore, who died in 1967, helped invent the A-hed, it's also true that the form was still very much a work in progress into the 1960s. On many days, the A-hed resembled that very first one—a short business story with a quirk. (One example: a piece on how World War II was very good for the greeting-card industry.) Alternatively, it was often a news feature. When the Soviet Union's Nikita Khrushchev visited the United States in September 1959, his travels and doings occupied the A-hed spot for five days running—an occurrence entwined with a bit of Barney Kilgore lore. Or, as Fred Taylor, a *Journal* managing editor who was aboard then, recalls: "The late, great Barney Kilgore was gadget happy and had just got one of the first car phones. So the reporters trailing Khrushchev used Barney's car, calling in their stories on the wonderful phone to the extent they ran down the car battery and got stuck somewhere in Iowa."

The success of the A-hed owes as much to the quality of ideas as it does to good writing, and the idea factory itself owes much to *Journal* culture. Page One has always been famously picky about A-hed ideas, yet famously egalitarian about who comes up with them. It is still very much a decentralized art. Any reporter at the paper can pitch and write an A-hed for Page One, as can (and have) news assistants and interns (with proper guidance and editing, of course). Once an idea is accepted, the paper gives the lucky scribe what most metro newspapers would consider a languid amount of time to report and write a story that is usually under 1,500 words in length. True, many A-heds are done in a day or two, but it isn't uncommon for A-heds to take a week to report and a week to write—even longer. Consider that when *Journal* staffer Carrie Dolan alighted in the San Francisco bureau as a fresh-faced college graduate in 1982, she soon found herself in conference with Ken Slocum, the taciturn Texan who was bureau chief at the time. A clever features man, Mr. Slocum had a Texan's bias against what he considered fancy, overpriced, big-city hotels. He inexplicably shoved a note across the desk to Ms. Dolan that mused that it was probably possible for a person to travel across country for the price of a single night in the more expensive hotels in the *Journal*'s headquarters city of New York.

Carrie was starting to wonder what that had to do with her when Ken drawled: "So Carrie, you better get goin'"—and then broke into a chorus of the Willie Nelson song "On the Road Again."

And off she went, in an account that appears in this book, driving for a week coast-to-coast in a cheap rental car, trying to prove Mr. Slocum's theory in the A-hed column.

Ms. Dolan's story shows what comes of a quirky set piece, well executed. The A-hed's history is also filled with stories of opportunity—reporters in exotic, remote, even dangerous locations putting their well-honed features eyes to the ground around them and coming up with gems. Barry Newman, unquestionably the current dean of *Journal* A-hed writers, was banging about the Australian Outback in the spring of 1978 when he realized that the Aussies had built a barbed-wire fence longer than the Great Wall of China to separate sheep-eating dingoes (wild dogs) from the nation's wool crop. It was certainly an A-hed but there was a small hurdle: A New York editor, who could not envision the splendor of such a fence from so far away, cabled Mr. Newman to say that such a story probably wasn't worth spending more than $200 on. So Mr. Newman rented exactly

$200 of air time from a local pilot with a small plane and got the color he needed from above.

Tony Horwitz, who won a Pulitzer Prize for the paper in 1995 for his coverage of workplace issues, recalls covering the conflict in Serbia and realizing that there were probably A-heds even in that madness. So one night, at considerable risk, he crawled up a hill above Sarajevo and into a Serbian sniper's pit where he spent time with Serbian gunmen discussing Isaac Bashevis Singer stories while the Serbs sporadically sprayed sniper fire on Croats below. (Mr. Horwitz, now a full-time author on leave from *The New Yorker,* got his story; it was impossible to tell whether the Serbs got any of their targets.)

Adventure, pathos, humor, irony—this is the stuff of storytelling and the elixir of storytellers. If *The Wall Street Journal* were a house, the A-hed would surely be our front porch—a place where stories are spun out with a kind of spare exuberance, for an audience of clever listeners.

So pull up a chair and enjoy!

—KEN WELLS

CHAPTER ONE

THE WAY WE ARE NOW

---

1. *Phone Hex*

It was a first date, and Lee Cruz was necking in the car. In midtussle, she jostled the cell phone in her purse and, without realizing it, she triggered speed-dial No. 2, which rang up her ex-boyfriend.

He answered and listened in. For 22 minutes.

One thing she says struck her cavesdropping ex as especially memorable: "No, no," she told the new beau. "You're a married man."

Introducing yet another unforeseen hazard of the Information Age—the SEND or TALK button on your wireless phone. On many portable phones, hitting SEND will automatically redial the last number you called or someone on your speed-dial list. So it takes just the tiniest slip of the finger to broadcast the audio track of your life to someone you know who wasn't supposed to hear it.

"He didn't have to sit there and listen to it," moans Ms. Cruz.

But they almost always do sit there and listen.

"Of course I want to hear this," says Andrea Carla Michaels, owner of Acme Naming, a San Francisco product- and company-naming firm.

A few years back, Ms. Michaels was treated to a half-hour answering-machine recording of her boyfriend at the time, Matt Palmer. Mr. Palmer, who had inadvertently pressed SEND on his cell, was discussing women with four male friends after a night of drinking at the Comet Club.

She could have erased the tape once she realized what was going on. But why on earth would she do that?

Ms. Michaels was 37 years old; Mr. Palmer was 27. Would Mr. Palmer's friends make fun of the age gap? "I'm much more in the camp of wanting to know the worst than not wanting to know something," she says. "There's nothing I don't want to know."

In the end, Ms. Michaels herself was unmentioned in the taped conversation. But the next day she called Mr. Palmer and played back a few choice bits.

Mr. Palmer, who now runs MP8 International, an Internet telephony sales and marketing firm in Ketchum, Idaho, considers himself lucky. "It could have been a lot more incriminating than it was," he says.

Few cell-phone nightmare scenarios come close to what Wendy Harrington inflicted on herself last summer. She had been fending off a particularly persistent suitor for weeks, but when he invited her for an island weekend, she accepted, on the condition that her roommate come along, too.

En route on the ferry, Ms. Harrington called her host from her cell phone and left a message giving him her arrival time. Then, as her phone sat in her purse, she apparently hit the SEND button just as her roommate was prodding her to explain why she wasn't attracted to the guy. Ms. Harrington mentioned a few positives. But the 20-minute deconstruction soon turned brutally frank, touching on his habit of practicing his golf swing without a club and the two women's general disinclination to like men who wear cologne and say "shucks." Pouring on the salt, they discussed intimate details of Ms. Harrington's previous relationship with someone she describes as the "kinky doctor."

"I could not imagine a more emasculating conversation," she says. Only as they prepared to step ashore did she realize her phone had been engaged to her host's voice mail all the while.

"I hit END, feel a wave of dread—the kind that seems really bad at first and then just keeps getting worse," she recalls, speaking on condition that her suitor, the island and her hometown not be named. "My stomach is now churning with the knowledge that I might really hurt this nice man who has shown me nothing but adoration."

The poor fellow met the two women near the dock, and his uncomplicated smile suggested that he had yet to listen to the message. The three then headed for a restaurant, and he checked his voice mail. "Wendy, it sounds like you called me from the boat," she remembers his saying. "It sounds like you're having a great time."

She dreaded the denouement, but he stayed on the phone only briefly and said he would get back to the message later.

That set the tone for the rest of the weekend. He received several other phone messages, always skipping over hers to listen to the new ones. They went waterskiing. They ate in restaurants. "The whole weekend his phone is terrifying me," she says.

Finally Sunday arrived, and the women left for home. It was only then, apparently, that her message got through to her gracious host. "We never talked again," Ms. Harrington says. One lesson she learned from the harrowing experience: Lock the keypad on your phone when you put it down.

But the more that wireless phones proliferate, the greater the chances of embarrassing faux pas. Not long ago, Ed Salvato, senior editor of PlanetOut.com Travel, a gay Internet travel site based in West Hollywood, Calif., and some friends were in a car having a very graphic conversation about the sexual adventures some men they knew had at a desert resort.

A half-hour later, Mr. Salvato's mother phoned him. That wouldn't be unusual, except that Mr. Salvato's cell phone was new, and, while he had his parents' number programmed into speed dial, they didn't have his number. They did, however, have a new Caller ID device, and the two technologies colluded against Mr. Salvato. He had unwittingly dialed his parents, who overheard smatterings of the conversation and, after disconnecting, called back the number on Caller ID.

"Did you hear what we said?" Mr. Salvato asked his mother, alarmed. She just claimed to have overheard some "joshing."

"She had 'mother's ears' on," he says with relief.

Some telephonic mishaps aren't about sex. Robbie Herzig was deep into a job interview in Denver when a friend called. Ms. Herzig thought she was sending the call to voice mail, but instead accidentally answered it. The friend overheard her detailed pitch for more stock options and a bigger salary.

Ms. Herzig got the job, and now does strategic planning at Client-Logic, which provides marketing and other services for e-commerce companies. But she has never told her boss about the cell-phone incident.

"I work for a technology company," she explains. "You don't want to admit that you can't work technology."

—MICHAEL M. PHILLIPS, May 2000

2. "Nothing Personal. We Sue All Our Friends."

SAN FRANCISCO—There was romance in the resumes: She, a computer consultant turned fashion model; he, an Apple Computer engineer turned Silicon Valley entrepreneur. They were young, beautiful, wired for love.

But caution fell between them. During a yearlong courtship, Alfred Tom held back, wary of revealing too much. Then it happened. After an afternoon with friends, Mr. Tom took Angela Fu back to his car. There, on the front seat of his 1994 Integra, he went for it.

"Naturally, I flinched a bit," Ms. Fu says. But in a stroke, it was done: a signed nondisclosure agreement, or NDA, in the parlance of the Net set. Henceforth, Ms. Fu would be sworn to silence about her boyfriend's trade secrets.

DNA, meet NDA, your twisted, alphabetical cousin in the world of baser instincts. Long the province of lawyers, investment bankers and other traffickers in corporate secrets, nondisclosure agreements have gone mainstream.

Propelled by the Internet frenzy, an epidemic of secrecy pacts is spreading through personal relationships, passed between lovers, friends, relatives, roommates, even business partners.

The documents surface at dinner parties, weddings and sushi counters. One entrepreneur NDAed his rabbi, then his rabbi's wife. Bill Gates NDAed the carpenters working on his home. Quincy Smith, who ran corporate development for Netscape before becoming a venture capitalist, fields NDAs from his parents' friends, attached to business ideas.

Ask young and breathless Net heads at a picnic or family barbecue what they're working on, and you'll probably get back some blather like, "An end-to-end solution for e-commerce personalization in the business-to-business space."

Ask what that means, in plain English, and out comes the NDA, materializing from breast pockets and knapsacks, PalmPilots, picnic baskets and glove compartments. "It's one of the critical items for a date: car keys, credit cards, condoms and an NDA," says high-tech consultant Mark Macgillivray.

Most of the forms involve one or two pages of standard legalese, pledging the signatory to silence concerning the bearer's "intellectual property." Judges have ruled NDAs enforceable in all 50 states, lawyers say, but good luck bringing tongue-waggers to court. Proving that somebody leaked proprietary information is seldom worth the time and expense it takes, attorneys say. Still, the truly paranoid—and indiscreet—collect hundreds of sworn secrecy pledges before their businesses ever earn a dime.

Philip Lee, co-founder of SportBug.com—"performance feedback over the Internet using satellite tracking"—usually makes people add their signatures, petition-style, to a two-sentence NDA he keeps scribbled on the back of his notebook. But caught unprepared at a restaurant recently, he dashed off a fresh secrecy oath for some business-school buddies on scratch paper, with his lawyer, who happened to be dining with him, adding "syllables and threatening language over my shoulder," says Mr. Lee, 31 years old.

"The NDA is the 21st-century equivalent of the medieval wax seal," says Kent Walker, associate general counsel of Netscape. "It's a mystical incantation people rely on, when in fact the only real security is to keep your mouth shut."

Mr. Tom tried that with Ms. Fu, until things heated up. At first, when his girlfriend asked about his work, "he said he'd tell me eventually," Ms. Fu, 29, recalls. Finally, after dating a year or so, he popped the form. "I didn't even read it," she says. "I totally trusted him and I knew he trusted me."

Really? After Ms. Fu signed the NDA, "I still didn't tell her much," says Mr. Tom, 30, who, suffice it to say, is developing a wireless-communications product. "But at least she could feel part of the conversation."

Techies accept NDAs as part of the landscape. Some people from other walks of life, however, still bridle at being asked to commit their loyalty to a legal document to catch up with old friends.

Internet entrepreneur Eddie Lou—"We're a first mover in a large, business-to-business vertical space"—had no problem getting his roommates, friends and girlfriend to sign NDAs. He keeps extra forms in his car.

But recently, two college buddies in the East, in separate phone calls, hung up on him when he told them they'd have to sign NDAs before hearing about his business.

When he called back one of them, a close fraternity brother who works in finance in New York, it happened again. "He said, since he's not signing the NDA, he's not in a position to talk to me, and hung up," says the 28-year-old Mr. Lou. "Everybody here says 'Give me the NDA,' but people outside this area don't understand."

In most gatherings of digerati, wielding NDAs confers an aura of value on a start-up, even when, as in many cases, there isn't any. But spring one on the wrong person, like a venture capitalist, "and it's like writing on your forehead, 'Look at me, I'm clueless! I don't know how the game works,'" says Silicon Valley financier Guy Kawasaki.

That's because the bigwigs of the Internet crowd—the professional investors, consultants, securities analysts and top technology writers—scoff at NDAs and don't sign them on principle. They say they see too many similar ideas, dozens or more a week, to have their tongues tied by any single one. Instead, they preach the honor system to prospective entrepreneurs.

Yet horror stories abound of venture capitalists and others who said "trust us," only to use secrets gleaned from one business plan to help another.

"Not only are NDAs important, but I think start-ups should go a step further," says Internet tycoon Sabeer Bhatia, who doesn't even tell hires for his latest company what they're working on until they show up for work. Mr. Bhatia, 31, credits secrecy with giving his first start-up, Hotmail, a decisive six-month lead on the competition, paving the way for its sale to Microsoft for a reported $400 million in stock.

For Hotmail, Mr. Bhatia collected more than 400 NDAs in two years, from employees, friends, roommates—but no girlfriends. "A beautiful woman is a beautiful woman," he says. "I just don't tell them about my business."

Mr. Macgillivray, the consultant, was chatting with friends at a crowded party recently, when somebody piped up with his latest business idea for an obscure computer-graphics process. "Two sentences into it," Mr. Macgillivray says, "he pulled out the NDAs. Even the other Valley people looked at him and said,'You've got to be nuts! We're at a party, pal.' He looked at us with disgust, more convinced than ever we were all there to rip him off."

Jim Busis, co-founder of Wishbox.com—"a universal gift-registry for Gen Y" based in Pittsburgh—brandished several NDAs at the end of a small dinner party in his honor, taking several old friends by surprise. "Here's a man to whom I confided many of the most intimate details of my bizarre divorce, swearing secrecy from me?" says Liz Perle, editor at large of publishing-house Harper San Francisco and a friend of Mr. Busis's since college.

Mr. Busis, 43, explains NDAs are nothing personal, just a legal formality. He also NDAed relatives and friends in town for his daughter's baby-naming ceremony last spring, he says. The rabbi who officiated at the ritual, and the rabbi's wife, signed in Mr. Busis's car on the way back to their hotel.

"At first I giggled and thought, 'Who does Jim think I'm going to tell about this?'" recalls Rabbi Lennard Thal, vice president of the Union of American Hebrew Congregations in New York. "Then I was sort of flattered that he might actually have thought, in the circles I run, anyone would be interested."

—PETER WALDMAN, November 1999

3. *Men Will Be Boys* . . .

TEMPE, Ariz.—A champagne-colored Lincoln Town Car cruises the fringes of nearby Arizona State University, pulling into the parking lot of McDuffy's. It's a popular student hangout with neon beer signs, perky waitresses and sports games blaring on multiple TVs. Four guys in shorts and sneakers pile out and head for the entrance.

"Uh-oh, it looks like I'm going to get carded," says Dave Protz. The joke lasts as far as the door: After all, he is 44 years old.

Mr. Protz has come all the way from Plymouth, Wis., for five days of spring break—spring break for adults, that is. Grown-ups of all ages are taking advantage of a booming economy to whoop it up in the sun. Only instead of family vacations, these folks—mostly middle-aged men—are trying to relive their college days with outings that can resemble the rowdiness of the Fort Lauderdale beach scenes of lore.

Myrtle Beach, S.C., for example, has about a dozen new bars now catering to this special kind of March madness. For the mature spring-breaker, there are bikini contests, 75-cent draft beer and hairy-chest competitions. On a recent night, Jason Rice, a Myrtle Beach Area Chamber of Commerce official, happened to drive by Xanadu, a loud nightclub that advertises wet T-shirt contests; he saw a sea of people, many of them with gray hair, waiting to get in. "At this point, nothing surprises me," says Mr. Rice, who estimates that one-third of the town's $2.4 billion in tourism revenue pours in during the spring season.

For many of these post-college spring revelers, golf is the beard— that is, ostensibly the main attraction, and a convenient excuse to spouses and significant others left at home. The Tempe-Scottsdale area and Myrtle Beach have nearly 150 golf courses between them. And another magnet of the seven-iron set, Hilton Head Island, S.C., finds itself not coincidentally another of the places where the over-the-hill gang hangs out for spring kicks. The entertainment is somewhat high-brow in the town of 29,000, but a club called Monkey Business is still packed nightly, even if it requires shirts with collars.

Here in the Scottsdale area, some residents complain about aging revelers racing through town or streaking nude at hot-tub parties. "They're obnoxious," says Debi Gaitens, an executive recruiter who shuns downtown this time of year because of the crowds.

Granted, most of these baby-boomer retreats are hardly the stuff of MTV highlights; some aging spring-breakers declare defeat after one night of heavy drinking.

But on a recent weekend, Mr. Protz and his three buddies, all brothers-in-law from the same Wisconsin town, head straight from the airport to the liquor store to buy three bottles of Absolut vodka, which they promptly drink, stirred into tonic water, in the hot tub at their luxury condo. They groggily call it a night, but not before reminiscing about their own college spring breaks years and years ago. Only today, instead of six to a room in a dumpy beachside motel, they are staying two to a room in a $300-a-night condo.

The next evening, happy hour finds them at McDuffy's, where the presence of a large number of college girls doesn't seem to be a deterrent. "Why should the college kids have all the fun?" asks Mr. Protz, an impish salesman and self-appointed ringleader. A few months ago, he announced to his wife and three children that he deserved a chance to cut loose from the winter stress.

One of the brothers-in-law, Dean Wesenberg, needed a little arm-twisting to persuade him to tag along. "I've never done anything like this," says the clean-cut 35-year-old Mr. Wesenberg, sitting awkwardly on a high stool at McDuffy's.

Around him are bouncers in full referee gear who have had to eject older tourists for getting too fresh with the college girls. "They're pretty harmless but you have to keep an eye on them," says Jake Guzman, a manager at McDuffy's.

Mr. Protz and company, though, take the attitude that, when in Rome, do as the Romans do. The next night, at a club called Giligin's, the group finds itself alone at a table, watching the rest of the crowd dance and throw napkins at each other. They have run out of Monica Lewinsky jokes when two of them finally approach a couple of women at the bar about doing "Jell-O shots."

This, according to a 19-year-old caddie they have met, is a popular game played by college students in bars here. The etiquette, such as it is, goes like this: The shot, a cube of Jell-O saturated in vodka, is placed upon some part of the anatomy. The imbiber then licks it off. Consent is highly advised.

Mr. Protz, in fact, jokingly offers to throw his own body into play.

But the women, both youngish lawyers, laughingly decline, although one slurps up the spiked Jell-O from his hand.

Nearby, California lawyer Michael Lonich and 11 other buddies are shuffling about to the Doors' '60s anthem, "Break on Through," while a DJ announces the next special on tequila shots. Each of them is pushing—or well past—40. "This place is perfect for adult spring break," Mr. Lonich says. His group has spent five days watching spring baseball, playing video games in bars and drinking the night away. They have also played a round of golf a day—which Mr. Lonich says was the primary reason so many of his friends could slip away from their families.

As further proof of this, travel companies that specialize in booking golf vacations say they detect a surge in interest among their mostly male clients in being booked into places where opportunities to play the 19th hole match the challenges of the first 18. "One of the first questions my clients always ask me is where the bars are," says Jeff Savage, president of Tee Time Travel Inc. in Scottsdale.

In fact, a government survey for the greater Scottsdale and Phoenix region found that, except for scenic beauty, golf was the No. 1 reason tourists said they came. But the sport ranked only seventh in activities tourists actually did. Two spots higher on the list: nightclubbing.

Beyond that, at least one campaign to lure golfers trades on the fact that some of the good old boys who go on golf vacations don't mind ending up in places with lots of pretty girls. One ad for a Myrtle Beach golf package shows a young woman on a beach, poised in a sporty golf outfit.

Still, despite complaints in some corners of Scottsdale that the aging spring-breakers indulge in boorish behavior, most people here see the upside. There's little danger the place will turn into a hot spot of middle-age rowdiness: Scottsdale's high-priced hotels and green fees averaging $140 a round deter the honky-tonk tourists. "These aren't kids," says Richard A. Bowers, manager of the city of 190,000 residents. And among the estimated two million golfers who visit Scottsdale annually, most still come for golf.

It's also not entirely clear whether Mr. Protz and the Wesenbergs, having gotten their spring break, will get a break back home. While the men are cavorting about Scottsdale, the Wesenberg wives and Doreen Protz are stuck back in six inches of snow, sipping Tom Collinses and plotting their revenge: Their own trip to Las Vegas. Or maybe Germany?

"He's dead meat," Lisa Marie Wesenberg says of her husband, Dean, who left for the trip on her birthday and hasn't called since. Pam Wesenberg is also perturbed by the male exodus. "I don't think husbands and wives should take separate vacations," she says.

But not to worry. After two nights of bar-hopping and drinking, the spring-breakers opt for condo-cooked dinners, the hot tub and bed by nine. "I'm tired, I want to go home," says Duane Wesenberg, complaining of body aches and a hangover.

—NANCY KEATES, March 1998

4.   . . . And Some Boys Will
  Stay That Way

HOFFMAN ESTATES, Ill.—Carole Olis doesn't know what to make of her 23-year-old son, Rob. He has been living at home since his graduation from college more than two years ago. Her six older children returned to the nest for just a few months and then bolted.

"I ask him, 'Why don't you move out with your friends?'" says Mrs. Olis, shaking her head. Rob has a ready answer: "They all live at home, too."

Rob Olis and most of his buddies are launching their adult lives back at the homes where they used to play with LEGOs. Across the country, this new breed of mama's boys—confident young men with jobs, college educations and girlfriends—bonds around refrigerators full of mom's leftovers. And, when they are out partying, they remind each other to call home when it gets late.

And what of their female counterparts? More so than men, they are out on their own. Consider the statistics: Two decades ago, the percentage of men and women who spent at least part of their 20s living at home was equal—about 40 percent. Today, some 45 percent of men in their 20s return to the nest, while only about 35 percent of women do. And the gap may be widening, say Frances and Calvin Goldscheider, demographers for the Population Reference Bureau, a nonprofit group in Washington.

Among the twentysomethings of Generation X, the trend is spawning bizarre changes in mating rituals and lifestyles. In the hip bars of Denver, 24-year-old live-at-home Sean McDermott has learned to flirt—with no hope of inviting over a young woman later. "I evade the issue," he says. Scott Tennery of Bedford, Texas, doesn't necessarily want to invite anyone over, even if he could. His parents turned his bedroom into a guest room when he went away to Southern Methodist University. Now, back at home, he has a floral bedspread. Says Mr. Tennery, also 24: "It's not very manly."

Why are so many young men flapping back to the nest? Perhaps because it is stress-free. Dads keep them on a loose leash and moms do their cleaning. Daughters, meanwhile, get lectured and nagged. Young men are increasingly more willing to forgo independence in exchange for extra cash and mom's doting. Some scholars say it is an odd re-creation of times past, when men often sought marriage right out of school with nurturing, nonworking women.

With delayed marriages and fewer girlfriends today willing to pick up wet towels, men "get a better deal at home," says Pepper Schwartz, sociology professor at the University of Washington.

Women don't fare so well. While a few parents of live-at-home sons turn their backs to intimate visits from girlfriends, they are almost never so liberal with their daughters and their boyfriends. At the same time, contemporary late-night etiquette makes it more imperative for women to live independently, says Martha Farnsworth Riche, demographer for the Population Reference Bureau. Generation X couples typically prefer to go back to the woman's place after a night out—because it is usually cleaner for one thing. It is also considered to be more politically correct: Men now think they will get further, and in less trouble, if trysts are conducted on the woman's turf.

Mr. Olis's live-with-mom friends here in middle-class suburban Chicago get together for football and softball games and beer fests, sometimes with parents. This is hardly the way recent films like *Reality Bites* paint young graduates' lives: messy coed apartments with romantically involved roommates.

Charlie Harrigan, a 23-year-old computer programmer who is the only one of this circle to have his own apartment, finds his friends' live-at-home lives curious and confining. But he stubbornly stands by his crowd. "They're my friends, regardless of the choices they make," he says of the group, many of them Illinois State University graduates.

For his part, Mr. Olis says he sees no reason not to stick around home another year. An affable man, he sits down to family dinner at 6 p.m. after a day on the job marketing pagers. He likes to watch *Seinfeld* on television upstairs with his parents, though he has his own separate room in the basement.

So why, then, are his female friends cutting the umbilical cord? "I think," says Mr. Olis, surrounded by his mother's doll collection in the living room, "women feel like they have something to prove." He reflects on this, hunched over a Lite beer, when suddenly his mom calls from the kitchen: "Robby! Get the coasters out!"

Moms of this generation, many of them divorced, seem mostly glad to have their sons back in the fold. The guys keep them company and help out with chores men often handle, such as mowing the lawn. Mrs. Olis, who isn't divorced, offers another benefit: "He makes me laugh all the time," she says fondly of Rob, her youngest son. His father, John Olis, notes that the $100 a month Rob pays in rent covers his expenses, and his presence isn't much of a bother since he comes and goes as he pleases. "Robby has complete freedom," Mr. Olis says.

Living at home is cushy. Merrilyn Baldassano, deemed one of the "coolest" moms by the suburban set, gets up at 1 a.m. to cook meals for 24-year-old Danny when he is hungry. "He's spoiled," says Mrs. Baldassano. She is pleased, though, that he often requests her meatloaf.

Of course, Danny says he can't be as affectionate with his girlfriend, Trish, as he was in his apartment at college. But for now, good food and clean laundry are acceptable trade-offs for "half control of my life," he adds.

Like Rob Olis and most of his live-at-home friends, Mr. Baldassano hasn't been driven back home by the economy. A steel-screw salesman, he earns about $30,000 a year. "I could make it on my own," he says. But if he paid hundreds of dollars a month for rent and bills in Chicago, he would have to cut back on his four-night-a-week pub crawls, $35 concert tickets and his $1,000 Las Vegas jaunts with friends.

Many of these X-ers want the extra cash to buy expensive toys. Denny Hennessey, a pleasant 28-year-old who recently moved home after six years on his own, is saving to trade his Pontiac Firebird convertible for a Jeep Cherokee. "All of my buddies are moving back. Why shouldn't I save my money?" asks Mr. Hennessey, an account representative for a transportation firm. Other treats—like Cap'n Crunch cereal, a childhood favorite Mr. Hennessey's mom recently tucked in the pantry—are just icing, he says.

Patrick Scialo thinks the money he saves living at home will eventually earn him a home of his own. He is 26 now and in no hurry to leave—he is targeting 30, the same age as his live-at-home brother. "I'm very content where I am," says Mr. Scialo, a real-estate agent.

The young women in the suburban Chicago crowd, meanwhile, seem to value freedom over possessions. On visits to Chicago, the guys sometimes swing by the two-bedroom apartment of high-school friends Robin Templet and Robin Taglieri—and enter a different world. A portable CD player substitutes for a stereo. An ironing board serves as counter space in their sparse kitchen.

Yet liberation from rigid dinner schedules and nosy parents hasn't freed them from live-at-home men. JoAnne Egan, whose relationship with Mr. Olis ended not long ago, is dating yet another live-at-home boyfriend with no plans to move out. Ms. Templet's 26-year-old brother has lived at home for some time now.

Ms. Templet has become quite adept at separating the men from the boys. As a waitress at Chicago's Gin Mill bar, she tests a well-groomed lad tipping her big bills one night by delivering the crucial question: "So, you live downtown?"

"Nah," he says. "I'm, like, from the suburbs." Ms. Templet translates—this is Generation X code for: "I live with mom." Later, out of hearing of her would-be Romeo, Ms. Templet flips her long blonde hair and declares: "Total turnoff."

—CHRISTINA DUFF, October 1994

5. *Not Your Mother's Cemetery*

ST. LOUIS—Some people want to go quietly. Dorothy Schaffer wants to go digital.

"I didn't want my kids to remember us as old tired Mom and Pop," she says.

It's a good bet they won't. She and her husband, Lester, have enshrined their final message on the closest thing yet to a talking tombstone, a computer at Belle Rive cemetery here that functions as a kind of ATM of the dead.

It's a stainless-steel obelisk, in a public room off the cemetery's central office, with a computer screen bearing the mathematical sign of infinity. Mrs. Schaffer, a talkative grandmother of 84 years old, has no plans to die soon, but is dying to show off her digital memorial. She taps out S-C-H-A-F on a touch-screen pad, as visitors will do one day, and an image of the couple appears on the screen. Her voice, in stereo, emerges from the machine: "Whenever you listen, you'll hear the voices of your ever-loving mother and dear dad . . ."

Mrs. Schaffer contemplates the effect on her family as they punch her up when she is no longer around: "I can hear them say, 'Oh, Mom!'"

The memorial kiosk is only the newest, most futuristic example of tombstone technology that promises to transform cemeteries from places bound by granite into playgrounds of the imagination. Beyond computerized databases of the departed, vendors are offering small, battery-operated computers embedded in tombstones themselves. One of them, known as Viewlogy, is capable of displaying a digital scrapbook of photos and text. On top of that, computer-aided design and laser carving tools are making stonecutting and tombstone design cheaper, easier and more creative than ever before.

A decade ago, only the rich could afford chiseled busts of themselves or ornately carved epitaphs on headstones. Now, diamond wire saws hooked up to computers enable stonecutters to design complex shapes and cut them swiftly and precisely. As a result, some cemeteries, once quiet gardens of stone, are becoming libraries of quirky letters to the world. Columns and urns are giving way to mouse ears and motorcycles and other crypt kitsch.

Jeff Martell, president of Granite Industries of Vermont Inc., estimates that a 3-foot-high shamrock he sells for $2,000 wholesale would have cost as much as $3,500 before the new technology. His Barre, Vt., company has sculpted Harley-Davidsons detailed down to the model year for several people killed in motorcycle accidents, a statue resembling Mickey Mouse for a child, a sea turtle, cars, pianos, airplanes, and "all the toys we have in our society today," he says.

There's a tombstone shaped like a life-size baby elephant in Moultrie, Ga.; a giant stone clothespin in Middlesex, Vt., ordered up by the head of a clothespin-making company; and a spectral golfer in Bedford, Ind., carrying his clubs.

New laser tools also enable tombstone designers to draw intricate portraits on stone, with resolution of 200 dots per inch, comparable to a basic ink-jet printer. Schott Monument Co. in Cincinnati has etched guitars, horse heads, cats, and an image of a computer monitor and keyboard on tombstones.

For those embracing the new technology, one allure is the ability to get in not just the last word but a long last monologue. W. Odell Goodman of Dover, N.C., had Joyner's Memorial Inc. design a 20-foot-long tombstone covered with 27 paragraphs of text detailing his personal philosophy, life story, genealogy and a few other tips. "I, W. Odell Goodman, am inviting the U.S. people and people of the world to visit Maplewood Cemetery, Kinston, N.C., 28501 . . . and learn how our sacred federal law, government and quota controls will save the U.S.," it says.

Clyde Chamberlin, a Zephyrhills, Fla., tombstone enthusiast who has photographed this and other unusual stones, calls them "messages to the world." Plus, he says, "you can't argue with it."

Irene Kirchner, 67, has had portraits of her five Pekingese dogs copied from photos onto her tombstone (leaving room for future dogs). Across the front, she asked Trademark Etching of Carthage, Ill., to draw a train, representing the 30 years she spent working for a railroad company. "I'd thought about it for a long time," she says. "I just thought it would be best if I did it myself, because when I'm gone they wouldn't know how I wanted it."

Ms. Kirchner isn't alone. "People think, 'What I do is important.' They refuse to be buried where they can't express themselves," says Helen Sclair, a Chicago cemetery historian. She has noticed more tombstones popping up with recreational themes—knitting needles, bingo cards and Scrabble boards. Others point to the popularity of the Peace Light, a solar-powered light that adds an ethereal atmosphere to tombs.

Some experts say the new technologies seem serendipitously timed, coinciding with a boom in personalization by a generation obsessed with making personal statements. "When the baby-boom generation gets here, look out. They're going to be individuals in death just as in life," says Dan Majestic, marketing manager at the bronze division of monument maker Matthews International Corp. of Pittsburgh.

But others say technology is simply an invitation to an impulse that dates back beyond the Egyptians. "Back then, people wanted to preserve food and pets," says Paul Saffo, a technology forecaster at the Institute for the Future. "Once upon a time, they wanted to preserve bones, then their memories, then their information."

That doesn't mean everyone is ready for cutting-edge memorials. Many cemeteries still impose size and style limitations on tombstones. Still others are slow to embrace the new computer technology, worrying that futuristic kiosks will jar with the lugubrious dignity of cemeteries and funeral homes. Tom Daly of Boston's St. Michael's cemetery notes that when he contracted with Intera Multimedia, a Montreal maker of memorial kiosks, he insisted on encasing the unit in mahogany.

And some people fear that computerized memorials won't withstand centuries of bad weather and vandalism, leaving future cemetery visitors to puzzle over a 2001 landscape of silent monoliths. But Forever Enterprises, the Belle Rive cemetery owner and a computer memorial provider, points out that it backs up its information in archives and gives extra videotape or CD-ROM copies to the families. Leif Technologies, Lebanon, Ohio, encases its Viewlogy tombstone units, costing about $4,000, in a stainless-steel box with a hinged cover; it ships them with a battery that doesn't need changing for about ten years. Still, Deac Manross, Leif's founder, sees the point. "I'm nervous about an eternal guarantee," he says.

What's next? Holograms. At the moment, the technology is simply "prohibitively expensive" but "it's within the five-year picture," says Bill Obrock, a salesman at Forever Enterprises. More futuristically, Mr. Obrock envisions tombstone computers, operating on "fuzzy logic" technology that would "emulate" a deceased person's personality, allowing visitors to have a virtual dialogue with the dead.

Now that all data can be converted into digital format, "you could certainly find immortality as a bit stream passing through space," says Mr. Saffo, the futurist. He conjures up an orbiting crematorium. "Have it beam out a digital signal so we can listen to Uncle Ernie as he passes over every night."

But most customers have an audience in mind. "Anyone can walk in and see it," says Mrs. Schaffer. "It makes you feel kind of good." The Schaffers paid $700 for a funeral-home package that included the video memorial and the cost of donating their bodies to a nearby research center; their only grave will be on the computer.

The Schaffers' computer file allows viewers to choose among options like "Scrapbook," which calls up an array of family photos, and "Tribute," which shows clips from an interview. They tell stories about their courtship, which included a ride on an elephant in a St. Louis park, and show mementos of their New York honeymoon. Mrs. Schaffer says she wanted to soften her children's grief. "I don't mind dying so much when you can laugh about it," she says.

At the end of the video, the couple kisses—a long kiss. "So, kids, have fun with what your mom and dad said. Consider it an adventure and we in heaven will be much pleased, and we'll be waiting for you," Mrs. Schaffer says as the image fades out.

—ELIZABETH SEAY, March 1998

6. *Why the Girl Scouts Sing the Blues*

LAFAYETTE, Calif.—Something is missing at Diablo Day Camp this year.

At the 3 p.m. sing-along in a wooded canyon near Oakland, 214 Girl Scouts are learning the summer dance craze, the Macarena. Keeping time by slapping their hands across their arms and hips, they jiggle, hop and stomp. They spin, wiggle and shake. They bounce for two minutes.

In silence.

"Yesterday, I told them we could be sued if we played the music," explains Teesie King, camp co-director and a volunteer mom. "So they decided they'd learn it without the music."

Watching the campers' mute contortions, Mrs. King shakes her head. "It seems so different," she allows, "when you do the Macarena in silence."

Starting this summer, the American Society of Composers, Authors & Publishers has informed camps nationwide that they must pay license fees to use any of the four million copyrighted songs written or published by Ascap's 68,000 members. Those who sing or play but don't pay, Ascap warns, may be violating the law.

Like restaurants, hotels, bars, stores and clubs, which already pay fees to use copyrighted music, camps—including nonprofit ones such as those run by the Girl Scouts—are being told to ante up. The demand covers not only recorded music but also songs around the campfire.

"They buy paper, twine and glue for their crafts—they can pay for the music, too," says John LoFrumento, Ascap's chief operating officer. If offenders keep singing without paying, he says, "We will sue them if necessary."

No more "Edelweiss" free of charge. No more "This Land Is Your Land." An Ascap spokesman says "Kumbaya" isn't on its list, but "God Bless America" is.

Diablo, an all-volunteer day camp that charges girls $44 a week to cover expenses, would owe Ascap $591 this year, based on the camp's size and how long it runs. Another composer group, Sesac Inc., which owns copyrights to such popular tunes as Bob Dylan's "Blowin' in the Wind," says it plans to ask camps for another set of royalties this fall.

So far, Girl Scouts of the U.S.A., the national organization based in New York, isn't playing along with royalty demands. But the American Camping Association, in Martinsville, Ind., which includes many Scout camps, advises members to comply. Diablo's regional Girl Scout Council in Oakland is low on cash and decided its

20 area camps can't afford the extra expense. Rather than risk a law-suit, the council told all the camps to scratch copyrighted songs from their programs even though only a few received warning letters.

"At first I thought, 'You guys have got to be kidding,'" says Sharon Kosch, the council's director of program services. "They can't sing the songs? But it's pretty threatening. We were told the penalty can be $5,000 and six days in jail."

So, the camp's directors have scrutinized its official "Elf Manual" and, in the section headed "Favorite Songs at Diablo Day Camp," have crossed out the most popular copyrighted tunes with black Magic Marker. The Scouts know about only a few of the banned songs because Ascap hasn't mailed out a complete list; it comprises four million songs and runs 70,000 pages. Ascap says it has, how-ever, put a list on the Internet.

After finishing off hot dogs and s'mores for lunch, the Elves—senior Scouts charged with helping younger campers—gather in a circle with directors to decide what they can sing.

"Is 'Row, Row, Row Your Boat' copyrighted?" asks Holly Foster, a 14-year-old Elf with a turquoise happy face on her cheek. "Row, Row, Row Your Boat" may float, the directors decide, but "Puff the Magic Dragon" definitely is out.

"How about 'Ring Around the Rosie'?" another Elf asks. The di-rectors veto it.

"We wanted to sing 'Underwear,' but it's set to the tune of 'Battle Hymn of the Republic,'" says Mrs. King, the co-director. "We're not sure if that's copyrighted; so, we don't sing it."

"When in doubt don't sing," advises Site Director Leslie Shan-ders.

Even harder than figuring out which songs are which, directors say, is explaining it all to young Brownies. "They think copyright means the 'mean people,'" says Debby Cwalina, a 14-year-old Elf. Holly explains it to them this way: "The people who wrote it have a thing on it. A little 'c' with circles around it. There's an alarm on it. And if you sing it, BOOM!"

That explanation doesn't always sink in. Alissa Fiset, age eight, crinkles her nose when asked why she can't sing "Puff the Magic Dragon." While squirting a friend with a water bottle, she says: "They did a rewrite on it. A copy thing. But why can't they just take the 'c' away?"

Ascap, which is based in New York, defends the royalties. "Songwriters are small-business people who write songs to make a living," Mr. LoFrumento says. "The royalties allow them to send their kids to Girl Scout camp, too."

The federal copyright act allows composers and music publishers to demand royalty payments for any public performance of copyrighted material. The law defines a public performance as "where a substantial number of persons outside of a normal circle of a family and its social acquaintances is gathered." Although the law has been on the books since 1909, Ascap began notifying large music users, such as hotels, only a little over a decade ago and more recently has worked its way down to small users, such as rodeos and funeral homes. This year, it negotiated a reduced annual fee of $257 with camps enrolled in the American Camping Association. For camps, such as Diablo, that aren't association members, the fees are higher, ranging from $308 to $1,439 a year. Small camps that last two weeks or less get a special rate of $77.

Penalties for noncompliance can be stiff. The law sets fines up to $25,000 or a year in prison, or both, for major infringements. According to Mr. LoFrumento, Ascap, which sends monitors around the country, has successfully sued restaurants, retailers and private clubs. While the law hasn't been tested on camps, copyright attorneys say even little girls would lose.

"If you make an exception for the Girl Scouts, you could set a practical precedent," says Russell Frackman, a Los Angeles copyright lawyer. "You give the impression that a particular use is not an infringement, and that can be used against you in the future."

Ascap contends that its members have contributed heavily to the Scouts over the years. In 1940, Irving Berlin donated all future royalties from his "God Bless America" to the New York City Boy Scout and Girl Scout councils. Although the Scouts still get royalties from it, Mr. LoFrumento concedes that, nevertheless, they can't sing it without paying the fee.

So, it's back to black Magic Markers.

After finishing the Macarena at the Diablo sing-along, one mother whispers that today is the sixth birthday of David Warneke, a camp volunteer's son. "We're not allowed to sing 'Happy Birthday,'" warns Debi Jansen, a co-director.

Huddling with the Elves, the directors come up with a plan: Sing a modified "Happy Birthday" to the tune of "Ninety-Nine Bottles of Beer on the Wall."

But Mrs. Jansen is worried. "I hope that's not copyrighted, too," she frets.

—LISA BANNON, August 1996

7. *Pity the Toad*

SAN FRANCISCO—For the record, Mojo Nixon says neither he nor any member of his rock band, Mojo Nixon and the Toadliquors, has ever actually licked a toad.

Still, with a name like that, Mr. Nixon's band can hardly help but attract attention from what authorities say is a small but growing segment of the drug culture that has taken up the bizarre practice of ingesting venom squeezed from live toads. "People come up to us all the time and ask if we get high licking toads," says Mr. Nixon, who calls the very idea "insane."

Mojo knows. He read something about toad-licking in the underground press about four years ago, and his band, the Burger Eaters, became the Toadliquors. Although tales of getting a buzz from lapping toad squeezings have circulated through underground lore since the 1960s, drug authorities on both sides of the law agree on one thing: Toad-licking is not just weird but dangerous.

Toad venom contains dozens of chemically active compounds, including enough poison to kill dogs that sometimes catch the homely little hoppers and try to eat them. "I would think you could poison yourself pretty badly before you got high licking toads," says Andrew T. Weil, an ethnopharmacologist at the University of Arizona's College of Medicine in Tucson.

Thus, after a spurt of experimentation, toad-licking tapered off.

Toad-smoking, on the other hand, seems to be less risky and is on the rise, says Cecil Schwalbe, a research ecologist for the Interior Department. Dr. Schwalbe says the heat from smoking venom appears to break down the toxins while retaining the psychedelics. "The people who believe in better living through chemistry found out you could get the same hallucinogenic reaction from smoking toads as from licking them," he says.

Dr. Weil, a physician and drug-culture researcher, says that when he and a fellow researcher smoked dried venom from a Colorado River toad, it produced "a sense of wonder and well-being."

Dr. Weil's report, published two years ago in an obscure anthropological journal, *Ancient Mesoamerica,* apparently sent a smoke signal through the drug underground.

Arizona wildlife authorities recently raided the home of an unlicensed reptile-dealer near Tucson and discovered dozens of football-sized Colorado River toads sitting placidly in the man's living room. (State law does allow possession of up to ten toads if you have a fishing license.) John Romero, law-enforcement program manager for the Arizona Department of Game and Fish, says his agents puzzled awhile over why anyone would have toads around the house. "Then the light came on," Mr. Romero says.

On the Southern California drug market these days, drug agents say a healthy toad can fetch up to $8. One alleged dealer was arrested for illegal trading in wildlife last fall after he ran an ad in the University of Arizona student newspaper seeking a toad supply.

"Cane Toads," a 1989 documentary film that describes smoking toad venom in Australia, has become a cult-video favorite. Toad-licking also came up recently on the television series *LA Law* (which mistakenly showed a bullfrog instead of a toad) and in an MTV *Beavis and Butt-head* cartoon. "The show reflects what's going on in the youth culture," explains a *Beavis and Butt-head* spokeswoman.

Still, the whole toad thing is so bizarre that even critics are hard pressed to maintain a straight face. South Carolina lawmakers giggled when a bill was introduced four years ago that would have made the state the first to outlaw toad-licking. Rep. Patrick B. Harris, finding the practice "repulsive but amusing," proposed sentencing violators to 60 hours of public service in a local zoo.

Toads made the news again last month when California drug agents arrested Robert Shepard, a 41-year-old Boy Scout troop leader in Angels Camp, Calif., about 100 miles east of San Francisco. Mr. Shepard was charged with several drug offenses, including possession of bufotenine, a chemical constituent of toad venom and a recognized hallucinogen. The agents also impounded Mr. Shepard's four Colorado River toads—Brian, Peter, Hans and Franz.

Gregory Elam, the officer who made the arrest, says Mr. Shepard was so contrite he helped drug agents make a training video showing how venom is squeezed from kidney-shaped parotoid glands on the back of a live toad, then dried and smoked. "It was pretty disgusting," says Mr. Elam, who has a big photograph of a toad on his office wall. "This is not something you would brag about to your mama."

Mr. Shepard won't talk to a reporter about toads or anything else. But James Webster, his attorney, says he himself had never heard of toad-smoking. "I've heard of a princess kissing a toad," says Mr. Webster, misremembering the story of the frog prince. "I guess these days she'd be busted, too."

Narcotics agents say Mr. Shepard may be the first person ever arrested on toad-smoking charges. Bufotenine, as a hallucinogen, has been on federal and state dangerous-drug lists for years, and its possession is illegal.

In his *Ancient Mesoamerica* article, Dr. Weil reported that toad skins and artifacts depicting toads have turned up at Indian ceremonial sites in Mexico and Central America dating back more than a thousand years. The researcher and others speculate that Mayans, Aztecs and other ancients may have used toad venom as an intoxicant in their rites.

Dr. Weil and his co-author, Wade Davis, theorize that the Colorado River toad has become the smokers' choice not because of bufotenine, but because it contains large amounts of the chemical compound 5-MeO-DMT, a powerful psychoactive drug.

Experts describe the toad as a shy amphibian found mostly in the Sonoran desert in northern Mexico and in the southern parts of Arizona and California. The toads live underground most of the year, emerging only during the brief rainy season in midsummer.

The Colorado River toad, Dr. Weil says, is a virtual psychedelic factory, whose venom produces a 20-minute high that is so intense it can be frightening to the uninitiated. "I've seen people take one deep puff and fall over backward as they exhale," he says.

Toad puffers, Dr. Weil says, usually are unresponsive for five minutes or more, making little noise until they open their eyes. Mr. Davis, a Washington anthropologist, calls the effect "a magical slap in the face."

That may be pleasing to toad-smokers, but it could mean problems for toads in the wild. Dr. Weil says he has already received telephone calls from Californians eager to visit southern Arizona, where the critters are plentiful, to catch Colorado River toads. "This looks like it could be a trend, and the toad is the one that will suffer," says Mr. Romero, the Arizona Game and Fish official worried about depleting the toad population.

The toad's protector, say officials, will probably be environmental laws, not drug laws. California, for example, began implementing a law last week that makes it a misdemeanor to possess any of the shrinking population of Colorado River toads in the state.

"Eventually," says Mr. Elam, the Angels Camp drug agent, "you'll probably see a much stiffer penalty for possession of a toad than for a controlled substance. The environmentalists have more clout than the cops."

—BILL RICHARDS, March 1994

8. *Ruff! Ruff! Ruffage! Here, Rover, Have a Nice Bean Sprout!*

Lions may be evolutionary predators, gorging on meat, blood and guts. But Teresa Gibbs finds these ancient carnivorous stirrings unacceptable for her own member of the feline family.

So Ms. Gibbs has turned Yoko, her black, longhair cat, into a vegan—the strictest kind of vegetarian. Every day, Yoko feasts on garbanzo beans, lentils, split peas and broccoli—with a pinch of garlic. On special occasions, she nibbles asparagus spears.

"I don't think she misses meat in any way, shape or form," says Ms. Gibbs, herself a vegan. She takes a swipe at conventional cat food: "This is much better than . . . dead animal parts sitting around with flies on it all day long."

Yoko is a pioneer—and critics would say a guinea pig—in a controversial new movement that unites vegetarianism and animal-rights activism: vegetarian pets. Thousands of American pet owners have joined the movement, tossing out the Purina and Alpo and introducing Fido and Fluffy to nutritional yeast and wheatgluten flour.

The vegetarians purr about the benefits of a meatless pet diet, crediting it with curing all sorts of animal ailments from allergies to diabetes. Some even swear that cats on tofu and bean sprouts become so mellow that they stop chasing mice and birds.

"The health benefits are just incredible," insists Lorraine Sheppard, a Colorado massage therapist who converted her two dogs to vegetarianism five years ago. "The pets have more energy, more clarity of mind and a real peacefulness."

Such claims aside, some worry that the veg-pet people are barking up the wrong tree. "Dogs evolved on a high meat-based protein diet, and cats are truly carnivores," says Arleigh Reynolds, a clinician at Cornell University's College of Veterinary Medicine.

Thus, to deprive canines of meat invites a host of medical problems. Dr. Reynolds says he has treated a number of vegetarian dogs suffering from poor coats, lost muscle mass and liver problems. And cats—which require taurine, a nutrient found only in animal flesh—are susceptible to reproductive, growth and heart problems on a meatless diet. Dr. Reynolds says that, while some vegetarian pets are fed supplements to make up for possible nutrient losses, he knows of at least one cat death related to vegetarian taurine deficiency.

As for the claim that a vegetarian diet purges cats of predatory instincts, Francis Kallfelz, another Cornell veterinarian and nutritionist, is skeptical. "I don't think it's possible for natural instincts to be changed by feeding procedures," he says.

None of these concerns make much of a dent on vegans, who hail animal vegetarianism as a final break from the flesh-eating world. "In a small way, I'm trying to make a difference," says Mary Currier, a vegan and leading advocate of vegetarian pet diets.

Ms. Currier is helping more than most. The onetime suburban housewife has turned pet vegetarianism into her life's work, providing sanctuary for 32 vegetarian cats and five vegetarian dogs.

In her remote, battered New Hampshire farmhouse, Ms. Currier has accomplished what most owners of finicky felines would consider the impossible. As four cats snooze peacefully on a crowded kitchen table, two others eagerly attack and eat half of a cantaloupe on a countertop. "Little Fancy Feast loves fake hot dogs, and I have to hide the potatoes from Beethoven," says Ms. Currier, peeling a cucumber and feeding pieces of it to Polar Bear, a white longhaired cat.

Buying chickpeas and olive oil—among many ingredients in her homemade vegetarian pet chow—for 32 cats requires some sacrifice. "It's really difficult," says Ms. Currier, who devotes $450 a month to her animals and hasn't gone to a restaurant since last Christmas. "But if you have a dream, you get by."

Not that coaxing genetic meat-eaters onto vegetarian diets is without problems. Ms. Currier's success aside, Ms. Gibbs says it took her two months of experimentation before she found a garbanzo bean, lentil and split pea stew that her three cats could swallow. Temptation is a constant worry. Ms. Sheppard says she is happy that her dogs nibble almonds and grapes but has no doubt that, offered a steak, "they would eat meat."

Vegetarian pets also seem susceptible to stomach upsets, often requiring anti-gas remedies. Karen Porreca, a librarian for People for the Ethical Treatment of Animals and owner of four vegan dogs, regularly adds a few drops of Beano to their nightly rations that include brown rice and split peas. "One of them really needed it," she confides.

If the vegetarian pet movement is political to some, it represents opportunity for others. Wow-Bow Distributors Ltd. of Deer Park, N.Y., is among a half-dozen companies that have sprouted up to make commercial quantities of dog and cat health food. Wow-Bow's dog biscuit is baked from stone-ground whole wheat, yeast, fresh garlic, parsley and eggs (from free-range hens). Wow-Bow's logo: A Chinese Shar-Pei with a carrot dangling from its mouth.

No one knows how many pets—"companion animals" in animal-rights parlance—have gone vegetarian.

Pet Foods in Corona, Calif., says sales of its vegetarian dog chow jumped 24 percent to an estimated $2.4 million last year. That is enough of its soybean, rice, barley and carrot concoction to feed 19,000 canines. And the fourth edition of *Vegetarian Cats and Dogs*, published by a Montana maker of vitamin supplements for vegetarian pets, sold 2,000 copies in 1993—as many as in the previous six years combined.

For some, the vegetarian pet movement reflects a deep mistrust of commercial pet-food makers. Among a litany of accusations, one is that some meat in commercial pet food is unfit to eat; another is that some pet food is actually made from euthanized cats and dogs.

Both claims are untrue and the latter is "a rumor that goes around every ten years or so," says Mark Finke, director of nutritional research for Alpo Pet Foods Inc., a unit of Grand Metropolitan PLC. "We try not to buy our materials preground, so you can tell what they truly are." He admits that most pet-food companies, including Alpo, use meat and entrails from animals (horses, cows and other farm stock) that have died of disease or old age. But Dr. Finke says that high-temperature processes used in making and canning pet food kill any pathogens. (Ralston-Ralston Purina Co. and Nestlé SA, also major pet-food makers, declined comment.)

Furthermore, pet-food makers say that, vegetarian revulsion aside, dogs and cats find animal parts paw-licking good. "Dogs happen to love lungs," says Alpo's Dr. Finke. Adds Cornell's Dr. Reynolds: "If you watch a lion when it goes out and kills, the first thing it eats are the guts."

Which is why even some vegetarians think the vegetarian pet movement is misguided. For Donald Garber, a vegetarian and veterinarian, his cat Vlackavar is a natural carnivore who shouldn't be deprived of his birthright by human notions of a "politically correct" diet.

"I don't have the right to impose my will on another creature," says Dr. Garber. "Vlackavar is a cat and cats eat meat."

—SUEIN L. HWANG, October 1993

9. Bambi Deconstructed

PRINCETON, N.J.—With a periodicity coincidental to the orbital revolution of the sun's third nearest planet, an anomalous perturbation occurs at the Institute for Advanced Study, where people think about stuff, as Albert Einstein did here, without socks, for 22 years.

The perturbation, or "P," can be stated as: $P = RMd + (GMr)^2$, in which "RMd" represents a memo from Allen I. Rowe, associate director for administration and finance, that begins, "Re: Deer Control Program" and "$(GMr)^2$" is the resulting flurry of anonymous deer memos—some sincere, some facetious—from some of the institute's 184 resident and visiting geniuses.

In terms of density, the Institute for Advanced Study undoubtedly is close to its carrying capacity for geniuses. The mail slots read Kennan, Dyson, Geertz, Bombieri and Weil, intellectual superstars all. There is Piet Hut, who thought up Nemesis, the "Death Star," to explain the asteroid strike that may have done in the dinosaurs, and there is Edward Witten, the super-string theorist (don't even ask). And while there are people in residence who only think about Star Wars and Just Wars, there are obviously others who are prepared to fight Deer Wars—albeit anonymously.

Princeton Township has been increasingly overrun with deer since 1972, when it banned the discharge of firearms and, thus, deer hunting with shotguns. Estimated deer population then: 220. Now: 1,200. The institute first allowed deer hunting with bows and arrows in 1984, and it alerts its residents with a low-key annual memo announcing the hunt. This year, the memo went out on Sept. 30 and in it, Mr. Rowe stated that to keep the deer population at a "reasonable and sustainable level," a small number of expert bow hunters, duly authorized by Ramon Pressburger, "our Wildlife Control Officer," will be in the institute's 640 acres of woods and corn and soybean fields "beginning today" to cull the herd. A day later, the mailbox of at least one faculty member contained Mr. Rowe's memo, on which someone had drawn a deer's head, with an arrow through it, and blood, in red ink, dripping from the wound. It appeared to be the opening shot in Deer Wars '89.

By the middle of last week, a new memo was in circulation. This one cited a Harvard "study" proving that a deer "bristling with arrows and plunging about in a vulgar display of agony will effect more damage (to foliage and property) per square foot than a normal, unpunctured and unstimulated deer. . . ."

A graph showed increased damage in square-foot increments as a rising S-curve for each arrow in a deer. "Note: behavior of deer containing more than 36 arrows tended to level off," the memo tweaked. It was signed by the pseudonymous "Prof. Nomo Mentum." It is said that the 23 permanent faculty members, 11 emeritus professors and roughly 150 visiting research scholars here think so hard that they can't think for very long. And since they are here strictly for thinking—they have no students, classrooms, laboratories or exams to grade—people presume that they have plenty of time for frivolity and non-academic controversy.

But a random telephone survey of the professorial ranks turned up no one who would admit authorship of any memo. Not the "Interested Party" proposal a few years back that suggested the importation of a breeding pair of timber wolves, which would not only limit the deer supply but also the number of children and dogs on institute premises. Nor the "In Defense of Hunting" memo, which argued that the woods were already so dangerous because of Lyme-disease ticks, poison ivy, bikers, joggers, dogs, the "occasional flasher" and "some ferocious Princeton [University] students" that a few days of hunting weren't so terrible. Nor even the eyewitness account memo: "The arrow went through the doe's neck. We all saw it strike. . . . We came to several pools of blood with prints of her knees beside them."

One well-known treatise, contrasting the no-waste, in-accord-with-nature deer-killing and skinning ways of the noble Navajo with the wasteful-racist-savagery of the white man, is attributed, by those who heard it read, to an anthropologist who visited a few years back.

The institute's administrators say that the deer dither is no more than a neutrino-sized blip in the serenity of this thinking man's nirvana. Physics profs profess almost zero-gravity attraction to the issue. Astrophysicist John N. Bahcall, who thinks a lot about how the sun shines (the "solar neutrino problem"), says his kids are "deeply opposed" to the deer hunt, but he has no opinion himself. Freeman Dyson, a physicist who thinks about and usually has opinions on almost everything, just laughs.

Prof. Emeritus George F. Kennan, the distinguished historian, is staying mum. Prof. Emeritus Albert O. Hirschman, the distinguished economist who noticed in 1984 that he didn't receive a memo warning that the hunt was on, reasons wryly that this was a clever design by the administration to cull the ranks of the professors emeriti, who might stroll innocently into the woods.

The mathematicians may stand accused of rushing daily to the 3 p.m. tea and gobbling the cookies before the physicists, historians and social scientists arrive, but they show some compassion for the deer.

"I like them. I let them eat the plants in my garden," says Enrico Bombieri, the IBM von Neumann Professor of Mathematics. "The population is too large, but I don't think bow and arrow is a very effective way of reducing it."

"After seeing *Bambi,* nobody wants to kill a deer," says Prof. Luis A. Cafferarelli, whose current major interest is free boundary problems in differential equations. "Maybe they should catch and move them," he suggests.

"Too expensive," says John Kuser, who teaches forestry at Rutgers and heads Princeton Township's ad hoc deer committee. "You need heavy snow and starving deer, and it still ends up costing $300 per deer. You'd need to catch 500, and since the deer population can double annually you'd have a yearly bill of $150,000," he says. "And no place to send them. You can't give them away."

Deer polarization has neighbors warring across eastern U.S. suburbs. And in Princeton it spreads well beyond the institute. There are the deer lovers, the so-called Bambi-syndromists, and deer haters, the so-called deer-are-long-legged-rats-with-big-ears school, who tend to side with deer hunters, the so-called Rambo Fascist Pigs. Stan Waterman, the underwater filmmaker who shoots sharks with a movie camera, walks two black French poodles in the institute woods most afternoons and makes plenty of noise, which doesn't sit well with the camouflaged hunters he occasionally spots in tree notches. "I find it appalling," he says. "It's the Rambo mentality."

Fellow resident and diver, Peter Benchley, author of *Jaws,* says local deer are "wretched, sickly creatures starving to death" and need to be culled. One wrecked his wife's car a few years back, and, he says, deer are rooting around in people's garbage cans all over town. "If only they didn't have those saucer eyes and Walt Disney behind them. The Bambi complex seems to have taken over around here."

James A. Quitslund, associate director and spokesman for the institute, doesn't track pro- and anti-deer sentiment, but he thinks that visiting scholars, especially those with children who come from places with few or no deer, tend to view them fondly, whereas many longtime residents tend to despise the whole species, especially since the arrival of Lyme disease spread by deer ticks. He says the subject is "a little sensitive."

Mr. Pressburger, the wildlife control officer, says, "I've got to be careful what I say," his nonpaying job being one that requires heaps of diplomacy. He will say that his hunters are screened for temperament as well as safety skills and that they are mostly cops and "working people," who usually hunt before and after work, ten at a time maximum, in specifically assigned areas away from walking trails.

So far, he says proudly, there hasn't been a single confrontation or complaint, and 92 deer have been "harvested." Some institute scholars yukked it up over reports that only one deer was killed during the first hunting year. But that was on purpose, says Mr. Pressburger. Instead of hunting, the hunters walked the woods showing themselves to strollers and joggers, meeting institute people, chatting them up, being polite and friendly and explaining their safety consciousness and why what they were doing was best for the deer in the long run. They did this to avoid triggering a backlash among institute scholars and their families.

"You know, we're not dealing with a bunch of dummies here," Mr. Pressburger says.

Franz Moehn, described in a recent book as one of the institute's most revered figures, undoubtedly has the most experience in actual deer-handling. He is the institute's chef, and among the buffet platters he arranged for a fall reception last Friday were slices of succulent venison. From New Zealand, he says, not from out back.

—JAMES P. STERBA, October 1989

10. *The Deeper Meaning of Mail*

NEW YORK—Emma Thornton still shows up for work at 5 a.m. each day in her blue slacks, pinstripe shirt and rubber-soled shoes. A letter carrier for the U.S. Postal Service, she still dutifully sorts all the mail addressed to "One World Trade Center," and primes it for delivery.

But delivery to where and to whom?

Since Sept. 11, as many as 90,000 pieces of mail a day continue to flood in to World Trade Center addresses that no longer exist and to thousands of people who aren't alive to receive them. On top of that is another mail surge set off by well-wishers from around the U.S. and the world—thousands of letters addressed to, among other salutations, "The People Hurt," "Any Police Department" and "The Working Dogs" of "Ground Zero, N.Y." Some of this mail contains money, food, even biscuits for the dogs that were used in the early days to help try to sniff out survivors.

The mix of World Trade Center mail and Ground Zero mail represents a calamity for the U.S. Postal Service, which served 616 separate companies in the World Trade Center complex whose offices are now rubble or relocated. On a cavernous floor of the James A. Farley General Post Office in midtown Manhattan, the nine carriers, including Ms. Thornton, who once walked the World Trade Center routes have been brought together to help sort this out.

Her route in the North Tower has been transformed into a 6-by-6 steel cubicle (called a "sorting case") surrounded by tall metal racks of pigeonholes. She and co-workers have been told by supervisors to keep busy, and workers know they shouldn't concern themselves with whether anyone will pick up the mail they are sorting, or if the names correspond to any of the missing. But they do. She often sees faces behind the names on envelopes—people she saw five days a week and joked with in the elevators.

These days, lots of people she bumped into every day are still unaccounted for, and looking at a company's address, or merely the floor number, can plunge her into tears. She worries about a kindly woman named Sonia who ran the freight elevator at the Windows on the World restaurant and often gave her snacks and lunch. Cantor Fitzgerald, Marsh & McLennan and Windows on the World were on her route—companies now seared in the public consciousness because they were high up in the tower. Like any good carrier, Ms. Thornton can rattle off their floors and suite numbers by memory.

"My whole career was at the World Trade Center," Ms. Thornton, 57 years old, muses. "I was at the World Trade Center when it went up, and I saw it when it went down."

Technically, the Postal Service's "return to sender" policy dictates that uncollected mail be immediately sent back. Since the vast majority of people who worked in the Twin Towers are still alive and most of the companies are still operating elsewhere, the Post Office is planning to hold on to all mail for at least three months, giving stunned companies and individuals more time to claim it. But the mountains of mail have already swamped normal mail bins, and the Postal Service has had to bring in Dumpsters and rows and rows of big plastic crates to store it all.

As for the "Ground Zero" mail addressed to "The Dogs" or "The Firefighters," the Postal Service isn't sure yet what to do with it and has sought advice from disaster authorities. It's "overwhelming," says Pat McGovern, a Postal Service spokeswoman.

Before Sept. 11—and before an anthrax scare that has put postal workers on the front lines of another bout with fear—Ms. Thornton had exactly the job she wanted. A chatty, down-to-earth person now widowed, she migrated to New York from Columbus, Ga., in her early 20s looking for work. She craved a secure job. After taking a series of civil-service tests for New York's mass-transit department and even the police department, she opted for the Post Office. Her reasoning: "I thought, 'Oh, if the government goes broke, that is the end of the world.'"

She started in 1971 and since 1974 has delivered mail from the

77th floor to the 110th floor of One World Trade Center. Some mail carriers shun high-rise work, citing fear of heights and elevators. Some postal workers specifically avoided the World Trade Center because its upper floors were known to creak and sway in stiff winds.

"Nobody wanted this route," Ms. Thornton recalls. But she had watched in admiration as the Twin Towers went up and decided it was the only job she wanted.

She took to it readily, despite the daunting logistics and the need to change elevators frequently, and she considered her route, with its own zip code, 10048, a "small town in the sky." She had numerous chances to give up lugging mail for a desk job but turned them all down, even after a brush with catastrophe in 1993, when terrorists first struck the World Trade Center and killed six people. Ms. Thornton had been in the building 15 minutes before that attack and despite it, vowed to carry on. "It was a way of life, and I got used to it," she recalls.

To her, the tower's firms were more than addresses. These were her friends and customers, people who plied her with steaming cups of coffee and Danish in the morning, and invited her to their Christmas and office parties. "They would give me food. I partied with them—good people," she says. Postal supervisors say so many carriers like Ms. Thornton are breaking down on the job every day that they've had to organize regular counseling sessions for them.

The morning of Sept. 11, Ms. Thornton was sorting mail at the Church Street Post Office a block away when the first hijacked plane struck. Recalling 1993, she didn't wait for instructions. She began to run and didn't stop till she arrived at City Hall, about seven long blocks northeast of the disaster. Only then did she look back at the towers in flames. She watched from afar as the offices she had known so well collapsed into a roaring avalanche of rubble.

She is still incredulous: "There is no building. After 30 years, there is no place, there is nothing."

The next day, she and other World Trade Center carriers, plus an additional 60 or so relocated from the Church Street station, were summoned back to work at the ancient Farley building on Eighth Avenue and 31st Street. Ms. Thornton decided to take a few days off, however. "I couldn't take it," she says. "I stayed in my house."

At the Farley building, there were already piles of mail to sort— the charred, dusty pieces recovered from Church Street station, itself inundated by debris and dust from the collapsing towers, as well as new mail that continued to arrive, unaffected by the disaster.

Together the carriers have recreated in miniature a semblance of their old route. The World Trade Center buildings were allotted sorting areas ringed with dozens and dozens of beige and gray metal pigeonholes to accept the buildings' mail. Ms. Thornton's cubicle is marked with a large sign that reads 1 WORLD TRADE CENTER in bold black letters. Each of the companies on her old route has its own pigeonhole. She sits in this cramped, dim space for eight hours a day sorting mail. When a pigeonhole fills up, workers come and dump the overflow into large, marked crates.

Ms. Thornton says she doesn't want to feel ungrateful. After all, she is alive and getting a paycheck. But most days, she feels lost and disoriented. She misses the din of the building, the rush of the elevators, the friendly chats in the lobbies. "I have no place to go," she says. "It is like I am homeless."

She is also obsessed with the missing. In the first days after the explosion, few companies came to pick up their mail. Then, in a trickle, people began to show up, even from the hardest-hit firms such as Cantor Fitzgerald, which lost an estimated 700 of its 1,000 employees, and Marsh & McLennan, an insurance company where almost 300 people died. For weeks, the mail to Windows on the World, where an estimated 166 people, including scores of diners, were killed, continued to pile up. At last, a week ago, someone arrived for the first time to get it. "It took people a while to get themselves together," Ms. Thornton figures.

Some companies still have sent no one, and latecomers often carry bad news. "There's that sad situation on 79," she says of a company called International Office Centers Corp., a provider of furnished office space that occupied some of the 79th floor and leased most of the rest. "They had a Christmas party every year and invited me," Ms. Thornton says.

The company had been in the North Tower for 22 years, almost as many years as Ms. Thornton had delivered there. She was friendly with an assistant office manager whose nickname was "Bisi." They chatted almost every day, Ms. Thornton recalls.

An International Office official came by not long ago to claim mail and confirmed what Ms. Thornton feared. Bisi, whose real name was Olabisi Yee, died with three other workers on duty that day and six tenants who rented space from the company. Says Sean Keegan, whose wife, Burdette Russo, owns the company: "Nobody got out of our space."

There are some happier endings, too. Ms. Thornton had worried about employees of a small firm called Alliance Continuing Care Network, a nursing-home concern on the 77th floor. Two weeks ago, a postal colleague came up to Ms. Thornton with a business card from a man named John David Smith of Alliance who was there to pick up mail. Ms. Thornton barged out screaming with glee and hugged Mr. Smith in the hall.

"Oh, my God, I wondered what happened to you," Mr. Smith said to Ms. Thornton. Mr. Smith, who confirms the reunion, calls Ms. Thornton "a very wonderful woman" who always had a cheery word when she delivered the mail.

And then there's Sonia. Ms. Thornton finds herself preoccupied with the woman who ran Windows on the World's freight elevator. They chatted often as Ms. Thornton moved the mail up and down between the 106th and 110th floors. They were roughly the same age, had much in common, called each other "mommy."

"She was such a kind woman," Ms. Thornton says.

The woman's full name was Sonia Ortiz. She had immigrated, impoverished, from Colombia and loved her job so high above Manhattan. Her son, Victor Ortiz, says his mother was thrilled to be working in a place where she'd gotten to meet stars such as Michael Jackson and Eddie Murphy, among others.

She was "home there," says Mr. Ortiz.

Sonia is missing and presumed dead.

—LUCETTE LAGNADO, November 2001

11. *Luck Among the Ruins*

NEW YORK—Monica O'Leary thought her luck had taken a turn for the worse on Monday afternoon when she got laid off from her job.

But the fact that she didn't go to work on Tuesday turned out to be nothing short of miraculous for Ms. O'Leary. She had worked as a software saleswoman for eSpeed Inc., a technology company with offices on the 105th floor of the World Trade Center.

Ms. O'Leary, 23, is still grappling with memories of her last visit with co-workers on Monday afternoon. "I worked with a lot of guys, so I kissed them on the cheek and said 'goodbye,'" she says. "Little did I know that it was really goodbye."

For hundreds of people in New York, Washington and other cities affected by the deadly terrorist assault, Tuesday morning turned out to be an incredibly lucky time to oversleep, reschedule a meeting or take time off to sneak in a haircut. By doing so, they managed to sidestep the almost unimaginable fate that befell their co-workers and friends in the devastating attacks on the World Trade Center and the Pentagon.

Greer Epstein, who worked at Morgan Stanley & Co.'s offices on the 67th floor of the World Trade Center, escaped possible injury by slipping out for a cigarette just before a 9 a.m. staff meeting. Bill Trinkle, of Westfield, N.J., had planned to get an early start on his job as sales manager for Trading Technologies Inc., a software concern with offices on the 86th floor of the World Trade Center's Tower One. But after fussing with his two-year-old daughter and hanging curtains in her bedroom, he missed the train that would have gotten him into the office about a half hour before the attack. Instead, he took a later train directly to visit a client company, where workers hugged him as soon as he walked through the door.

Joe Andrew, a Washington lawyer and former chairman of the Democratic National Committee, had a ticket for seat 6-C on the ill-fated American Airlines flight 77 from Dulles International Airport to Los Angeles, but switched to a later flight at the last minute. "I happen to be a person of faith," says Mr. Andrew, "but even if you aren't, anybody who holds a ticket for a flight that went down . . . will become a person of faith."

In some cases, it was simply a good day to sustain seemingly bad luck. Nicholas Reihner was upset when he twisted his ankle while hiking during a vacation to Bar Harbor, Maine. But it was the reason he missed his Tuesday morning trip home to Los Angeles from Boston on the American Airlines flight that was hijacked and crashed into the World Trade Center.

"After I sprained my ankle, I was bellyaching to my hiking companion about how life sucks," says the 33-year-old legal assistant. "I feel now that life has never been sweeter. It's great to be alive."

Then there's George Keith, a Pelham, N.Y., investment banker who had a meeting at 9 a.m. Tuesday on the 79th floor of the World Trade Center. While he was driving through Central Park the night before, however, the transmission of Mr. Keith's brand-new BMW sport-utility vehicle got stuck in first gear. The breakdown forced him to cancel the morning meeting. But by the time he called the BMW dealer Tuesday, he was anything but furious. "I told them it was the best transmission problem I'll ever have," he said.

David Gray, a compliance officer for Washington Square Securities, lives in Princeton, N.J., and was due to arrive by commuter train at the Trade Center for a meeting with one of the firm's brokers just at the time the first plane hit. But a few days earlier, Mr. Gray, the husband of New York City Ballet principal ballerina Kyra Nichols, broke his foot while jumping rope at home. Mr. Gray said he had been feeling very "sheepish" about the nature of the accident, but now says, "Thank God I was a lousy jump-roper."

After he broke his foot, he rescheduled the meeting for later in the day so that he could drive into Manhattan instead of taking the commuter train. "So I was on the New Jersey Turnpike watching the World Trade Center go up in flames, instead of being in it."

In some cases, a chain of unlikely circumstances added up to a collective near-miss. For Irshad Ahmed and the employees of his Pure Energy Corp., the circumstances were these: A postponed meeting, a delay at a child's school, and a quick stop at the video store. Mr. Ahmed, president of the motor-fuels maker, had been set to attend a 9 a.m. meeting in the company's 53rd-floor conference room inside Tower One. But last week, the participants decided to push the meeting back. As a result, none of Pure Energy's nine employees were at work when the terrorists struck. Some were at a New Jersey lab. Others were out at appointments. Mr. Ahmed's secretary was running late at her child's school. As for Mr. Ahmed, he decided to stop off and return a couple of Blockbuster videos. "It's one of those little decisions you make that lead up to big events in life," he says.

For others, a decision to defy orders proved lifesaving. Michael Moy, a software engineer for IQ Financial Inc., was at his workstation on the 83rd floor of World Trade Center Tower Two getting ready to write software when the first jetliner struck Tower One. A few minutes later, he says, building security came on the speaker and instructed occupants to remain in their offices, saying that it would be more dangerous in the streets due to falling debris from the other building.

Disobeying those instructions, Mr. Moy and his boss told the 15 or so employees in their wing to start heading down the stairs, Mr. Moy says. Once again an announcement came over the speaker system, instructing employees to return to their respective floors. A few employees decided to do so and headed toward the lobby's elevators.

Just then, the doors of several elevators exploded, apparently because the second hijacked airplane had slammed into the building just a few floors above them.

Pandemonium followed, but being familiar with the stairway systems in the building, Mr. Moy and his boss directed co-workers to a little-used stairway that was relatively empty. As a result, dozens of people were able to hurry downstairs and escape into the street. "I'm glad we acted the way we did," says Mr. Moy, "otherwise I wouldn't be having this conversation with you."

In Washington, a woman who has spent years advocating tighter security controls at U.S. airports learned first-hand Tuesday just how close a brush with death can be. Marianne McInerney, executive director of the National Business Travel Association, would have been on the doomed American Airlines flight from Dulles if not for a last-minute flight change.

Ms. McInerney, a stickler for not paying more than $1,000 for business flights, had reluctantly booked a ticket on the ill-fated flight. But last Friday, she managed to find a less expensive ticket out of Washington's National Airport.

Ms. McInerney, 38, says she intends to use her position with the NBTA to raise the issue of lax security more forcefully with the airlines and Congress. "We have thought for so long that we are six degrees separated from any instance [of terrorism] we see. But yesterday we became separated by one degree, if that."

Marya Gwadz can thank her unborn son for being away from her 16th story office in Tower Two. Ms. Gwadz, 37, a principal investigator for the nonprofit National Development Research Institute, usually gets to work as early as 8:45 each morning. But on Tuesday, 8½ months pregnant with her first child, she was feeling tired so she caught a later subway from her Brooklyn apartment, and got out a stop early. "It was a beautiful stop and a beautiful day," she recalls. Then she saw the flames, and later watched her own building crumble. "At that point, I grabbed my stomach and started to run," she says.

In some cases arising from Tuesday's tragedy, the questions of survival and guilt are unusually complex.

Convicted of a 1986 robbery and killing, Texas inmate Jeffrey Eugene Tucker was scheduled to be executed Tuesday evening. Instead, he got a last-minute, 30-day stay from Gov. Rick Perry because the U.S. Supreme Court was closed, preventing last-minute appeals.

His lawyer, Robert C. Owen, of Austin, Texas, says he was relieved. "You can't imagine the feeling of dread you get from representing someone when your court of last recourse has just gone into hiding and isn't answering phone calls."

> —ROBERT TOMSHO, BARBARA CARTON
> and JERRY GUIDERA, September 2001

CHAPTER TWO

STYLE

12. *The Art of the Perfectly Awful*

SAN JOSE, Calif.—It is the best of lines, it is the worst of lines; it is mountains of majestic purple prose; it is parody—"call me, Ishmael, anytime"—and lush, languid, lilting alliteration; it is metaphor mixed, nay, chopped and pureed, in the Cuisinart of the mind, and lousy similes that can still come out smelling like a rose; it is sentences that run on, and on, and on—and on!—for it is the Bulwer-Lytton Fiction Contest.

In short, a contest for bad writing.

"We didn't really want *bad* bad writing," asserts Scott Rice, a professor of English at San Jose State University and the contest's founder, conceiver, originator, creator, designer—in short, the guy who started the thing. "Bad bad writing, nobody wants to see. What we were really looking for was *good* bad."

Consider this entry, a somewhat twisted version of the frog-prince tale. Like all the other eligible entries, it is what the author imagines to be the first sentence of the worst of all possible novels.

"The sun oozed over the horizon, shoved aside darkness, crept along the greensward, and, with sickly fingers, pushed through the castle window, revealing the pillaged princess, hand at throat, crown asunder, gaping in frenzied horror at the sated, sodden amphibian lying beside her, disbelieving the magnitude of the toad's deception, screaming madly, 'You lied!'"

About 3,000 people entered the contest from around the world— from around the very globe! They submitted over 6,000 entries that, with skilled ineptitude, punished the English language. Many entered the first lines of famous novels—after some injudicious fiddling. "We got a lot of 'call me Ishmaels,'" avers Bill Burnette, a San Jose State lecturer. "We got a lot of 'best of times, worst of times.'" Some contestants even submitted whole unpublished manuscripts. "Maybe they sent them along to show there was indeed a rotten novel behind the first sentence," muses Mr. Rice, who will unveil, disclose and unfrock the winner tomorrow.

The contest filched its name from Edward Bulwer-Lytton (Lord Lytton), a 19th-century author who wrote *The Last Days of Pompeii*, coined the phrase "The pen is mightier than the sword" and wrote prose as thick as pea-soup fog, so thick you could cut it with a knife. Snoopy, Charles Schulz's literary canine, owes Mr. Lytton a great debt, for it was the good lord who began one of his novels thusly:

"It was a dark and stormy night; the rain fell in torrents except at occasional intervals, when it was checked by a violent gust of wind which swept up the streets (for it is in London that our scene lies), rattling along the house-tops, and fiercely agitating the scanty flame of the lamps that struggled against the darkness."

But was Lord Lytton really so bad at writing that the contest should take his name? Bill Burnette pauses a moment, considers the question, and answers slowly, in his drawl: "Yes, I'm afraid so. If he'd just stuck with 'It was a dark and stormy night,' he'd have been okay. That isn't a bad opening. He just didn't stop while he was ahead."

The author of the best worst sentence stands to win an autographed four-panel Peanuts strip featuring Snoopy clacking out "It was a dark and stormy night." The runner-up will win a set of 28 volumes of Bulwer-Lytton's work, bought from a woman who unloaded the books for a buck apiece. There will also be a group of "dishonorable mentions for people who had written bad stuff that was quite bad but not quite bad enough to be put in the hall of fame or enshrined."

The winner, however, won't necessarily be a truly bad writer. After all, it takes talent to write poorly, contest judges contend. "The better sentences are acts of literary criticism or language criticism," argues Mr. Rice. Nancy Heifferon, a San Jose State lecturer and a contest judge, agrees: "There's no doubt that whoever wins this contest will be a good writer."

Contestants see no shame in entering. "It's just fun," observes Mary Brown of Ventura, Calif. Steve Garman, the city manager of Pensacola, Fla., explains he would be delighted to win the thing: "In a perverse sense it's an honor to win a bad-writing contest."

One entrant believes that winning could help his career. He is Scott Davis Jones, a Sausalito, Calif., free-lance writer who submitted this simile, seeking, as similes do, to relate the unfamiliar to the familiar: "The surface of the strange forbidden planet was curdling like cottage cheese gets way after the date on the lid says it is all right to buy it." Mr. Rice opines: "He relates it to something so familiar it's absolutely banal."

This remark would not displease Mr. Jones. "I'm writing a whole book that's poorly written," he discloses. "I mean purposely poorly written." The book, begun ten years ago to ease the tensions of trying to write well and entitled *The Crumwall: A Fetish in Three Parts,* is a third-person, historical, fabricated, inaccurate, prevarication-full—indeed fake—account of how a fellow named Fred Crumwall gets along in a village struck by the plague in 1348. (For that is when the plague struck the hapless village.)

"I'd really like to win this," he concedes. "It would be a real feather in my cap. It might help me sell the book." But what if he loses? "Losing this fiction contest? I don't know, maybe that's a selling point in itself." He plans to ship the first 100 pages of his book to his agent soon. "That should be enough to give her a good idea," he declares, "or is it a bad idea?"

The judges in this contest aren't playing any games—they're playing hardball. Nearly all are university instructors and veterans of lousy student writing that flows like traffic on a Friday night, or like coagulating blood, drying like mud the moment it reaches the reader's eye, but not exactly. "I've had six years of experience reading a lot of terrible compositions," confides judge Nancy Heifferon, recalling how one of her students wrote of a "doggie dog" world, instead of dog-eat-dog. "The judges aren't exactly jaded," intones Scott Rice. "That means too much of something pleasant. Let's say appalled."

We join these judges now in a house high atop a not-ungreen hill in the not-unsteep foothills rimming the Santa Clara Valley, where 14 judges, from teaching assistant to vice dean, all from San Jose State, sit in groups of three or four reading entries out loud, picking bests for different categories, sipping wine from glasses now dulled with fingerprints, and at one point digressing from the matter at hand to talk in low tones of how the raccoons will eat a domestic cat and leave only the claws, and where occasionally, amid the periodic pauses, critical comments rise upward from this scholarly assembly.

"That's *gross!*"

"We're done. We want something dirty."

"Is lack of clarity good?"

"Whoever wrote that—I'd like to meet him and point out his zits to him. There's too much contempt for humanity in that one."

Three judges by the window, including the vice dean and English Department chairman, begin by gagging over this entry in the "vile pun" category: "Pamela's heart beat fast and her hands trembled a lot as she listened to the intermittent knocking on the front door of her shanty located near the railroad tracks, beside a hobo jungle, and she thought, 'That is a bum rap if I ever heard one.'"

Over on the not unrust-colored couch, another group guffaws over an entry in the contemporary-realism category: "The camel died quite suddenly on the second day, and Selena fretted sulkily and, buffing her already impeccable nails—not for the first time since the journey began—pondered snidely if this would dissolve into a vignette of minor inconveniences like all the other holidays spent with Basil."

The same group takes on this one: "It was a dark and snowy night as he studied the feminine silhouette faintly outlined in the window—the lovely tapered fingers, small shaped waist and trim derriere—then he realized it was his own reflection."

"Isn't that wonderful?" ooohs one judge. "I like that one," ahhhs another.

For one instant—a fleeting, transient, ephemeral, evanescent, awfully short moment—one entry captivates the judges. It is an entry from a Jesuit priest, read aloud: "You name it, I've seen it—the depths, the pits, the bottom; Vic Steele's the name and proctology is my game." To which the judge cries: "Oh God, I like that one!"

And thusly did the day wane—after all, it was a waney day. The shadows crept on cat's feet into the valley. As the sun died slowly, frogs began croaking in the pond outside the window. And one judge looked up quizzically, cocked her head, shifted her gaze to another judge standing before the window, and asked: "Was that you, Dan, or was that a real frog?"

—ERIK LARSON, May 1983

13. *Roasted Porcupine and Basil, With a Hint of Tire Mark*

ABERDEEN, N.C.—With its back arched and its head cocked, the brown squirrel appears poised for a scamper as Tom and Frances Squier gaze at it through the cool mist.

"They don't get freezer burn if you leave the fur on," Mr. Squier explains.

His wife glares into the open freezer at the critter, which looks surprisingly chipper, considering that her husband found it dead on the highway.

"Whether you get it with a gun or a Goodyear, it's still the same meat," says Mr. Squier.

Mrs. Squier should be used to this by now. After all, being married to a Green Beret turned backwoods Paul Prudhomme is no picnic— at least not the usual kind. As the author of an offbeat outdoors column that appears in five area newspapers, Mr. Squier, a brawny 45-year-old with eyebrows as thick as shrubs, is known for his recipes for cactus quiche, cattail muffins and Christmas tree (pine needle) jelly. A frequent ribbon-winner at state fairs, he also brews a mean dandelion coffee, spices his stir-fry dishes with crunchy cicadas and stuns yellow-jacket nests with a fire extinguisher so he can "harvest" the larvae for soup.

Then there are his meat dishes. Mr. Squier's self-published *Living Off the Land* cookbook includes recipes for braised porcupine, sauteed crow and beaver-tail stew, as well as down-home dishes like "Mom's Baked 'Coon and Sweet 'Taters" and "Old Tough Rabbit Baked in Milk." For more formal occasions, he offers armadillo stuffed with wild rice, muskrat simmered in sherry and groundhog baked in sour cream, spiced mustard and a bit of rosemary.

"There's nothing that he wouldn't eat that's not poisonous," marvels Thomas Pope, Mr. Squier's editor at the *Fayetteville Observer-Times* in North Carolina.

Well, almost nothing. "I haven't eaten any bats," says Mr. Squier, "and I prefer not to eat kidneys just because I don't like the smell."

Still, he praises rattlesnake as "the other white meat" and uses it to make Chinese snake soup, faux "seafood" salad and chicken-fried snake. In fact, Mr. Squier rarely goes anywhere without a cooler and a pillowcase for scooping the dead reptiles off the highway.

Fans of Mr. Squier's column regularly show up at his rural home with dead animals found on local roads. Mr. Squier admits that determining whether a roadkill is fit for the oven can be tricky—forget the details. He advises that they keep longer in the winter and that the freshest ones are those found on a stretch of highway passed a few hours earlier.

Mr. Squier learned about wild plants and game at the knee of his Cherokee grandfather, a hunter, herbalist and connoisseur of opossums, snapping turtles and other entrees foraged from North Carolina's rivers, swamps and woodlands.

After high school, he worked as an alligator wrestler in Silver Springs, Fla., and lived in a tree in the nearby Ocala National Forest, where armadillos were his culinary mainstay. Later, as a Green Beret, he served in Vietnam, Honduras and South Korea, gaining a reputation as a soldier who relished toasted beetle grubs, deep-fried anaconda and almost anything cooked by locals. "Fresh monkey and dog-meat stew," he says, almost wistfully, recalling his Vietnam years. "It was more tasty than the canned stuff."

A U.S. Army Special Forces master sergeant and senior medic, he has appeared in military training films foraging for wild plants for food or medicine, and recently he helped the military devise a computer program for identifying plants. He also revised the field survival manual.

Mr. Squier does fish and hunt. But true to his Indian heritage, he won't kill an animal without using all of its parts, a belief that has spawned recipes such as scrambled eggs with venison brains and a bullfrog soup that uses parts most cooks would never dream of.

When he isn't looking for food, Mr. Squier repairs the shells of injured turtles with epoxy glue and regularly scampers across four-lane highways to rescue animals that he releases in the wild. Still, as he writes in his book: "If I can't save them, I am going to saute them."

"His kitchen is the 'Roadkill Cafe'" says Rocky Gonzalez, a chief warrant officer and fellow Special Forces survival trainer. "What's really amazing is that it is so tasty. It borders on haute cuisine, or even higher than that."

Indeed, Mr. Squier has become a hot item at herb festivals and wild-food gatherings from Colorado to Canada. Locally, his lectures and tastings at the Weymouth Woods Sandhills Nature Preserve frequently attract crowds of 100 and more. "He has groupies," says Kym Hyre, a Weymouth Woods ranger.

Some fans travel around the state to hear his talks about edible wild plants and game cooking. "Oh, he's really made an impression," gushes Louise Thomas, of Wadesboro, N.C., who has developed a fondness for day lilies stuffed with cream cheese since she began attending Mr. Squier's talks. "I've never considered eating weeds before," adds Cynthia Little, whose garden club recently followed Mr. Squier on a weed-eating tour.

Because Mr. Squier looks at dandelions and chickweeds the way most people regard onions and parsley, his yard probably won't be a featured attraction for Ms. Little's garden club. He won't cut the grass and only lets his wife mow parts of their otherwise overgrown five-acre plot. "And it took a while for him to trust me to be out here alone," she notes.

Of course, not everyone admires Mr. Squier's culinary skills. Literary agents have advised him to drop the roadkill recipes and, locally, some newspaper editors have spurned his dinner invitations and urged him to tone down his more unusual recipes. "He brings in pictures, too, which kind of makes it worse," says Jan Howard, food editor of the *Moore County Citizen News-Record*.

At home, one sister-in-law brings a cooler of food on visits and if some family friends can't persuade Mrs. Squier to cook, they insist on seeing the food wrappers before sitting down to dinner. With that in mind, Mr. Squier sometimes tries to help people get over their "food prejudices" by reading a list of the odd body parts that are ground into many of the sausages, hot dogs and cold cuts found at the supermarket. "Sometimes, it makes them stop and think," he says. "Most people would rather have a dead squirrel off the road than the lips off a cow."

—ROBERT TOMSHO, June 1993

14. *Domes of Resistance*

Man's fight against baldness rages on many fronts. There are shaved heads, buzz cuts, baseball-cap cover-ups, fuzz from Rogaine and Propecia, hair implants, scalp pulls and toupees.

As these methods flourish, however, the most elegant baldness remedy of all recedes: the comb-over.

So, when ABC newsman Sam Donaldson stands up on the White House lawn, or New Mexico State University's basketball coach, Lou Henson, paces courtside, viewers might not realize it, but on display is the fading glory of the well-coiffed balding man.

"Twenty years ago, of the guys who were balding, I'd say 50 percent combed over," says Sal Cecala, who has long manned the corner chair at Chicago's Civic Opera Salon. "Now," he adds wistfully, "it's one percent."

Oh sure, some will say good riddance to the comb-over, calling it a ridiculous act of self-deception. But actually, the tasteful comb-over—subtly moving hair from where it is abundant to where it no longer grows—is a remarkable act of self-reliance. No rugs. No plugs. No drugs. Just a man and his comb.

And the great ones are proud to talk about it. "I've always taken a little and done a lot with it," says New Mexico State's Mr. Henson.

Two trips to the NCAA Final Four, and a hairstyle known nationally as the "Lou-Do," attest to that.

"My advice," Mr. Henson says, "to guys like me who are losing a little: Wash it, blow it dry. Use a fine-tooth comb and comb it and wrap it around. And then spray it."

Though on the trailing edge of fashion, the comb-over remains unbeatable in its versatility. The classic side-to-side comb-over covers everything from a high forehead to a stark-naked crown. Front-to-back covers the so-called monk's patch. Back-to-front softens a widow's peak. And most impressive of all is the U-turn, such as Mr. Henson's, starting above or behind one ear, sweeping out over the forehead and veering back toward the opposite ear.

Give the U-turn a little lift in front and it achieves a spectacular rings-of-Saturn effect. "I'm covering nine miles of scalp with six miles of hair," boasts late-night television host Tom Snyder.

Julius Caesar ruled the Roman Empire with a back-to-front comb-over, and in his later years added a wreath. "The historical version of the baseball cap," says Thomas F. Cash, a psychology professor at Old Dominion University in Norfolk, Va. And when Napoleon Bonaparte's hair met its Waterloo, the French emperor, too, reached for his comb, Dr. Cash says.

Why not glory in baldness? That's easy for guys with lots of hair to say. Hair loss through the ages has been hurtful to self-esteem. A full head of hair is symbolic of youthful virility. Yet about half of all men thin out on top. Thus, the urge to comb over. "Thirty to 40 years ago, what was the alternative? Nothing," Dr. Cash says.

When America's fighting men came home from World War II, and their hair began to thin, peace and prosperity gave them time to raise the comb-over to new heights. Little noticed among the long-hair hippies of the day, the comb-over reached its zenith with the 1968 release of the Mel Brooks movie *The Producers*.

In it, Zero Mostel plays Max Bialystock, a washed-up Broadway producer whose hair, in the opening scene, snakes out from behind an ear and clings to his scalp like a rotten banana peel. It says: Max has hit bottom. But as Max's fortunes improve, his hair miraculously grows into a seamless, even sexy, comb-over.

A comb-over "shows ingenuity and character," Mr. Brooks, the director, says. "Zero had a lot of hair, but it was all behind his ear. It took an extra hour every day to get Zero's hair from the back to the front."

The style remains popular in Congress, where good fashion sense always comes first. "We have quite a few," says Nurney Mason, a 15-year veteran of the House of Representatives barber shop. For thinning men considering a move to comb-over, Mr. Mason has this advice: "It's easier to do with straight hair. You can stretch it further. And spray is very good because, wherever you put [the hair], it will stay right there for the entire day."

Using hair spray is a sign of a man who has made peace with his comb-over. Those who don't spray risk the fallen comb-over—long locks of thin hair hanging about the shoulder.

Choice of spray is important, too. Women's aerosol hair sprays, used by about 80 percent of men who use a spray, come out of the can like gangbusters and can blow a carefully built comb-over right off a man's head, warns Mike Puican, director of marketing at Alberto Culver Co. His company's Consort men's hair spray "just kind of falls on your hair," Mr. Puican says. "We've tested a lot of spray rates."

Former Buffalo Bills quarterback Jim Kelly could've been the man to take the comb-over into the 21st century. Thinning on top, in 1994 he began to "slick it back" in a way that, quite unintentionally, partly hid his bald spot. "I wasn't doing it to cover up," he says. But it went over well. "People told me it looked good," Mr. Kelly says. With time, it could have become an honest and intentional comb-over—the best kind.

But Pharmacia & Upjohn Inc., the maker of Rogaine, would have none of that. "The company came to me," Mr. Kelly makes clear. They offered him money to use Rogaine and be one of its spokesmen. "And I said, why not? It's definitely working," Mr. Kelly reports.

Propecia, a Merck & Co. pill used in larger doses (and called Proscar) to treat prostate enlargement, is in smaller doses applied to kill the comb-over. Merck is proving that hair means a lot to a guy. About 3.8 percent of men using Propecia in a study reported some sort of sexual dysfunction. But maybe that's not such a big deal: 9 percent of men in a Pharmacia & Upjohn survey said they would consider using a baldness treatment that results in impotence.

Yet even inside Merck, the comb-over endures. Its chairman and chief executive officer, Raymond V. Gilmartin, sports what appears to be a classic side-to-side comb-over. His public-relations assistants wouldn't pass along to Mr. Gilmartin a request to talk about his hair.

Once a comb-over, always a comb-over? For public figures known to be thinning on top, the sudden appearance of a full head of hair would be implausible. Could that explain the speculation in Washington that ABC's Mr. Donaldson, whose hair does a U-turn dip over his forehead, wears a piece? "If it's a piece, it's a comb-over piece," John T. Capps III, a Morehead City, N.C., printer and founder of Bald Headed Men of America, observes admiringly.

"People have been making fun of my hair for years," says Mr. Donaldson, who prefers to keep the world guessing.

—JEFF BAILEY, September 1998

15. *The Agonies of Miss Ag*

CHICAGO—The queen of the cows is the very model of a farmer's daughter. "Heavens," she says with a sigh, "I'm the fifth generation to milk Guernsey cows on this farm."

The princess of pork, in her pigskin sash, has equally impressive lineage. "But most people in urban areas don't know about farming," she laments, "because not even their grandparents grew up on farms."

The queen of honey—a beekeeper whose name, Melissa, means "honeybee" in Greek—says she has dreamed of winning her royal title since she was "an itty-bitty girl."

But now these young women—the National Guernsey Queen, the National Pork Queen and the American Honey Queen—have a chance for still greater celebrity. They are in the big city today to vie against seven other farm-belt finalists for a comprehensive crown: the title of Miss Agriculture.

The contest is a first. Followers of the many and various commodity queens have long felt there needed to be a showdown among them, a way to determine which of the rural royalty shall truly reign. Now, in a competition jointly promoted by 12 farm magazines, more than 45,000 farmers have cast the ballots that narrowed the field to these ten pretenders to the throne.

Unlike those eliminated—including an egg queen, a wheat queen and a corn queen—most of the finalists had big promotional campaigns behind them. Sweet-potato farmers unearthed support for the Louisiana Yambilee Queen. Sheepherders rounded up enough votes to land two of their own in the finals, the Lamb and Wool queens of both Pennsylvania and North Dakota.

Each finalist carries her title with a fetching, down-on-the-farm wholesomeness. But beauty isn't the issue here, say the contest's sponsors, and there will be no parading around in bathing suits.

Rather, in the two days of intense competition that will end when the winner is named tomorrow night, contestants will be judged on their knowledge of agriculture. The princesses will give speeches on the product they represent and then hold conversations with one another, while five judges observe to see who best articulates the farm spirit. "They want the queen of the queens," says Susan Gesling, 19, whose title is Maryland Dairy Princess.

After the contest, part of which will later be televised on a syndicated show called the *U.S. Farm Report,* the winner will go to Washington for a reception with Agriculture Secretary John Block on Tuesday—National Agriculture Day. Then she will travel the country as spokeswoman for agriculture, earning an expected $15,000 in speaking fees.

The finalists all seem, so to speak, sprouted from the same stalk. They share a rural idealism that sets them apart from their city sisters. "What's agriculture?" asks North Dakota Lamb and Wool Queen Debra Bredahl, 18. "It's the beauty of the land and the sight of a full table. It's the people working side by side. It's more than cows and plows: It's a way of life."

They are unabashedly patriotic. "I hope there's always room in this country for small family farmers because they built America," says Guernsey Queen Angee Mohr, 19.

They also seem defensive about farmers' image. Their fathers aren't pitchfork carriers in grimy overalls, they stress. And they often add that city people ought to stop complaining about food prices or about "freeloading farmers" who harvest government subsidies. "People don't realize the expense and investment involved," says the National Pork Queen, 20-year-old Julie Unverfehrt. "They don't appreciate what a bargain food is in America. They don't understand the risks a farmer takes."

Ohio Queen of Beef Valerie Parks, 20, snaps, "People shouldn't gripe with their mouths full."

But though these earnest young women are champions of the farm belt, they realize that city people often aren't sure what to make of them, in their rhinestone crowns and livestock-skin sashes. "Some people think I'm bizarre," admits Melissa Hart, the 20-year-old Honey Queen.

Each has endured a measure of ribbing. Miss Hart says crowds at parades buzz like bees when she rides by. Wherever the Ohio Queen of Beef goes she hears the line from the Wendy's hamburger ad: "Where's the beef?" And the National Pork Queen is often called Miss Piggy, though she is far more svelte than that zaftig Muppet. "People expect a pork queen to be large and overweight," she says. "They don't realize that the fat content in pork has decreased 50 percent since 1955 through improved genetics and selection."

Some queens, though, are from places more attuned to the idea of agricultural royalty. In Louisiana communities, more than 100 young women reign over such commodities as strawberries, rice, sugar cane, shrimp—even petroleum. The state's Yambilee Queen, Kristina Bordelon, 19, says she has befriended many of the others at festivals where they appeared together. Several tutored her in the fine points of their special crop or critter to prepare her for this weekend's contest.

These Louisiana women share some common frustrations. "All the queens down here have problems with their crowns," Miss Bordelon says. Some crowns are so bulky "you get a dent in your head and a migraine headache," she says.

Another burden of nobility Miss Bordelon has borne is having to promote yam-eating by example. "I'd have these sweet-potato pies," she says, "and people wouldn't eat a piece until I ate one first. I must have gained 12 pounds. I looked like an ox."

She has since shed the pounds. And after a year of glorifying Louisiana yams ("the Cadillac of sweet potatoes"), she says she is well suited to represent, if not consume, all the bounty in Miss Agriculture's cornucopia.

The other nine finalists say they are equally willing to forget loyalties to the product that got them where they are. "Miss Agriculture can't favor her original industry," the Guernsey Queen says solemnly.

Still, some feel an almost spiritual link to their commodity. Melissa Hart, the Honey Queen, says her father's happening to give her a name that means "honeybee" was the greatest coincidence of her life.

As the competition gets under way in a Chicago hotel today, several of the finalists are planning to bolster their chances with props. Expect anything, they say, from bees to sides of beef. The queen of Guernsey cows, Miss Mohr, jokes that her show-and-tell routine will feature her teeth—Hollywood white from all the milk she drinks.

Pennsylvania Potato Queen Tammy Zimmerman, 19, has brought along a three-foot-tall walking potato in a black top hat. "It's my six-year-old nephew," she says. "I made him the costume and he has gone everywhere with me."

The finalists also have been sizing up the competition. They have read one another's resumes, each brimming with 4-H achievements and Future Farmers of America awards. And even though beauty isn't supposed to be a factor, the young women say they are realistic, and they have studied one another's pictures, too. "She's a darling," one says of another contestant. "But hopefully she won't know too much or speak too well."

One thing they all have is poise. Several first won farm-queen contests as peppy and determined young girls. Their titles took them out of the pastures and into the spotlight, molding them into experienced public speakers. Now, five are majoring in agriculture communications at college.

They also have acquired certain more-specialized skills that a future Miss Agriculture might need. For example, Miss Mohr, the Guernsey Queen, has learned she must speak loudly and energetically when she addresses farmers at evening gatherings. "They get up so early that if you aren't saying something they want to hear, they'll nod off," she says.

And the reigning milkmaid has found a special way to introduce urbanites to life in the barnyard. At shopping-mall promotions, she doesn't just shake the hands of city folks. "I milk their fingers like I'd milk a cow," she says, "just to give them the feel of what it's like."

—JEFFREY ZASLOW, March 1984

16. *And the Winner for Placing the Most Bras Is . . .*

Tom Hanks is still mulling it over, but the Hush Puppies people are hopeful. They have a pair of custom-made shoes they want him to wear on Monday night when he picks up his Oscar as best actor, if he wins one. They are breathable black, brushed-pigskin oxfords like the ones Forrest Gump wore in the movie.

The 67th annual Academy Awards have Hollywood in suspense. What the winners will be wearing has fashion designers in a dither. This is the biggest photo opportunity of the year for them. Getting winners and the luminaries who present awards to wear their threads has been on their minds for many months.

Designers and garment manufacturers have been badgering nominees and presenters. For the past week, the faxes and media advisories have been flying thick and fast with news of each new conquest.

"Sharon Stone is confirmed," exults Valentino's publicist, Carlos Souza, spreading the word that the actress will wear one of the Italian couturier's designs. Gianni Versace, who uses Madonna in his print ads, says he has lined up best-actor nominee Morgan Freeman and *Pulp Fiction* director Quentin Tarantino, not to mention the perennial front-row sitter Sylvester Stallone, one of whose girlfriends was a Versace model.

Calvin Klein's obsessions are Mr. Hanks (above the shoes) and best-actress nominee Jessica Lange, both of whom have indicated they will be wearing their Calvins. So will supporting-actor nominee Samuel L. Jackson. But there is a contest still in progress for John Travolta, who is also up for best actor, and Uma Thurman, a supporting-actress nominee. Mr. Klein wants them, but so does Giorgio Armani, and the actors, so far, are noncommittal. And sometimes actors don't even show up in what they have promised to wear.

Otherwise solidly in the Armani column are the show's host, David Letterman, and best-actress nominee Jodie Foster.

As designers fly in on their own dime to supervise final fittings, Hollywood is snickering about all the inducements the luminescent ones get to wear what they wear. It's a given that the biggest stars get their gowns and tuxes free, and that the lesser lights will be returning loaners on Tuesday.

And if free stuff isn't motivating enough, purveyors sometimes play to a star's kind heart. Should Mr. Hanks wear those custom-made Hush Puppies—and he hasn't promised that he will—the manufacturer, Wolverine Worldwide Inc., will make a donation, the size of which it won't discuss, to his favorite charity.

The official line from the big fashion houses is that they don't have to stoop too low, certainly not so low as to offer rumored cash payments or gifts of year-round wardrobes. What the stars choose, designers wish us to believe, is "a friendship" thing. "Calvin has always been associated with the stars," says Mr. Klein's spokeswoman. And, from Armani's spokesman in Milan: "Armani is very much against the idea of buying stars."

But the backstage hustling proceeds shamelessly. *True Lies* star and Oscar presenter Jamie Lee Curtis says she had at least a dozen requests from designers this year. "I'm amused to receive the attention," she says. But she thinks the fashion gab distracts people from the achievement awards. "The first thing the media ask you is, 'Whose dress are you wearing?'"

Ms. Curtis turned down the blandishments, having already taken a free gown from Pamela Dennis, the Seventh Avenue designer who sells her most of her clothes. For her, it is a "professional friendship" thing.

Dressing the stars may shine a klieg light on designers' egos, but they say the buzz doesn't always do much for the bottom line. "The publicity I've gotten hasn't translated into dollars," insists Vera Wang, who in past years has dressed Sharon Stone and Marisa Tomei.

This year, Ms. Wang made Holly Hunter's Oscar gown for the second year in a row. Ms. Wang figures the dress cost her at least

$25,000. She will use some of the design touches in her ready-to-wear line.

Last December, the Donna Karan organization made its pitch to dress *Forrest Gump* producer Steve Tisch. "They made it very clear to me that, if we were to be nominated, they wanted to dress me. . . . I was really flattered," Mr. Tisch recalls. He got a free tux to wear to the recent Golden Globe Awards and a different one for the Oscars. And Ms. Karan gave his girlfriend, Jamie Alexander, two free dresses, including a spectacular six-kilo beaded number for Monday night.

"I'm trying to get up the courage to ask Donna for a suit for my niece's bat mitzvah next month," Mr. Tisch jokes.

By Valentine's Day, when the Oscar nominations were announced, the promotional pace picked up. Angela Bassett (a best-actress nominee last year for *What's Love Got to Do with It?*) read the names of this year's nominees in a red pantsuit by Escada. This fashion factoid got at least six media mentions. Ms. Bassett wore Escada at last year's Oscars, too.

"We just love Angela. We've gotten advertising that money can't buy," says Sandy Graham, Escada's New York publicist. She says this year Escada's design team sent all nominees a wooden box sealed with wax containing sketches of gowns and a handwritten note: "We would love the opportunity to dress you." Valentino sent all the actress nominees congratulatory bouquets, accompanied by notes offering couture gowns.

If some fashion designers are coy about seeming to be publicity-hungry, that is hardly true of the diamond trade. "The Oscars are a marvelous public-relations opportunity," says Cri Cri Solak-Eastin, the West Coast supervisor of the Diamond Information Center. The trade group has gathered some $25 million in diamonds from Harry Winston and Van Cleef & Arpels that will be lent to stars for Oscar night. Mr. Tisch got a free .4-carat diamond stud for his bow tie. In 1989, the diamond people gave Jack Nicholson a bat-shaped stud because of his role as the Joker in *Batman*.

But that Liz Taylor dripping-in-diamonds feeling will be fleeting for most. The diamond people and their security guards will be there at evening's end to take back their gems. Says Ms. Solak-Eastin: "It's kind of like Cinderella—you turn into a pumpkin."

—TERI AGINS, March 1995

17. Men in Brown

People at Nike got a bit suspicious when professional runner Lynn Jennings started ordering new sneakers every week, always asking that they be sent UPS.

As it turns out, it wasn't the shoes she really wanted. It was Dave Hill, her UPS man.

"He looked like Kevin Costner in brown," she sighs, recalling their long talks on the doorstep.

Four years—and hundreds of packages—later, Dave and Lynn are husband and wife.

"I'm the woman who finally ran away with the UPS man," she says.

Not that others haven't tried. UPS men—the humble couriers in tight brown polyester uniforms driving clunky package trucks—have become sex objects of the service world.

Brown-collar fantasies have spilled over into books, plays, television shows and rock songs. In the new movie Boys on the Side, Drew Barrymore's character remarks on the sex appeal of men in uniforms—"especially UPS uniforms." A tune called "Drive by Love," performed by the Bobs, a California pop group, describes a romance between a UPS driver and a Fotomat clerk and has this refrain: "I can't get that driver out of my head. He honks his horn and my face turns red."

UPS, officially known as United Parcel Service of America Inc., gets frequent requests at its Atlanta headquarters to license deliveryman calendars, including one that was to be called "The Buns of UPS." The company turns them down but doesn't mind that people find its deliverymen cute. (About 93 percent of its deliverers are men.) UPS has used sex appeal in its advertising: One of its TV commercials has several businesswomen rhapsodizing about Bob, their UPS man. "Tall, dark and handsome," says one. "He's got brown eyes," whispers a second. A third admits: "I think I have a crush on him."

Even the company's phone number is provocative: 1-800-PICK-UPS.

So what's the attraction? UPS men do have to be in sort of good shape to deliver more than 200 packages a day. And they are unattainable, always on the run. For a few women, the allure is more basic: "He's the only man I see here every day," says Michelle Ryals, a shipping manager at Santa Fe Jewelers in Santa Fe, N.M.

Competitors ask what UPS has that they don't have. Federal Express Corp. insists its drivers are much more stylish than the men of UPS. "Sure, I guess those guys are attractive if you like big sweaty guys in brown shirts," says a Federal Express spokesman, but Federal Express drivers look far more "presentable in pressed white and navy."

Female Federal Express couriers have been objects of sexual interest, too. Patti Anderson, a Federal Express courier in New Jersey, says she has received flowers on the windshield of her delivery truck and has been propositioned by dock workers—none of which particularly bothers her.

Ms. Anderson herself admits to wanting to run off with the UPS man on her former route. And such fantasies are widespread. Just ask Sumita Sinha, a Washington attorney. She recalls that as a teenager working at her mother's store in Morgantown, W.Va., she and a friend would wait every morning at 11 for the UPS man—a tan, blond, muscular hunk.

"We scheduled our whole morning around it," she says. "He looked so cool in the uniform, and he always rolled his sleeves up so his muscles would show. He talked a little bit, but never too long."

Karen Canavan, a 29-year-old marketing executive in Atlanta, first observed the UPS effect as a student at Georgia Southern University, where the campus UPS man was the talk of her friends. "We would all just stop and watch him jump in and out of his truck," she says. More recently, Ms. Canavan says, she has taken a liking to a UPS man who works out at her gym.

Rose Davadino, an office manager at Bragman Nyman Cafarelli, a Beverly Hills, Calif., public-relations agency, says she and a man in her office rush to the front desk in the morning to catch a glimpse of their UPS man, Frank. Similarly, Philip Brenton, a buyer at IF, a Manhattan boutique, says he and his saleswomen have developed a special bond with their UPS man, Rene. "We love to talk dirty to him," he says.

The highly charged atmosphere makes some drivers uncomfortable. Scott Serpa, a 17-year veteran driver in Seattle, says he recently had to change routes after a woman started coming on too strong. "I kept telling her I'm married."

George Kieffer, a driver in Denver, says he is all for spending time with customers—but there is a limit. "It can be a pain in the neck," he says. "They're customers, so you can't really be rude. But it's like we're a listening post. Women go on about their hair, and problems with their boyfriend, and their bodies."

Still, many drivers say they do like to play along, so long as they can make their delivery quotas.

That sense of purpose, that devotion to duty, may be one more thing that makes these men sexy. "Here's a man I can count on—even if I can't count on any other men in my life. He meets my needs and then he's gone," says Nan DeMars, a consultant to executive secretaries in Minneapolis. "He's a made-to-order fantasy."

Because UPS men are so reliable, Deanna McKay, an insurance adjuster in Fort Lauderdale, Fla., became quite attached to hers, a tall fellow (6-foot-5) named Jamie Connell. She would call UPS to ask about him whenever he failed to show up. Now, she calls him at home. "The replacement guys are nice, but they're not Jamie," says Ms. McKay, who has an enlarged photograph of him on her office wall. He is flattered by the attention.

Sharyn Wolf, a New York psychotherapist and author of the book *Guerrilla Dating Tactics,* has some special insight into the phenomenon: She grew particularly fond of her previous UPS man, Tony, and has started warming to the new guy, John. Her mother is also a professed UPS lover, recently describing a "spiritual connection" to her deliveryman in Florida.

"Maybe it's genetic," jokes Ms. Wolf, the therapist. "But there's that moment, when he's handing you the package, and you're both holding it . . . It's very meaningful."

Especially for home-shoppers. In a recent episode of the CBS sitcom *Dave's World,* a mother and daughter both were having affairs with their UPS drivers. "You know what a big catalog shopper I am," said the mother, played by Florence Henderson.

Whatever the animal magnetism a UPS man might possess, the uniform seems to be a big part of the appeal. Jeff Sonnenfeld, a professor at Emory University and consultant to UPS who drove for the company as part of his research, dons his UPS browns a couple of times a semester to make points about corporate image-making. He says students invariably then flock to him after class and in the hallways to compliment the outfit.

"Some of them ask me to wear it the rest of the year," he says. "Believe me, I've thought about it."

—ROBERT FRANK, February 1995

18. *Poetic Justice*

> Should the state make proclamation
> Of a Poet's Day creation
> Is the latest burning question of the day.
> Or, is poetry worth a penny
> In the daily lives of many
> Is a means of putting it
> Another way.
>   [Esther York Burkholder]

And that pretty well sums up the situation. Gov. Ronald Reagan of California is refusing to declare next Monday Poetry Day in his state, and so the poets have asked Californians to inundate the governor with pennies to finance an official proclamation.

It all sounds rather silly, except the poets insist they are serious, and they are making veiled threats of Poet Power at the polls. The governor is serious, too, and he is refusing to yield. And so nearly every poet in the state—the number has been wildly overestimated at up to two million—is sending off a penny and a poem in protest.

It could only happen in California.

> Dear Guv—
> Relent, old boy!
> This fabulous day
> Poetry must have its way!
>   [Goldpan Gus Garretson]

The Guv insists he has nothing special against poets. Rather, he is just against proclamations. He stopped issuing all official proclamations in 1970 as part of his well-publicized economy-in-government drive. A spokesman for the governor says that in 1969 Mr. Reagan signed 192 proclamations proclaiming everything from Welded Products Month to California Wheelchair Games Day. "The cost to the already overburdened taxpayers" was $2,815.12, the spokesman adds. What's more, it takes at least a half dozen bureaucrats to research, type and produce each scroll, he says.

That works out to about $14 and six bureaucrats per proclamation, and the poets thus are asking for pennies to pay for all this and thus avoid further burdens on the already overburdened taxpayers. But the governor isn't being swayed by either the pennies or the accompanying poems, most of which have a simple message. Like:

> To the Governor:
> Here's a penny.
> Please bestow it
> On the long-neglected poet.
>   [Pegasus Buchanan]

The idea of pennies for poetry originated with Scholer Bangs, an editor of an industrial magazine and a part-time poet, and other poets quickly took up the cause. "We would hope the governor would take into account the importance of poetry in California, where one out of every five published poems in the U.S. originates," says Charles Welch, a school principal in Chula Vista and president of the California Federation of Chaparral Poets. "A proclamation is an acknowledgment that poetry exists, that it has meaning in human life," he adds.

For the past three years, the governor has sent along letters saluting Poetry Day, without proclaiming it. But the poets want more than a salute this year. "That just says 'good luck' and 'bully for you,' but it isn't *significant* enough," says Mr. Welch. "For too long, we poets have had the image of being ineffectual and unconcerned with the realities of the world around us, but then when we speak out people think we're some kind of nuts."

So the poets will settle for nothing less than a proclamation. Here's how a Beverly Hills cocktail waitress–poet puts it:

> Pennies flooding, bright and fair;
> Flowing in from everywhere;
> Show our Governor the way
> To once again proclaim the day

And urge that all be made aware
Of Poets' words and all they say.
[Maria Martinez]

An implication of possible political reprisal comes from poetry federation officials in a stream of statements. Mr. Bangs, for example, insists that a proclamation wouldn't be a trade-off for poets' votes in next month's election to decide the fate of a Reagan-backed tax plan. And the very denial, of course, could be interpreted to mean that poets would consider a trade-off.

Frances Clark Handler of Miami Beach, who heads the national Poetry Day committee, is aghast at the California uprising. (Governors in four other states also have refused to proclaim Poetry Day, but poets there don't seem to care.) "This doesn't do poetry any good," she says. "It's just a bunch of little gray-haired ladies who want a proclamation to show off at their little teas."

In other words:

A proclamation, to a writer,
Shouldn't cause a major fight. A
Proclamation's aimed to please
Sneakered ladies at their teas.
[Anon]

—STEPHEN J. SANSWEET, October 1973

19. *Hair Wars*

DETROIT—The city that gave the world tail fins and the Supremes is suddenly giving it something else.

A new definition of Big Hair.

Consider the contribution of Willie Robinson. Competing in one of a recent spate of hair-styling competitions, Mr. Robinson, a local stylist, paraded on stage with his model. She was perhaps 5-foot-2. Her hair was perhaps 2-foot-5, and bound together by a zipper. It swooped upward in a towering wave known as a French roll.

Then Mr. Robinson unzipped the 'do. He retrieved, from within, a live, four-foot python; last time it was two white doves, and a bottle of champagne with two glasses.

Explains the 39-year-old Mr. Robinson in classic understatement: "You have to do different things to entertain the crowd."

Michael Turner, another Detroiter, was unfazed. At the same event, he introduced the world to the "Hairy Copter." His model sported a style that, with the aid of tiny battery-powered motors, included flashing lights and miniature rotating helicopter blades. Mr. Turner's creations have earned him the nickname "Mr. Motor Hair."

The catalyst for this burst of hirsute ingenuity is "hair wars," a series of hair-fashion shows set to music and aimed squarely at the nation's 31 million African Americans. "There are two powerful circuits in the African-American community—the church and the hair salon," says David Humphries, 39, a local disk jockey who cooked up the idea as a night club gimmick ten years ago.

From a local lark, the genre, also known as fantasy hair, has tumbled across the urban landscape like Rapunzel's locks, making Mr. Humphries a kind of Henry Ford of the hair set. Competitions have sprouted in Los Angeles; Columbus, Ohio; and Flint, Mich. Next year, Miami, Dallas, New York, Atlanta, Washington, Chicago—and Tokyo—are all expected to join the hair-wars fray.

These are contests with no formal winners or prizes beyond the oohs and ahs of audiences, which sometimes number in the thousands. The shows are meant to be fun and campy, though they have a commercial side as well. Salons and hair-product concerns often underwrite them, and use the events to promote new products and their hair artistry. The bottom line, however, is pushing hair design to the outer limits. "In hair wars, anything goes," says Karl Reed, 35 and owner of the Utopia Salon in Southfield, Mich., who has participated in a number of the contests.

To see what Mr. Reed means, consider the recent scene at the

Plaza Hotel in suburban Detroit, where Motown's fantasy-hair stars are matching wits and 'dos with fledgling fantasy-stylists from Chicago. About 300 models, representing some 100 salons or independent designers, are competing. There is definitely a home-court advantage.

African Americans spend an estimated $2 billion a year on hair-care products and services, and Detroit has long been recognized as the nation's black hair capital. The city's 14,400 licensed cosmetologists and 1,742 barbers outnumber the city's social workers, real-estate brokers, builders, dentists or doctors. And that doesn't count the thousands of unlicensed hairdressers working in kitchens and basements around town.

Out of this critical mass comes the fantasy-hair movement, which is making hair the new idiom for hip. Contests aside, the genre is showing up at Detroit clubs, as well as its street corners and even its shopping malls. "This is the new Motown," declares Mr. Humphries, now a full-time hair impresario who travels around promoting the shows. "And you are only as hot as your latest hit hairdo."

In a sprawling room off the Plaza Hotel's lobby, *hot* is among the operative words. Lights glare. Models primp. Stylists frantically comb, tease, lacquer, dye, press, curl and glue hair into unimaginable shapes and positions. Hairspray wafts through the room like a fog. Given the reach of some hairdos, which climb as much as three feet above the scalp, designers often have to supplement the model's hair with hairpieces, some of them real hair, some synthetic.

One woman's burgundy hair peeks out from under a fluorescent purple head wrap that matches her tennis shoes. A dozen women in red, skin-tight, patent-leather halter tops, boots and minishorts stroll through the crowded room. One sports gigantic, swerving spiral curls; others have perpendicular, multicolored, two-foot-long ponytails.

Some of these styles take two days to create. Yet many will be washed out later that night. They are impossible to sleep on and, in the case of Wanda Saxton, "a little too flamboyant for my job." By day, Ms. Saxton, 25, punches data into a computer for a Detroit burglar-alarm concern. Tonight, she is modeling for La Parisian hair salon, wearing a leopard-spot miniskirt and a hairstyle that features a dizzying number of huge barrel curls tumbling off her head in all directions.

By show time, more than 2,000 people are jammed into the ballroom and surrounding halls, fans having paid as much as $20 a person to get in. The audience is very much a part of the scene. Mildred Roper, for example, came all the way from Minneapolis to watch. But the 29-year-old could be a participant, considering the three large horns of hair, bathed in gold sequins, that adorn her coif. Another woman in a lime-green sweater has woven intricate lime-green braids into her hair.

As the models parade down the runway, LaToya Pearson, a hair stylist for 30 years, provides a running commentary laced with rap and rhymes.

"Girl, I didn't come to play—work that runway," exhorts Ms. Pearson, urging a model to keep up her strut. Ms. Pearson describes the 'do as "a ponytail swinging in the air, accented with artistic octopus pin curls."

Next comes the "Flamingo Feather," a style that starts with a bald look in the back. About midway up the head, tiny curls appear. The curls gradually get larger until they flow forward into a feathered, bronze-colored frenzy. "Curl it, twirl it, bake it, shake it," Ms. Pearson chants.

The crowd roars at Ms. Pearson's quips. "That hairstyle is so hot that man over there is just fanning," she gibes. Later, she observes: "Girl, I'm so tired. Last night this man beat on my door all night long. Then, at 7:30 in the morning, I got up—and let him out."

The evening's show stopper turns out to be Raphael Isho, 45, a local stylist, who brings the crowd to its feet with his exotic basketweave look, featuring not only woven hairdos but also matching woven clothing made of hair.

One headpiece frames a model's face, making her resemble a

cobra. On another model, black and yellow hair braids match braids used for a fringe on her sleeves and skirt. Her bikini top and belt are made of hair—pressed to look like leather.

For Ms. Saxton, who is taking all this in, part of the appeal of being in hair shows is seeing the competition. But she is pleased that her profusion of barrel curls also gets lots of applause. "It's one big party and I like all the attention," she says. "I even get recognized on the street."

Among stylists who get lots of attention, Mr. Turner, 31, certainly qualifies. Some thought it would be impossible for him to outdo his "Hairy Copter." But at another show in Los Angeles where the copter got high-fives, he unveiled a style that some think did.

His model walked on stage with a ponytail pulled forward on her head. Mr. Turner grabbed her hair—and spun it around to reveal a whole new 'do.

The trick? Her coif was an ornate wig, styled differently back and front, that rotated along a miniature circular track mounted on her head.

—ANGELO B. HENDERSON, April 1996

20. *Rise Up, Ye Sleeveless Men!*

As scorching heat grips much of the country, the most uncomfortable creatures are the best dressed: big shots wilting under tight collars, neckties and suit jackets, their arms entombed in shirts buttoned snugly at the wrist.

But why pity them? Widely available is a cool alternative: the short-sleeve dress shirt. It can be worn with tie, optional jacket thrown over the shoulder.

Who cares if it is denounced by fashion plates and otherwise shunned? The sartorial arguments against it all boil down to an elitist sleevism.

"Civilized gentlemen do not wear short-sleeve dress shirts," says Derrill Osborn, director of men's clothing for Neiman Marcus, the snooty retailer. Neiman Marcus salespeople, he says, are taught to avoid "everyone they see with a short-sleeve shirt." And customers know better than to ask. "We have no short-sleeve dress shirts at Neiman Marcus. Not one," Mr. Osborn adds.

Despite the superior ventilation and wholesome look of the fashion, short sleeves are seen as hopelessly déclassé, the garb not of executives but of bus drivers, clerks and engineers. Working men, in other words.

Thus, Dilbert of the comic strip wears short sleeves, but billionaire Ross Perot? You must be kidding. Even under their robes, not one of the seven men on the Supreme Court wears short sleeves, according to the court's spokeswoman. Neither does Time Warner's Ted Turner. Nor does Jack Welch of General Electric. Not even Bill Gates. When the software billionaire dresses up at all, a Microsoft spokeswoman says, he is strictly a long-sleeve guy. "And," she adds sternly, "I think that gets him off the hook for being geeky."

Only a brave few in the conformist upper echelons of business dare exercise their right to bare arms. "A shirt and tie is a shirt and tie," says David Topczewski, a Milwaukee trial lawyer defiant about the short sleeves he wears year-round.

Scorn is heaped upon short-sleevers. Charles M. "Mike" Harper spent an enviable career as chief executive officer at ConAgra Inc., then at RJR Nabisco Holdings Corp. But some people recall only his forearms. At 6-foot-6, Mr. Harper is a giant among short-sleevers. He wears his with a tie, summer and winter, with a jacket and without.

At ConAgra, the big food processor in Omaha, Neb., a public-relations woman, Lynn Phares, "unbeknownst to me," Mr. Harper says, had an artist paint in a shirt cuff to show under the CEO's jacket in an annual-report photo. "I guess she was ashamed of me," Mr. Harper says.

Ms. Phares says she did the deed and is unrepentant. Her main regret is that the artist failed to paint a cuff on the other arm, too.

At RJR, the food and tobacco concern, Mr. Harper was invited to a cocktail reception for the company's personnel types. He realized ten minutes into the affair that he was being lampooned: The entire crew showed up in white short-sleeve shirts.

The case for short-sleeve shirts is this: They are air-conditioned, and they are practical. Accessorizing is a breeze. Forget those pretentious cuff links. If you are partial to bow ties, don't let sleeve length stop you. Suspenders? They don't look any sillier with short sleeves than with long. Pocket protectors? It's up to you.

Many short-sleevers work in such comfort they are oblivious to the slights of sleevists. Informed that the combination of short-sleeve shirt and tie is a fashion horror, Charles Ehrlich, a vice president at the Lafayette, Ind., truck-trailer maker Wabash National Corp., responds: "I'll be darned."

Don't be afraid that short sleeves will shorten your career. Wade Fetzer, an investment banker in Chicago for Goldman, Sachs & Co., has been a short-sleeve wearer for 26 years. The fashion statement, he says, puts him "right at home with Midwestern clients." But does he dare wear them on summer visits to Goldman's New York headquarters? "No problem," he says.

The fashion arguments against short sleeves seem just a tad arbitrary. They expose hairy arms, asserts Neiman Marcus's Mr. Osborn, who, with his long handlebar mustache, apparently prefers hair over the lip. They get all wadded up and wrinkled when a suit coat is pulled over them, says Tom Julian, who watches fashion trends for ad agency Fallon McElligott.

Most important, say fashion experts, long sleeves enable gentlemen to "show a little linen" beneath their jacket sleeve. Golly.

Apparel historians say that when gents began wearing suits in the 19th century, they never took them off in public. Shirts were considered underwear to be washed every day; white cuffs showed that the shirts were clean.

Although short-sleeve shirts were around in the 1920s and 1930s, they didn't take hold as business attire until after World War II. But, today, even their purveyors aren't particularly proud of them. Lands' End sells short-sleeve dress shirts in its catalogs but rarely shows them with ties and never with a jacket. Huntington Clothiers, another catalog company, pictures its "half-sleeve" shirt with a tie, but CEO Michael Stern says: "I can't come to its defense. It really is an inappropriate dress shirt."

Hollywood, meanwhile, plays to the ugly stereotypes. Homer Simpson, the hapless Fox Network cartoon character, is a safety engineer at the nuclear power plant in Springfield, U.S.A. His short-sleeve shirt and clip-on tie, says Mike Scully, executive producer of *The Simpsons*, are wardrobe shorthand to declare that Homer is doing "the bare minimum, and is damned proud of it."

Even Homer's wife, Marge, betrays sleevist sentiments. Heading off for a family portrait, she protests to Homer that he shouldn't wear that outfit. Homer's retort: "But Sipowicz does it."

Indeed, Detective Andy Sipowicz on the ABC police drama *NYPD Blue* is the thinking-man's short-sleeve wearer. The show's costume designer buys billowy long-sleeve shirts for actor Dennis Franz and then cuts the sleeves even shorter than the usual. More fleshy arm is revealed. No wonder Detective Sipowicz gets the shapely assistant district attorney.

Off camera, too, Mr. Franz wears short sleeves, with a suit even. And he has Sipowicz-like advice for critics: "Get a life."

Still, there are small signs that the fashion world is coming to its senses. Starting last year, men's fashion shows in the United States and Europe featuring tighter-fitting shirts, pants and jackets, slipped in some short sleeves. A few, egad, with ties.

The ties are mostly the same color as the shirts, sort of a retro gas station–attendant look. Short sleeves "are huge," says Carl Bethencourt, a vice president at Unionbay sportswear in New York. "It's big in the gay community and it's filtering down into the suburbs." With ties? "Still underground," he says.

Last spring, Brooks Brothers stores began carrying patterned and brightly colored short sleeves, and Jarlath Mellett, the chain's design director in New York, has been wearing them himself. "I think anybody can get away with it," he says. Still, short sleeves account for just 4 percent of the company's dress-shirt sales.

When the trend finally does bust out, as it is bound to do, Mitchell Quain, an investment banker at Furman Selz LLC in New York, will be ready. Mr. Quain, an engineer by training, was a happy short-sleeve guy until he arrived on Wall Street 22 years ago. He showed up for his first day of work, at the firm then known as Wertheim & Co., in suit, tie and short sleeves.

His new boss, Bud Morten, marched him across the street to Brooks Brothers and bought Mr. Quain five button-down, white oxford long-sleeve shirts. No more short sleeves for him, not in all these years.

But on hot summer days, Mr. Quain confesses, he feels a certain longing: "I'd love to wear short-sleeve shirts."

—JEFF BAILEY AND ROBERT L. ROSE,
July 1997

21. Men Are from Hardware Stores, Women Are From . . .

I will make a clean breast of it. Once my husband gave me a strainer for Christmas. This revelation staggers gift consultants, who busy themselves at this time of year selecting extravagant baubles for their clients.

To gift experts, the strainer misses on several counts. It is utilitarian. It's cheap. It's not romantic. And it's ugly. Linda Barbanel, a

Manhattan psychotherapist, even sees a hidden message in my strainer. She describes it as a "know your place" present. "I bet he never used it," she astutely observes.

But I am not alone. Once, Sunny Bates received a manhole cover from her husband, Scott Campbell. "He found it on the beach covered with tar," says Ms. Bates, who runs an executive-recruitment firm in Manhattan. "It had my initials on it." That was when they were newlyweds, and as far as gift-giving goes, she says "he hasn't improved over time."

Coaxed to recall presents best forgotten, women have long memories. Gift-giving between couples can backfire in either direction, of course. It's just that women tend to make a big deal out of gifts, and men don't. This can spell tension amid the tinsel.

Ms. Bates's manhole cover was followed, on other festive occasions, by a pickup truck, a front-end loader and a toilet bowl. "He buys me exactly what he wants," she laughs. "I think most men do. He just happens to lust after heavy machinery." Her computer-salesman husband also comes through with books of IOUs: "You know," she explains, "like when you were little and you promised your mother one vacuuming." But she hasn't redeemed many of his coupons. After all, she says, "It was never 'IOU a diamond.'"

Ms. Bates, who says even former boyfriends with impeccable taste always gave her insulting presents, bets that Zsa Zsa Gabor always gets exactly what she wants. "Some women are the kind that always get flowers," she says. "Other women get humidifiers." Long ago she took the advice of a friend and became what she calls "self-basting." When she wants to be lavished with something frivolous or extravagant, she buys it herself.

In some households, the ritual gift exchange is fraught with dark subplots. Bettie Bearden Pardee of Boston, an author and authority on entertaining, now laughs about one "catastrophic" Christmas in her youth that escalated into a sort of Yuletide night of the long knives.

"It was always a bone of contention in our house that my father couldn't carve," Ms. Pardee says. That year, her mother hit upon a solution: She gave him an electric carving knife. Her luckless father—a jokester who had steadfastly resisted learning how to carve—reciprocated with an expensive, bone-handled carving knife. "It was the final blow," Ms. Pardee says. "He was rubbing my mother's face in it, making it easier for her to continue doing something she hated—carve the meat."

Hours later, after what Ms. Pardee calls "the boudoir murmurs," her father came sheepishly to his daughter's room and implored, "Do you have anything in your jewelry box?"

"I was in my early teens," she says. "What would I have that my mother would want?" Instead, she thrust forward a favorite baby doll. "He got this look, and said, 'That could backfire.'"

Not only must a gift impress the recipient, in some circles it must withstand the scrutiny of finicky friends. "It's like show-and-tell," Ms. Pardee says of these post-holiday comparisons. Ruthie Watts, an Atlanta muralist, remembers the time she breathlessly told a friend that her husband had given her a microwave oven for Christmas. "I could see the concrete veil coming down over her eyes," Ms. Watts recalls. "She said, 'I always tell my husband never to give me anything that plugs in.' That's when I knew that one woman's perfume is another woman's poison."

Indeed. When a friend mentioned to New York socialite Mai Hallingby that she had been given a Range Rover by her husband, Ms. Hallingby joked: "That's like getting an electric knife."

Dawn Bryan, author of *The Art and Etiquette of Gift Giving,* says that the hunger for gifts is a "hunger for approval, importance, affection and love." To the extent that women are insecure in these areas, she suggests, gifts assume a loaded significance: "Women are saying, 'I'm of equal value, and you aren't paying.'" Men—probably because they have traditionally enjoyed greater economic status—"don't see gift-giving as so important and vital," she says.

When given gifts they hate, men generally shrug it off and get on with their lives. But they do resent chronic ingratitude. Don Kollmar, a New York therapist, finally broke up with a woman who consistently belittled the expensive jewelry he gave her. "She couldn't receive," he says. "I wound up feeling gypped."

On his tenth wedding anniversary, New York attorney Gerald McMahon raced out during a break in a trial and bought his wife an engagement ring, which he couldn't afford to buy before they were married. "It was a half-carat diamond," he says. "I figure she'll go crazy. She says, 'A half carat after ten years?' I was aghast."

How do men lumber into these minefields? One way is to confuse what a woman needs with what she wants. "It may be congenital," Sunny Bates speculates, "to be able to listen when she says she wants a humidifier and know she really wants maribou slippers."

When she was first married, Kevin White, an interior decorator in Santa Rosa, Calif., came home one Christmas after a long trip. Noting that there was nothing for her under the tree, she inquired about her gift. With great ceremony, her husband led her to her closet.

"My eyes were covered," she recalls. "I thought, this is wonderful—he's never bought me clothes before." But the visions of furs and filmy negligees evaporated when he unveiled the new lighting system he had rigged up for her closet. The next year he gave her a Dustbuster. "I didn't tell anybody," she confesses. "It was like high school—just make something up."

She has mellowed. "He was trying to make my life easier," she says. "When I thought about it that way, it was touching." Besides, she says, "It got better after that—he's moved on to jewelry." Nor are her own gift selections always on the mark. Her husband, an eye surgeon, routinely returns the clothes she buys him. He says he doesn't need them.

The worst gifts, consultants agree, are those that scream thoughtlessness. Author Dawn Bryan remembers that her ex-husband twice gave her expensive pierced earrings. The trouble was, her ears aren't pierced.

Such gifts provide plenty of grist for the therapy mill. Linda Barbanel says she uses gifts to assess "what's cooking" in her patients' relationships. She recalls a patient who had always received silver jewelry from her husband until the year he gave her a plastic barrette purchased from a street vendor. "Her initial reaction was that their relationship was going down the tubes," Ms. Barbanel says, adding that the patient brought the gift in to show her. "It wouldn't stay in her hair," Ms. Barbanel says. "This was an added insult." The patient now can laugh about the incident, Ms. Barbanel says, "but it took a year." The couple has now "settled into middle-aged marriage," she explains.

Sunny Bates may not be a therapist, but she offers a theory about why so many gifts go awry. Men, she contends, learn about gifts from their mothers, and those lessons are cemented for all time. "Think about it," she says. "The boy asks, 'Mommy, what do you want for Christmas?' Now, you don't tell a ten-year-old you want a feather boa. You don't say a ring—you're afraid you might get something made out of Popsicle sticks. So you say, 'Sure honey, those cookie cutters would be swell. Go down to the dry goods store and charge them to my account.'"

—ELLEN GRAHAM, December 1990

CHAPTER THREE

THINGS YOU MIGHT NOT KNOW

22. *The Fat Man Cometh*

NEW YORK—Why wait until the next story about coagulated fat in sewers comes along when you can read this one now?

District Council 37, the municipal employees union, has been putting up posters in the subway lately, praising the "everyday heroes" who work for the City of New York. The posters have pictures of a tree pruner, a museum guard, a dental hygienist. Do the guys who get rid of fat clogs in the sewers rate a picture?

Nah.

"Never got on a poster," George Markovics shouts above the oceanic roar of his jet-flusher truck. He is standing over a manhole in south Brooklyn, looking down. At the bottom of the hole, where raw sewage should be babbling along, a smear of sickly gray goop is blocking the pipe. "I like water, you know, sewers—I love it," yells Mr. Markovics, who works for the Department of Environmental

Protection. Positioning his rig near the hole, he bellows: "We do a lot for the city. We're the best. Hey, watch your back!"

Maybe Mr. Markovics, who is 40 years old, can qualify as a poster boy for the national sewer-fat crisis. America's sewers are in a bad way. Three-quarters are so bunged up that they work at half capacity, causing 40,000 illegal spews a year into open water. Local governments already spend $25 billion a year to keep the sewers running. The Water Infrastructure Network, a coalition of the wastewater-aware, warns that it will cost an additional $20 billion a year for the next 20 years to keep them from falling apart.

Roots, corrosion, cave-ins, bottles, broken stickball bats, rusty car parts—anything will divert sewage on its way to the treatment plant. But the blockages now are almost all wrapped up in fat. The perpetrator is fried food.

Fueled by the fast-food frenzy and an influx of immigrant cooks, America's appetite for eating out has bloated the national output of a viscous goop known as restaurant grease to three billion pounds a year. Where does used grease go? Traditionally, into the cauldrons of the rendering industry, which processes animal castoffs into useful products. But for reasons ranging from Malaysia's palm-oil boom to Mayor Rudolph Giuliani's crackdown on New York's garbage Mafia, more goop than ever is ending up in the sewer.

How it wends its way in—by pipe? by bucket?—is a matter of culinary mystery and governmental mystification. Once the goop arrives, the effect is clearer than mud: Grease and sewage don't mix.

Don Montelli stands over a manhole on another Brooklyn corner—a "notorious grease spot," he says, in front of a Chinese takeout. Mr. Montelli, a high-tech sewer worker, holds a video screen attached by wire to a robot camera down below. "What you're looking at right now," Mr. Montelli explains, "is grease down the sewer."

With colonoscopic clarity, the camera shows a pipe with a drippy coating of fat. Fat won't pollute; it won't corrode or explode. It accretes. Sewer rats love sewer fat; high protein builds their sex drive. Solids stick in fat. Slowly, pipes occlude.

Sewage backs up into basements—or worse, the fat hardens, a chunk breaks off and rides down the pipe until it jams in the machinery of an underground floodgate. That, to use a more digestible metaphor, causes a municipal heart attack.

Fat infarctions have struck of late in Honolulu; Columbus, Ohio; and Lake Placid, N.Y. A grease clot in Cobb County, Ga., recently set off a 600,000 gallon sewage surge into the Chattahoochee River. In January, the U.S. Environmental Protection Agency sued Los Angeles for allowing 2,000 overflows in the past five years; an EPA audit blamed 41 percent of them on fat.

New York's sewers run for 6,437 miles. Waste water and storm water mix in 70 percent of the system. When it rains hard, treatment plants can't cope with the flow, so regulators open and the mess gushes into rivers and bays. On dry days, the gates are supposed to stay closed, and do—except when grease gums up the works.

With 21,000 places serving food, New York gets 5,000 fat-based backups and several big gum-ups a year. Its environmental protectors have fingered greasy-spoon districts as suspects, not just Coney Island and Chinatown, but the area around Carnegie Hall. New York's greasiest sewers, however, lie in the section of the borough of Queens called Flushing.

Flushing is solidly Asian and restaurant-intense. Bouquet of deep-fryer wafts over streets abloom with signage. Crowds push past hole-in-the-wall stalls; fish and vegetable stands build mountains of perishing perishables. So much fat gets flushed in Flushing that last year it blocked the sewers 50 times. Three times at the end of 1999, it locked up floodgates and let raw sewage flush into Flushing River.

"We are subjected to the stench of sewer dirt to the degree that we are throwing up. This is not to laugh!" So said Julia Harrison, to laughs, at a special City Hall sewer-fat hearing. Ms. Harrison is Flushing's City Council member. "Restaurant people have been preached to, given literature, and still plead ignorance," she said. "It's not ignorance. It's up yours!"

"And down ours!" came a shout from the audience.

The city's plumbing code requires "grease-generating establishments" to have grease traps. A grease trap is a box. Greasy water flows into it and slows, letting the grease rise. The water drains into the sewer and the grease stays. The MGM Grand in Las Vegas has five 15,000-gallon grease traps; trucks pump them out. In big cities, traps fit under kitchen floors. They have to be emptied by hand.

Scooping out a grease trap is a job nobody wants to do after dinner. Often, nobody does. When a trap fills, greasy water races through it. A Chinese kitchen with four wok stations needs a 5,000-gallon trap or it may as well have no trap at all. Lots of places, Chinese and otherwise, don't.

Last year, New York kicked off a "Grease Outreach" campaign. A kitchen dragnet uncovered a 73 percent rate of grease-trap abuse. The city cracked down, first in Flushing, with fines of $1,000 a day. "We think we've been effective," says Robert LaGrotta, head of pollution prevention. Except that the sewers are still full of fat.

New York has six grease inspectors for 21,000 restaurants. It asks them all to recycle trap grease, but the city has only one trap-grease recycler. "We thought this was the future," says Livio Forte of A&L Recycling. It wasn't. Trap grease is too watery—expensive to boil down. In a month, A&L collects only 15,000 gallons of it.

Which recycles the question: Where does the grease go? Forget trap grease—it's a drop in the can. Most restaurant grease actually comes from deep-fat fryers. You can't pour gallons of that down the drain. The real issue is: What happens to the deep fat? Mr. LaGrotta admits he's out of his depth. "From my understanding," he says, "it has value, but I'm no expert. Better talk to some people in the business."

A place to start is Darling International Inc., a rendering company whose Web site says, "We are the grease team. We love it. We dream grease. Its color. Its . . . you know . . . greasiness."

"The value on this product is low," says Neil Katchen, who runs Darling's eastern region. "The cost of processing is high. Honestly, I've been in the business 30 years and prices have never been so bad."

Mr. Katchen is talking yellow grease. After Darling centrifuges french-fry particulates out of restaurant grease, yellow grease results. Once, yellow grease was animal fat; now, it's vegetable oil. It goes into animal feed but has uses in paint, face powder and adhesive tape. With oil costs rising, some renderers are burning it.

Yellow grease is an international commodity. On the exchanges, it's up against Brazilian soy oil and Southeast Asian palm oil, not to mention cocoa butter, Borneo tallow, meadowfoam oil and beeswax. Thanks to Third-World plantations, global oil-and-fat output has tripled since 1960 to more than 100 million tons a year. With this great grease glut sending prices ever downward, high-cost old fryer fat can't compete.

A grease pumper like Darling won't collect low-grade grease in New York. Darling gets it from scavengers willing to wrestle five-gallon jugs and 50-gallon drums out of cellars and back alleys.

"My family came here from Europe and got into grease because grease was good business," says Bob Sirocco, who is 42 and one of the grandchildren. His company is called American Byproducts. At 8 p.m., he's been wrestling grease since dawn. The price collapse has upset Mr. Sirocco's traditions: The grandfather paid for old fat; the grandson charges to haul it away.

"We don't charge enough," he says. "Maybe $30 a month." But his customers are in revolt. They don't have to hire grease collectors, so why should they? "They just, ah, do with the grease whatever they do with it," says Mr. Sirocco. "It's something I don't pursue."

This is where the Mafia comes in.

A grease disposal trick, restaurant people say, is to freeze it in plastic and chuck it into the garbage. Problem one: In summer, it melts all over the sidewalk.

Problem two: In 1996, Mayor Giuliani broke the cartels that fixed prices on garbage pickups. "One of the things they did," the mayor told the press at the time, "was to beat people up, bust their kneecaps and kill them." The city sent some perps to prison, asked national haulers to take over many routes and clapped a lid on prices.

That took care of the Mafia, not the grease. For pickups, haulers charge restaurants by the cubic yard; for dumping, landfills charge haulers by the ton. That means the profitable garbage is light and fluffy. Grease is heavy and dense—and putrid and sloppy. With prices capped and profits slim, haulers are raising a stink. They won't take the grease.

"No, absolutely not," says Bill Johnson at Waste Services of New York, a company with restaurant routes all around Flushing. "Grease is something we do not want to see in our trucks."

So? Where does it go?

"This is really reprehensible," says John Lagomarsino. "They dump it in the sewer at 1 o'clock in the morning." Mr. Lagomarsino, of J&R Rendering, is Bob Sirocco's cousin and a fellow grease man. "Look in the sewers," he recommends. "You see grease trails going into them. I mean, this is primeval."

Presented with this intelligence, a garbage collector in lower Manhattan drops a can and says, "Here, I'll show you." He walks to a corner sewer and points in. "See. That's grease." The basin is plugged solid. Lots of Flushing's are, too. One, on a restaurant-thick street, is so full even its grate is gunked up, and simple to sample: Sewer grease is gritty yet supple, sticky yet smooth, with hints of putty and beach tar.

"To me," George Markovics is yelling across the open manhole in south Brooklyn, "it's almost a concrete substance."

Mr. Markovics has lowered his flusher hose into the hole. Now he maneuvers its nozzle into the pipe, hits a lever and guns up the water pressure. The nozzle rockets into the blockage. Seconds later, sewage boils out, followed by hunks of fat riding the gusher toward the next floodgate.

"Know what this is from?" Mr. Markovics says as the flow returns to its usual ooze. "This is from good cooking. Good cooking—know what I mean? Whenever I see grease, that's what I think of. Good cooking and good food."

—BARRY NEWMAN, June 2001

23. *Prisons, Guns and Knickers*

To understand how Donald and Winifred Sonner turned a modest business making underwear for incarcerated females into a major force in the gun-cleaning-patch industry, it helps to know that there are no "delicate" cycles in prison laundries.

It was this knowledge that propelled the Sonners' Southern Bloomer Mfg. Co., of Bristol, Tenn., into heavy-duty undergarments for women's prisons and mental institutions.

"They have industrial laundries, and normal panties would just disintegrate," Mrs. Sonner explains. "So we started making them out of heavy 5.3-ounce knitted cotton, and they caught on pretty good."

But so did cheap imports, which the Sonners countered by branching into brassieres, nightshirts, T-shirts and men's garb for the larger inmate. "Our advantage is our range of sizes," says Mrs. Sonner. "We make panties with a 60-inch waist ($18.75 a dozen). Most importers sell bras in sizes 32A to 40C. But we go up to 56J ($52 a dozen)."

They built up a loyal customer base of about 125 prisons and mental facilities, selling roughly 1.2 million garments annually. But as volumes rose, scrap piled up. Roughly 22 percent of the piece of material used to make a pair of underwear ends up as waste. And by the early '80s, Southern Bloomer's landfill bills began to mount. Don Sonner, a 64-year-old who started out as a traveling socks salesman in the '50s, started thinking about recycling.

He tried mulching the scrap into pillow stuffing. No go; as knitted material, it clogged his machines. He mulled. Then one day in 1984, he followed his son, Stephen, into a gun store.

Gun-cleaning patches are squares of cloth, either store-bought or homemade from rags, that are used at the end of a rod with solvent or oil to ream down the inside of a gun barrel to clean and lubricate it. Stephen showed him some. "He's a buff, but I was ignorant of the gun business," Mr. Sonner says. "And when I saw one of those flimsy woven patches they sold that unraveled when you touched them, I said, 'Man, that's what I can do!'"

As gun-cleaning revelations go, it didn't stack up against the mysterious concoction the legendary Frank August Hoppe came up with in the shed behind his house in 1903: Hoppe's Nitro Powder Solvent No. 9—nine being the number of still-secret chemicals that go into each 4-ounce bottle ($4.95). Back then, reaming out barrels corroded by both old black powder and new smokeless powder was an arduous and irksome chore. And his brew eventually put Capt. Hoppe, a Spanish-American war veteran, into the Sporting Goods Hall of Fame—in 1982, 70 years after his death.

While Mr. Sonner doesn't expect to hear from the nominating committee anytime soon, his revelation turned Southern Bloomer around. "Underwear is the bottom of the garment industry and prison underwear is even lower on the totem pole," says Mr. Sonner. "The gun patch? The gun patch is the toilet paper of the gun industry. But it was the answer for us."

He explains his first move into the market. "I made some up in plastic bags with a copy-shop name tag and went to my local Wal-Mart," Mr. Sonner explains. "The manager said if he could sell them for $3.50 a bag, he'd take ten cases. I said, 'How much will you pay?' He said, 'I can pay $2 but I'd like to pay $1.75.' I thought about it and decided to sell them for 95 cents. I knew then that no one could touch me on price."

Soon, while shopping his underwear samples around to prisons, Mr. Sonner was visiting gun stores with the heavy-cotton patch samples. "It got to where I was selling $500 worth of patches a week." One day he stopped at the FBI Academy in Quantico, Va. They said they needed a more abrasive cloth for shotguns. Mr. Sonner made some from collar scraps. A year later, Southern Bloomer had FBI sales nationwide and a new motto: "Manufacturers of Quality Panties & the Finest in Gun Cleaning Patches."

Competitors ignored them. Indeed, the gun patch is such a humble accessory that when asked about sales, a spokesman for Brunswick Corp., the bowling-ball conglomerate that bought out Hoppe's two years ago, responds: "Can I ask you what a gun patch is?" A spokesman for Outer's, a patch seller owned by Blount International Inc., the lumbering-products and chain-saw people, says patch sales are proprietary. Both companies say sales are a minuscule part of their gun-cleaning equipment lines.

But patches are Mr. Sonner's only gun-cleaning product. And by selling cheap and making them out of heavy cotton, he was able to insert himself nicely into the business—especially after Hoppe's and Outer's came out with a polyester patch that costs more and, many gun buffs assert, absorbs less. Hoppe's and Outer's "just stepped aside and let us play through," says Mr. Sonner. "Sometimes small people can do things big people can't do."

One of Southern Bloomer's proudest moments came five years ago when its gun patches were embraced by the Green Berets, after rigorous testing against the patches of competitors.

"On behalf of the U.S. Army's 10th Special Forces Group (Airborne), I would like to extend our thanks for your assistance in deriving high-quality gun-cleaning products for our precision-weapons systems," wrote Staff Sgt. John M. Peterson III, a weapons instructor at Fort Devens, Mass. Southern Bloomer's patches, he said, were the "obvious choice" for cleaning the Green Berets' $5,000 sniper rifles, citing their "accuracy enhancement" qualities.

Mr. Sonner can't say how many patches he sells, but puts total sales of all panties and patches at about $1.5 million. "Our smallest patch runs 3,000 per pound, our biggest about 666 a pound, and I average 5,000 pounds a week," he says. "You figure it out."

He will say that patch sales now outstrip underwear sales 4-to-1, and he ran out of his own scrap long ago and must buy it from others to feed his huge patch-cutting punch presses. Southern Bloomer has 16 employees making patches in a 22,000-square-foot plant that also holds some underwear operations.

Besides the FBI, the Special Forces, the State Department and several other federal agencies he isn't at liberty to disclose, Southern Bloomer patches go to about 7,000 police departments and lots of chain stores.

"These are quality, very good, and they ship on time and are courteous people," says Margaret Savko, a buyer for the Maryland State Police, which uses Southern Bloomer exclusively.

"We do a lot of business around the globe now," Mr. Sonner adds. "We have distributors in Canada, Italy, New Zealand and the United Arab Emirates. But I'll tell you something, I don't know where all these patches go, who the hell uses them all. The Fort Worth police just bought 48,000, same with San Francisco. One account bought $7,000 worth in January. That's a lot of patches."

Southern Bloomer's namesake product, its underwear, continues to adorn female felons, famous and infamous, nationwide. One wearer was Lynette "Squeaky" Fromme, the Charles Manson disciple imprisoned for her 1975 assassination attempt on President Ford. In 1987, she escaped for three days from Alderson Federal Prison in West Virginia wearing Southern Bloomer underwear, Mr. Sonner says proudly. Prison officials can't discount the possibility, but "it's not something we normally document in our escape records," says Richard Russell, a prison spokesman.

—JAMES P. STERBA, April 1999

24. *But Will the Klingons* Understand *Deuteronomy?*

Citing deep philosophical differences with fellow scholars, Glen Proechel has resigned from his Bible-translation group.

"We have very, very different goals," says Prof. Proechel, a language instructor at the University of Minnesota. The rift will result in two translations of the Good Book for a civilization that, until now, has lacked the Word in its own language: the Klingon language.

Klingons, for those who have been off the planet for the past 30 years, are a fictitious alien race from television's *Star Trek* series. Prof. Proechel is now working alone on his Klingon translation, a paraphrase of the New Testament. Rivals are writing a literal translation of the entire Bible.

"It's not going to make any sense," Prof. Proechel says of the literal Klingon version. "It will be describing things that don't exist in their culture."

But Klingon literalists disagree. "You don't mess around with the Bible," even if the warrior-like Klingon vocabulary is void of biblical concepts like mercy and compassion, says Dr. Lawrence Schoen, a linguist overseeing the literalist translation.

Klingons, and *Star Trek*, have been on TV since 1965. But it was in 1984 that a linguist invented an official Klingon language for the movie *Star Trek III: The Search for Spock,* and it has been used in subsequent movies and TV episodes. For reasons that might escape some humans, Klingon has been picked up by avid earthling students, religious and otherwise.

The second annual Interstellar Language School, including a festival of Klingon poetry readings, will take place next month in Minnesota. There are Klingon newsletters, Klingon Internet conversation groups and audio cassettes with titles like "Conversational Klingon" and "Power Klingon." Weddings have been performed in Klingon. An estimated quarter-million copies of the Klingon Dictionary have been sold.

"Klingon is the first artificial language to be adopted by popular culture," says Dr. Schoen, a professor of psycholinguistics at Chestnut Hill College in Philadelphia and founder of the nonprofit Klingon Language Institute. The three-year-old KLI, which claims 750 members, is working on several Klingon projects, including language correspondence courses and translations of all Shakespeare's works. (It will soon publish a Klingon *Hamlet.*)

Speaking Klingon, Dr. Schoen says, "is no more bizarre than sports trivia, or knowing the details of engines of cars that haven't been manufactured in 20 years."

The KLI, based in Flourtown, Pa., is heading the Klingon Bible project, which could take up to five years. It involves ten scholars, led by a graduate of Yale Divinity School. They are getting help from a Lutheran Bible group; far from seeing the project as blasphemous, the group hopes it will draw attention to the challenges of translating the Bible for real people.

The scholars are translating directly into Klingon from Greek and other original biblical languages. Among the hurdles: the fact that the Klingons have no word for "God" or "holy," says Prof. Proechel. Conveying even basic concepts has proven difficult. "Their mode of thought is quite different," he says. "Things that are part and parcel of the Judeo-Christian faith—forgiveness, atonement—don't fit into Klingon thinking." (Klingon thinking does, however, allow for words like "choljaH," a ponytail holder, and "butlh," a phrase meaning "dirt under fingernails.")

Until recently, Prof. Proechel was part of the team, but he has since strayed from the flock. He is working on what he calls a "retelling of the New Testament in the world which the Klingons understand."

Consider the line from Mark "We have five loaves and two fishes." Klingon doesn't have words for loaves or fish. The literal camp uses the Klingon "tIrSoj," which means "grain food," and "bIQHa'DIbah," or "water animal." Prof. Proechel, translating the same sentence using things with which the Klingons are familiar, uses the Klingon "vagh 'Iwchab cha' ghargh wIghaj," meaning, "We have only five blood pies and two serpent worms."

That's where the rift developed. With only 2,000 words in the Klingon vocabulary to chose from, translators often disagree on the Klingon term closest to the meaning of the original. For instance, there are plenty of lambs in the Bible, but none in the Klingon world, so Prof. Proechel uses the word "targh"—a vicious, ugly, piglike animal. "But it is the most important animal to the Klingons, so it gets the message across," he explains.

Literalist scholars object to such substitutions, however in tune with Klingon culture they might be. "A targh bears about as much resemblance to a lamb as a charging rhino does," says Kevin Wilson, general editor of the KLI Bible project.

The Bible has undergone other unorthodox translations, of course. The American Bible Society says it has been translated into 337 of an estimated 6,000 languages and dialects spoken on earth. There are also rap translations, feminist versions, Cajun editions and a multimedia version in an MTV-like format. There are two versions of the Gospels in Esperanto, a turn-of-the-century language whose inventors hoped would become a universal tongue. (It hasn't.)

"A multitude of curious things have been done with Scripture," notes Gerald Studer, president of the International Bible Collectors Society. Mr. Studer has over 5,000 versions of the Bible, including the Gospels written in Liverpool slang, the New Testament supposedly corrected by spirits and the Book of Psalms written on 166 pages of animal skin. He eagerly awaits the Klingon translation.

TV's Klingons may not be particularly articulate, but Klingon's earthly scholars are quite picky about the Klingon language. Like the French government, they are dead set against polluting the alien tongue with earthly borrowings. "We are sort of like the Académie Française," the French agency charged with guarding the purity of French, says Dr. Schoen. "We're doing what we can to keep it pure." When faced with the need for a new Klingon word, translators are encouraged to simply recast the sentence using some of the 2,000 existing words. At last summer's Klingon language camp, for instance, players at a softball game had to work around Klingon's lack of equivalents for "safe" and "out." The solution: "yIn," which is Klingon for "to live," and "Hegh," Klingon for "to die."

Sometimes literalists break their rules. With no good substitute for "lamb," they are quietly using "SIp," Klingonifying the English "sheep."

When things get really desperate, scholars turn to Dr. Marc Okrand, Klingon's creator. Dr. Okrand has studied native American tongues, Chinese and Southeast Asian languages, but says Klingon's "collection of grammatical elements is unique. This is not an earth language."

Officially, the Klingon dictionary is limited to words acquired through interviews with a Klingon prisoner named Maltz captured in the 23rd century, says Dr. Okrand, who works at the National Captioning Institute in Falls Church, Va. But, in a pinch, Dr. Okrand can beam up a few new phrases. "From time to time," admits Dr. Schoen, the Klingon purist, Dr. Okrand "has agreed to review our wish lists and discover new words."

—CARRIE DOLAN, June 1994

25. The Steak Tender, the Soup Positively Rodentine

GUANGZHOU, China—The Cantonese people of south China are legendary for eating anything that moves—and some things that are still moving. The food market here features cats, raccoons, owls, doves and snakes along with bear and tiger's paw, dried deer penis and decomposed monkey skeletons.

Now, this rich culinary tradition, along with rising disposable income in this most prosperous city in China, has inspired kitchen utensil salesman Zhang Guoxun to open what is believed to be China's first restaurant dedicated to serving rat.

That's right: rat. Rat with Chestnut and Duck. Lemon Deep-Fried Rat. Satayed Rat Slices with Vermicelli. In fact, the menu lists 30 different rat dishes, even including Liquored Rat Flambé, along with more mundane dishes such as Hot Pepper Silkworm, Raccoon with Winter Melon, and Sliced Snake and Celery. And in the six months since the doors opened, customers have been scampering in at all hours to the euphemistically named Jialu (Super Deer) Restaurant.

"I was always eating out, but I got bored with the animals that restaurants offered," Mr. Zhang says during an interview over a plate of Black-Bean Rat. "I wanted to open a restaurant with an affordable exotic animal. Then I was walking home one night and a rat ran across in front of me and gave me this idea."

Mr. Zhang's restaurant is as trendy as they come in China. The 15-table, two-story eatery is a mixture of blond wood furniture, stucco walls and wooden lattice laced with plastic vines. Tonight's crowd includes a young couple who stroll in hand-in-hand and nestle in a quiet corner for a romantic rat dinner. Other groups include engineers, office clerks, salesmen and factory workers.

Tonight's special is Braised Rat. Garnished with sprigs of cilantro, the morsels of rat meat are swaddled in crispy rat skin. The first nibble reveals a rubbery texture. But the skin coats one's teeth with a stubborn slime. The result is a bit like old chewing gum covered with Crisco.

But other dishes are better. German Black Pepper Rat Knuckle (rat shoulders, actually; the knuckles are too small) tastes like a musty combination of chicken and pork. The rat soup, with delicate threads of rat meat mixed with thinly sliced potatoes and onions, is surprisingly sweet. Far and away most appealing to the Western palate is Rat Kabob. The skewers of charcoaled rat fillet are enlivened with slices of onion, mushroom and green pepper and served smothered in barbecue sauce on sizzling iron plates that are shaped like cows.

Also on the menu: a Nest of Snake and Rat, Vietnamese Style Rat Hot Pot, a Pair of Rats Wrapped in Lotus Leaves, Salted Rat with Southern Baby Peppers, Salted Cunning Rats, Fresh Lotus Seed Rat Stew, Seven-Color Rat Threads, Dark Green Unicorn Rat—and, of course, Classic Steamed Rat. Generally, the presentation is quite elegant, with some dishes served with lemon slices or scallions forming a border and others with carrots carved into flower shapes.

Experienced rat eaters, however, warn that this is no meat to pig out on. "Watch out," warns Wei Xiuwen, a factory manager eating at an adjacent table. "If you eat too much rat, you get a nosebleed." Several customers take off their shirts halfway through the meal because eating rat, like dog, seems to raise the body temperature for some reason. That's why rat is considered a winter food. In the summer, the restaurant does most of its business during the late-night and early-morning hours, after the weather cools down.

The restaurant is popular—Mr. Zhang claims profits of $2,000 a month—because it brings people back to their roots. The restaurant's cooks, and most customers, are originally from the countryside, where as children they ate air-dried rat meat. "If dried by a north wind, it tastes just like duck," Che Yongcheng, an engineer and regular customer, says wistfully of his favorite childhood snack.

For newcomers, Mr. Zhang has color brochures, featuring a photo of Rat Kabobs alongside a bottle of Napoleon X.O. In both the menu and brochure, the rats are referred to as "super deer" because Mr. Zhang says he wants to separate his fare from the common sewer rats that even Cantonese might find unappetizing. Mr. Zhang says his restaurant serves only free range rats, wild rodents that feed on fruits and vegetables in the mountains a couple of hundred kilometers to the north.

The brochure explains why rats are the health food for the 1990s. It says the rats are rich in 17 amino acids, vitamin E and calcium. Eating them promises to prevent hair loss, revive the male libido, cure premature senility, relieve tension and reduce phlegm. A rat's "liver, gallbladder, fat, brain, head, eye, saliva, bone, skin" are "useful for medical treatment," says the brochure.

The restaurant's basement kitchen is a Dante's Inferno where shirtless cooks sweat over huge woks atop howling gas-fueled stoves that shoot flames five feet in the air. Dozens of fat, ready-to-cook rats are piled in a bamboo basket next to a crust-covered pump that noisily slurps up a small river of scum that runs off the stove and across the floor.

The senior chef is not here tonight. An understudy, Huang Lingtun, clad in rubber sandals and pants rolled up to his knees, explains how the rats are rounded up. They're captured and cleaned by farmers who free-lance as rat bounty hunters. Some smoke the rats out by setting fields on fire and snaring the fleeing rats in nets attached to long bamboo poles. Others string wires across fields to stun unsuspecting rodents with high voltage charges. The rats, each about a half-pound, arrive at the restaurant freshly gutted, beheaded and detailed.

Mr. Zhang says that the traditional recipes on his menu were suggested by Tang Qixin, a farmer honored as a model worker by Mao in 1958 for his prowess as a rat killer. Rat eradication campaigns have been a staple of Chinese life since Mao declared war on the four pests—rats, flies, mosquitoes and bedbugs—in the 1950s.

In 1984, the last Year of the Rat, the government launched an all-out crusade in which an estimated 526 million rats were killed. In 1985, the government tried to maintain the momentum by promoting rat meat as good food, explaining that "rats are better looking than sea slugs and cleaner than chickens and pigs."

Like most successful entrepreneurs during these times of shifting political winds in China, Mr. Zhang is quick to highlight the patriotic nature of his business rather than the personal economic benefits. "I am helping the government by eliminating some pests and helping enrich some farmers," he says.

Mr. Zhang says he's too new to the business to think about a chain of rat restaurants. But he says he's unconcerned about anyone stealing his idea. "My quality is tops," he says, "so I'm not worried about competitors."

—JAMES McGREGOR, May 1991

26. The Sky, Sometimes,
Is Actually Falling

LONDON—Things happen. For instance: In 1980, a shower of peas fell on Trevor Williams in Dan-y-Byrne, Wales.

"I was cleaning out the goldfish bowl in the garden," says Mr. Williams, a gas-station attendant, now retired. "It was a clear day, a beautiful day. I heard this plop, plop. I couldn't make out what was happening. And the next thing I knew, a real good shower of peas came down. Dried peas."

How strange, thought Mr. Williams. He called the local radio station and reported it. The newspapers picked up his story. "All my mates were ringing me up, pulling my leg," Mr. Williams says. "Then this chap phoned from London. I'd had enough of it by then. I cut him short, I did."

The chap was Robert J.M. Rickard, archivist of the unexplained. When things happen, Mr. Rickard takes note.

He took note, a few years ago, of the piles of small stones Peter Lipiatt found on his farm, near Chipping Sodbury. Zoologists said birds couldn't have built them. They discounted furry creatures, too. "The only British mammal that does make small piles of stones," said a scientist at the British Museum, "is the Boy Scout." Mr. Lipiatt, for his part, found comfort in worms.

"If you go out in the night," he says, "they say you can actually see worms wrapping themselves around these stones and moving them. I'd go along with that, though I've never actually seen a worm do it."

But the worm theory didn't satisfy Robert Rickard. Neither did the notion that stones may move and grow and reproduce. "We take no sides," he wrote, chronicling the piles of Chipping Sodbury in a book written with John Michell, a student of the eccentric. Mr. Rickard doesn't explain. He records.

"I think of myself as a clerk, filing all these things away," he says one afternoon in the study of his house on London's eastern edge. "I have no urge to believe in explanations. If something drops out of the sky, I'm not surprised; I'm interested."

Politely, Mr. Rickard stands behind his desk-top computer while he talks with a visitor. The study has one chair and no room for another. Books jam the shelves, floor to ceiling: "Curious Facts," "Impossible Possibilities," "Enigmas," "Oddities." Folders spill from file cabinets and litter the floor with the accumulated evidence of anomalous events: mysterious oozings, freak plagues, invisible barriers, odd clouds, unusual darknesses, phantom smells.

The toad found in a chunk of coal, as reported by the *Times* of London in 1862, stirred Mr. Rickard's interest. So did last year's news that a bald farmer from Wiltshire began to grow hair again after a cow licked his scalp. Mr. Rickard has files on a New Guinea fruit bat that landed in Exeter and a Baltimore oriole that put down in the Isles of Scilly. He is keeping track of the unknown fungus growing on 3,000-year-old elk dung dug out of a Norfolk peat bog.

In case it ever amounts to something, Mr. Rickard has all the details on the rice, custard and mushy peas that recently fell out of a truck on the road from Gloucester to Bristol. He has put that item in the "accidents involving food" folder.

"I've got thousands of these things. The stuff just keeps growing," Mr. Rickard says. "It's crowding me out. It's taking over." He finds a loose clipping about an SHC (spontaneous human combustion) and throws it onto a pile.

Every few months, Robert Rickard rakes together 60,000 words or so of his collected stuff and puts out a magazine. He calls it *Fortean Times,* after Charles Fort, an American who "developed a view of reality," Mr. Rickard has written, "which seemed in his generation to be one of unprecedented craziness."

Mr. Fort, a giant of anomalistics, spent much of his life in the New York Public Library and the British Museum, scouring scientific journals for instances of the inexplicable and noting each on a scrap of paper. He died in 1932, at age 58, from "unspecified weakness," Mr. Rickard says. By then, he had published four volumes of anom-

alies, with 60,000 scraps to spare. Ultimately, Mr. Fort hoped, corre-
lations would emerge between such things as fireballs, alien big cats,
and the simultaneous filing of patents by total strangers.

"Not a bottle of ketchup can fall from a tenement-house fire escape in Harlem," he once said, "without affecting the price of paja-
mas in Jersey City."

In Charles Fort, Robert Rickard found a kindred spirit. Mr.
Rickard, now 40 years old and patchily bearded, was born in Deolali,
India, the source of the English slang word "doolally," which means
"slightly mad." But not until 1968, at school in England, did he come
upon Mr. Fort's opus. "I devoured it again and again," he says.

It was Mr. Fort's open mind that appealed most, exemplified by
his response to the 1890 report of a city appearing in the sky over
Ashland, Ohio. Some said it was the New Jerusalem, others Sandusky.

"May have been a revelation of heaven," Mr. Fort noted, "and for
all I know heaven may resemble Sandusky, and those of us who have
no desire to go to Sandusky may ponder that point."

Starting where Mr. Fort broke off, Mr. Rickard set out to compile
the peculiar. Two journals in America had sympathy, but no space,
for his torrent of oddities. So, in 1973, he launched the *Fortean
Times*. Today, it has a press run of 1,200, and vigilant anomaly spot-
ters in 17 countries, among them Jun-Ichi Takanashi in Japan,
Vladimir Rubtsov in the Soviet Union, and Ray Nelke in Missouri.

Like his idol, Mr. Rickard keeps an open mind. He doesn't buy old
wives' tales, like the one that says lightning never strikes twice in the
same place; it has already struck three times in the Primarda family's
backyard in Taranto, Italy. He doesn't even draw the line at "psychic
dentistry," in which teeth are unaccountably filled. But he doesn't resist scientific truths: When the Shenzhen Wildman turned out to be a
rhesus monkey earlier this year, Mr. Rickard willingly ran a retraction.

The only phenomenon Mr. Rickard does discount is the unsub-
stantiated explanation. He won't print "barefaced assertions" about
ancient astronauts, or the lost city of Atlantis, or remnants of Noah's

ark. The laws of magnetism haven't led him, as they have others, to think he knows why the fourth toe of the right foot of an American woman glowed for 45 minutes in 1869.

"For every expert," Mr. Rickard likes to say, "there is an equal and opposite expert."

The task of sorting genuine explanations from ingenuous ones, and fact from fancy, is complicated by Mr. Rickard's reliance on newspapers for much of his raw material. A respectable paper will reduce a werewolf to a filler. A sensational paper will make a giant earthworm out of a bulge in the road. "The standard of reporting is appalling," Mr. Rickard says. That is why he has a special interest in a more tangible kind of event: things that fall from the sky.

Rocks fall from the sky all the time. (They are called meteors.) A gopher turtle encased in ice came down on Bovington, Miss., in 1894. In 1969, there was a hail of golf balls in Punta Gorda, Fla., and four years later several thousand toads landed on the French village of Brignoles. Mr. Rickard has records of nuts and bolts falling out of the heavens, of nails, cookies, pennies.

Last year there was a fish fall in his own neighborhood, at Ron Langton's house.

"Some newspapers tell lies," Mr. Langton says, opening the front door of his row house in Newham for a newspaper reporter. "One said my lawn was covered with fish. I don't have a lawn."

No, Mr. Langton has a patch of paving stones in his backyard, along with a small vegetable garden and an old refrigerator. On the night of May 27, 1984, four flounders, three whitings and five smelts fell into the yard. Several more hit the roof.

Mr. Langton, a retired oil-burner repairman, was in the upstairs sitting room, watching television with his wife, Ellen. It was raining. "We heard things smacking down," he says. Next morning, they found the fish.

"The only place they could have come from was the sky," Mr. Langton says. "But how could anything of that weight just float up into the sky and come down in our garden?"

"When I was a kid, we had comics about men going to the moon," says Mrs. Langton. "We were told it was a load of bunkum. Well, it's happened, hasn't it? Things do happen, don't they?"

Mr. Langton called a newspaper, and a photographer came. Then Robert Rickard got wind of the fish fall. He visited the scene and carried the evidence to the Natural History Museum. The fish, he was told, were commonly found in the River Thames, two miles from the Langtons' house; they could have been picked up by a waterspout.

Mr. Rickard called the London Weather Center. He called the coast guard. Conditions, they said, were all wrong that night for waterspouts on the Thames. Apart from the easy answer of a prank, that left the bare facts: flounders, whitings and smelts in Ron Langton's backyard.

Mr. Rickard couldn't explain it.

—BARRY NEWMAN, September 1985

27. *The Offal Truth*

NEW YORK—Try this problem. You get this nice water buffalo as a house pet. It's rough getting food for it, and the neighbors are a bit squeamish, but you get by. Then one day your water buffalo comes down with something, and its day of reckoning arrives. Okay, now what do you do? There is no way you're going to stuff a water buffalo down the garbage disposal. And the ASPCA thinks you're kidding.

Here's how to get rid of it. Call the offal truck. The offal truck belongs to the New York Department of Sanitation, and it specializes in hauling away dead animals. Big dead animals. Like camels, water buffalo and whales.

While admittedly, not too many New Yorkers keep camels, water buffalo or whales around the house, disposing of large dead animals is not a trifling issue in the city. Every week, two or three horses drop dead somewhere in New York. With somewhat less frequency, so do hippopotamuses, orangutans, bisons, yaks and all the other assorted beasts that call New York home. "This is New York," says a man in the sanitation department, "so naturally you're always going to have an aardvark or a unicorn calling it quits someplace."

Last year, for instance, the offal truck (offal means animal byproducts) carted away 120 horses, four bears, four lions and a cow. That's about a normal year, give or take a moose and a couple of apes. Whether last year's collection is up or down from four years ago— when the truck scooped up 110 horses, six ponies, five deer, five mules, two camels, two sea lions, an elephant, a bison, a sheep, a wolf and a whale—depends in part on how you weigh, say, four lions and a cow against five mules and a bison.

The offal truck this year has already rounded up a herd of horses, four lions, three bears, three llamas, two calves, a cow, a polar bear, a donkey, a buffalo and a yak. With three months still to go, "it looks like one hell of a year," says a sanitation department man, who notes that "it's not every year that we get a yak."

You might wonder where the sanitation department finds these yaks and other large dead animals. Horses, which account for most of its business, come mainly from private stables, riding academies and Aqueduct racetrack. (Since the truck isn't sent outside the city limits, racetracks in the suburbs depend on private contractors to haul away their dead horses.) The rest of the menagerie comes chiefly from zoos.

Over the years, the offal truck has had to hoist a two-ton hippopotamus out of Prospect Park Zoo, fish a 1,000-pound turtle out of Bowery Bay and scoop a baby whale off the beach at Coney Island. A few years ago, it was called upon to pick up a nine-foot shark that someone apparently forgot at Park Avenue and 150th Street in the Bronx. Just a couple of weeks ago, it was summoned to cart away an ape that somehow ended up in a Brooklyn lot. "So far, nobody's missing it," says a sanitation official. "And it's really difficult to keep an ape around the house without the neighbors talking."

Parked at its station at Pier 70 at East 22nd Street and the East River, New York's—and perhaps the country's—only offal truck looks like a moving van. Light yellow in color, it's roughly nine feet wide, 20 feet deep and 12 feet high. It can hold as many as six horses at a time, and it sets the sanitation department back about $90 a day to operate. Inside is a winch with a steel cable. To pick up an animal, the back door of the truck is lowered, the cable is hooked around the hind legs of the animal and the winch is switched on to hoist the body aboard.

So far, the truck has never encountered an animal that couldn't be hoisted aboard. Elephants, however, have to be sawed in half. And the department figures the day is bound to come when it meets up with a full-grown whale. When that happens, it says, the Coast Guard is just going to have to tow it out and give it an appropriate burial at sea.

After being picked up, animals are taken to Spring Creek Park in Brooklyn, a landfill area where the bodies are buried. Money could be gotten for them at a rendering company, but all of those are outside the city, and the department doesn't consider it worth the trouble. After the animals are dumped, the truck is hosed down and sprayed with a disinfectant so that it smells almost normal again.

Not surprisingly, few sanitation men consider the opportunity to run the offal truck a big break in their lives, especially since the pay is the same $233 a week maximum that garbage collectors get. "It's not for the squeamish," says a sanitation man. "Just about nobody would volunteer to ride the truck."

But Hugh Collins and Andrew Slowe aren't nobodies, and they did volunteer to ride the truck. Formerly garbage collectors, they like the later hours (10 to 6) of offal-truck duty, and they claim that picking up zebras and yaks is a lot less monotonous than picking up tin cans and table scraps, even if it can be a lot smellier. "Boy, do you have to have a strong stomach," says Mr. Collins.

No other city is known to have an offal truck. Most big cities either depend on private contractors to haul away large dead animals or else leave it up to individuals to get rid of them the best they can.

Naturally, the offal truck doesn't hit the road on any old call. Someone always goes out ahead to verify calls, thus guarding against some crank who may ring the sanitation department to report that a dead rhinoceros is knotting up traffic around Seventh Avenue and 33rd Street.

In fact, some woman once called up and said precisely that. After suggesting that the lady have her eyes examined, the department checked it out anyway. Sure enough, it seems the circus had come to Madison Square Garden, and while the animals were parading around the street the time came for one of the big rhinoceroses.

—N. R. KLEINFIELD, October 1972

28. *Carrots, No Schtick*

NEW YORK—This morning we will discuss carrots.

Without carrots, flamingos in zoos would turn white. By eating too many carrots, some men have turned yellow (one turned orange, but he was mixing his carrots with tomato juice). There has never been a conspiracy to drive up the price of carrots (but there once was an onion conspiracy). Craig Claiborne and Dennis the Menace don't like carrots. Julia Child and Bugs Bunny do.

And carrots just might be (but probably aren't) responsible for the wage-price freeze, Phase 2 and all that.

Last things first. On the last consumer price index to be prepared before President Nixon froze wages and prices to fight inflation, carrot prices were the most inflationary of all. At that point, they were selling at 40.5 percent above the year-earlier quotes. Ironically, carrots aren't subject to the current controls—fresh vegetables have been exempt from everything—and now carrots are selling at about 35 percent above a year ago.

So what's up, doc? A conspiracy can be ruled out. "No," says a Department of Agriculture official, "that's not the reason." The reasons, he says, are drought and decreased plantings. Why are there decreased plantings? Because this is a good year for alfalfa and sour clover. Those two crops are rotated with carrots, and this year more farmers opted to go with alfalfa or sour clover than with carrots. Alfalfa and sour clover are not considered by humans as a tasty substitute for carrots.

At any rate, only 62,770 acres of farmland in the United States were turned over to carrots this year, down from 70,900 last year (and a record of 91,170 in 1963, a vintage year for carrots). Moreover, drought sharply cut the yield from the winter harvest in California and Texas, which accounts for more than half of U.S. production. (Carrots are harvested five times a year, but the other harvests didn't offset the winter drop.)

All of this means that carrots now sell for about 30 cents a pound retail in New York supermarkets. At that price, carrots still sell reasonably well.

Why do people eat carrots? the uninformed may ask. Little people eat carrots because big people make them. Carrots contain vitamin A, so parents force them on children to improve the youngsters' eyesight and to help ward off infections of the throat and urinary tract. Many children have noted that while their parents force carrots on them, the parents themselves take their nourishment other ways— such as from olives soaked in martinis. As a result, many children quit eating carrots as soon as they are big enough to drink martinis.

Since many big people don't eat carrots, they are not on the bestseller list at the local greengrocer's. In fact, they rank only ninth in value among the 28 principal vegetables grown commercially in the United States—behind potatoes, tomatoes, lettuce, string beans, sweet corn, onions, cantaloupe and celery. Of the better-known vegetables, in fact, only spinach seems to be less popular, which is understandable.

No less a cook than Craig Claiborne, former food editor of *The New York Times,* is cool toward carrots. Though he has written for the *Times* on "Elegant Endives," "Appetizing Artichokes" and "Ways With Maize," Mr. Claiborne never, to the best of his memory, wrote about carrots. "I stopped eating them some years ago," he says. "I guess that's why I wear glasses."

But Julia Child, the French Chef, is sure more adults would eat carrots if only they knew now to cook them. "Americans boil them in too much water," she says, "and then they throw out the water, which contains the goodness. It's insane." (It's unlikely, however, that she could convert Dennis the Menace. In a recent cartoon, he was saying to his mother, "Aw, you're just sayin' that. There isn't no such thing as CARROT COOKIES! Is there?" Sweat was pouring from his brow.)

Julia Child says carrots should be placed in a very small amount of water, to which butter and salt have been added, and allowed to cook until the water has evaporated and they can be sauteed in the butter that's left. After that, she says, they should be served with chives, shallots or finely hashed onion. She says carrots are also good when shredded and served in salad form, or glazed, pickled and mashed, or made into soup. She says one of the most delicious soups in the world is "puree a la Crecy," named after the town in northern France where the country's best carrots are grown.

Crecy is better known as the site of a famous French defeat at the hands of the English in 1346. But it's doubtful that the invaders invaded to get the carrots. Though carrots were discovered in Asia Minor at the dawn of history (that means nobody knows when), they weren't widely eaten by humans until the beginning of this century, according to the Department of Agriculture. All along, though, they have been used by people—to adorn the heads of English ladies, as a coffee substitute in Germany and as a sugar ingredient all through Europe.

For some reason, American Indians like carrots better than most other people do. According to a study prepared by the United Fresh

Fruit and Vegetable Association, "In 1855 surveyors for the Pacific Railroad reported that the Flathead Indians in Oregon were so fond of carrots they would steal them from the fields, although (they were) strictly honest as to other articles."

Rabbits also steal them from the field. But unlike Bugs Bunny, most rabbits eat the greens and only the exposed part of the root. (The root is the part that is usually eaten by people.) Mules also like carrots, which can be offered to them as an inducement to move when all else fails, including the whip. Thus the phrase, "The carrot and the stick."

Zookeepers everywhere feed carrots to flamingos and such birds as scarlet ibises to preserve the color of their feathers. In New York, the Bronx Zoo supplements the carrot diet with a chemical called "canthaxanthin," which is even more powerful than carrot juice. "Normally," says a spokesman for the zoo, "these two birds keep their colors by eating crustaceans such as shrimp and crab. But we can't feed them such an expensive diet." Without carrots and canthaxanthin, he adds, flamingos and ibises would turn white.

Administered in massive doses, carrots can do the same for man— as many a yellowing health-food addict has learned, to his surprise. Berton Roueche, who writes "Annals of Medicine" for *The New Yorker* magazine, recalled recently the case of a man from Alaska whose face had turned "a golden, pumpkin orange." In the course of a lengthy examination, doctors discovered he'd been eating carrots "the way some people eat candy" in the mistaken belief that they contained vitamin C, needed to ward off colds.

But they couldn't explain why the patient had turned orange instead of yellow until, that is, they learned he also drank heavy amounts of tomato juice. As Mr. Roueche, whose story "The Orange Man" has just been published in book form, observed: "Carrots are rich in carotene and tomatoes are rich in lycopene. Carotene is a yellow pigment and lycopene is red. And yellow and red make orange."

Someday we will discuss spinach.

—STEPHEN GROVER, December 1971

29. *Your Orthodontist and Ewe*

EDINBURGH, Scotland—First, pretend that you are a sheep.

And that you live on a diet of turnips and heather. And that, as a result, your teeth have become loose and you're afraid they might fall out. What to do?

Perhaps you should call Adam Thomson.

He is a dentist here. For humans. But in his spare time, he often thinks about sheep. And he has developed what he feels is the answer to the prayers of many a loose-toothed ewe:

Braces.

"Stainless steel—just like you'd put on children," says Dr. Thomson cheerfully. "It's no more uncomfortable than wearing braces is for a child. And it's much less trouble than dentures are for human beings. Sheep are less fussy than human beings, fortunately."

All this isn't as silly as it might sound. In the rugged Scottish hill country, loose-toothed ewes often develop Broken Mouth—an aptly named scourge in which a sheep's teeth break off or fall out, making it a feeble forager. Usually, such sheep are culled and sold for slaughter; they yield the farmer a considerably lower return than if they had a few more years of foraging—and, thus, lambing—in them.

The reason sheep get Broken Mouth is that their mouths are rather peculiar. All the front teeth are on the lower jaw. Upstairs, there's simply well-callused gum—with a toughness "like the bottom of your feet," says John Spence, who studies sheep teeth at the state-supported Moredun Institute here.

In itself, such an arrangement would make for stressful chomping—particularly on tough food, such as raw turnips and heather. But there's another problem: Because sheep don't brush their teeth, gum disease is common. That, too, weakens the teeth. As a result, when tooth meets turnip, the turnip often wins.

Broken Mouth is "quite an important problem" for local ewes—and therefore for local farmers, says Mr. Spence. Some farms cull more than 20 percent of their ewes each spring because of Broken Mouth. (It isn't a great problem for rams, because they're much more expensive than ewes and thus are pampered with gentler diets. As for the sheep that aren't kept as breeding stock, they go to the meat market long before dental problems set in.)

Which brings us back to Dr. Thomson. He is the son of a sheep farmer. A few years back, he had a sheep-farming patient, Robin Forrest, in his dentist's chair, and in keeping with the spirit of the occasion the two were discussing Broken Mouth. "As a joke," Mr. Forrest recalls, they decided to see whether they could develop a sheep denture.

The joke soon turned serious. Over the past three winters, the men have tried out three separate models (the Mark I, Mark II and Mark III) on Mr. Forrest's sheep. The last model was the best, and they've formed a company called Ewesplint Ltd. to market and sell the device. It is a modest little strip of stainless steel that is bent around a sheep's front teeth and cemented on with strong glue. It will cost the equivalent of $12 to $24, depending on the number purchased.

The most ambitious of the models was the Mark I—a cap of silver or gold alloy that fit completely over the sheep's eight incisors. Not only was it too expensive, it was too hard to fit; among other things, an impression had to be made. However, it was durable. Down on the farm, Mr. Forrest parts the lips of one woolly ewe to reveal a shiny set of lowers, now in their third winter. "Gold," he says, proudly.

Obviously, the splints don't have the same function as braces do on human teeth; few farmers seem terribly concerned about raising buck-toothed sheep. Rather, their purpose is to reinforce a sheep's wobbly incisors by bonding them to its well-rooted ones: "United we stand," in Dr. Thomson's words.

Most people think the brace will succeed in doing that. "Theoretically, it is promising," says Mr. Spence, the researcher. Similar devices have been reported elsewhere—apparently one was developed in Australia or New Zealand more than a decade ago—but they've been more complex than the Ewesplint.

Dr. Thomson figures his device can be installed in about a minute—30 seconds to put it on and 30 seconds for the glue to dry—but his estimate excludes the time needed to catch the patient. He guesses that a team of brace-setters initially would average 40 to 50 sheep a day, rising to 80 or 100 with practice. Ewesplint plans to supply the team—one glue-mixer, one brace-fitter—on all sales in this area.

Not everyone is convinced. "I just don't see many people wanting to go to the bother of sticking stainless-steel bands around the teeth of their sheep," says Sandy Cox, technical editor of *Big Farm Weekly,* a British publication.

James B. Outhouse, professor of animal sciences at Purdue University in Indiana, doesn't see the need for such a device in most parts of the United States because most American sheep have more gentle diets than those in Scotland do. "Our people don't feed as many turnips as over there," he says. However, he speculates that there might be some interest in the American West, where the grazing grass is often mixed with sand.

Still, the Ewesplint people figure economics are on their side. Most broken-mouthed ewes in these parts must be sold at age five or six, just when they're reaching their reproductive peak; ewe lambs to replace them cost the equivalent of about $150 apiece.

Ewesplint plans to begin selling and fitting the devices in a few months, after this spring's lambing. Farmers don't like their ewes to be handled when they're pregnant. The company says it already has more orders than it can fill and has had inquiries from as far away as New Zealand.

At first, though, it plans to concentrate on its local market—the notoriously hard-headed sheep farmers of southern Scotland. "We figure if we can convince the rural farmers around here that this thing works," says Dr. Thomson, preparing for a metaphorical plunge, "then the world is our oyster."

—ERIC MORGENTHALER, February 1981

CHAPTER FOUR

MEN AT WORK

---

30. *The Waning Days of Mr. Coke*

ICHAUWAY PLANTATION, Ga.—This place and its people are of another time.

Matched pairs of mules hitched in brass-studded harness still haul dog wagons with leather benches to the hunt. Black servants in crisp white smocks serve lunches of dove pie with nutmeg, corn pancakes sopped in sorghum syrup, and cold home-churned buttermilk in figurined ceramic mugs. Afterward, they stoop to offer moist Havana cigars from fine-grained humidors.

"I like it better than any place in the world," says Robert Winship Woodruff, the reclusive, 91-year-old American business legend who made his fortune selling Coca-Cola to the world. More than half a century ago, he carved this domain out of the wild south Georgia sage fields and forests, giving it the Creek Indian name for "where the deer sleep."

Today, the old tycoon spends his days in the rustic elegance of his big white-board country house. Outside, the tea-olives and giant live oaks draped in Spanish moss frame a gray-green peace. Beyond lie the kennels and stables, the servants' quarters, the bird-dog cemetery and a 30,000-acre sportsman's paradise. The fields are flush with game, the rivers thick with bass.

"The boss"—as he is known to everyone at Coca-Cola Co.—is nearly blind and deaf from age and all but crippled by stroke, but he hasn't forgotten his business. At noon, a favorite niece, Martha Ellis, interrupts his chat in the paneled gun room for a ritual stock reading: "Coke is plus one-quarter," she yells, "at 30½ and 13,000 shares. Pepsi is up, Dr Pepper no change. Royal Crown is up." The boss listens, blows a chain of thick blue cigar smoke rings, then takes a sip of Coca-Cola. To himself, he mutters: "Mmm. Good drink."

If anyone doubted that Mr. Woodruff is still "the boss" at Coke, he cleared the air just last year. Flexing his control of 17 percent of the company's stock, he overruled Chairman J. Paul Austin on a number of matters, including the embarrassing role of Mr. Austin's wife as company decorator and the selection of a new chairman (he chose Roberto C. Goizueta over Mr. Austin's reported choice of Ian Wilson, who recently left the company).

Later, Mr. Woodruff appointed his personal secretary, 68-year-old Joe Jones, to the Coke board. Mr. Jones, who as a constant companion has become practically an alter ego to Mr. Woodruff, says the boss was happier than he had ever seen him after picking up the reins at Coke last year. "Things now are working out the way he likes, the way he thinks bodes well for the future of the company," Mr. Jones says. "He feels comfortable with the new man."

"I'm free to do pretty much as I please now," says Mr. Woodruff, who "retired" from the company presidency in 1939 and is currently chairman of the finance committee. "I come and go. I have a very nice understanding with the company." When he travels, for example, he flies on one of three corporate jets whose cabins are decorated with bird scenes and whose tail numbers end in RW.

Now the boss, whose wife, Nell, died in 1968, spends even more time at his beloved Ichauway, riding the wagons to the hunts and sitting in front of the great stone fireplace recalling a life that was as full as they come. Reminders of long-dead friends are everywhere: translucent photo lampshades depict Mr. Woodruff hunting with President Eisenhower, riding the range in full cowboy regalia at his former Wyoming ranch (once owned by Buffalo Bill), and golfing with perhaps his closest friend, Bobby Jones. A big wild turkey slain decades ago by Grantland Rice stands in the dining room beneath woodcock, albino quail and coosa bass encased in framed glass bubbles.

Ike's favorite retriever—along with the boss's 17 other favorite bird dogs—lies outside in the dog cemetery; each has its picture on a tile attached to the headstone, and, as Mr. Woodruff notes, "You had to be pretty good to rate being buried in that cemetery."

Photos of ballplayer Ty Cobb and newspaper publisher Ralph McGill hang in the gun room. There also rests a shotgun with an inlaid gold profile of a quail, a dove and "Mike," a pointer whose tombstone declares: "He had everything." (The gun was a gift from John Olin, who headed Winchester Arms Co. and who, along with the Mellons of Pittsburgh and numerous other wealthy industrialists, built plantations near here after visiting Ichauway.)

"They were glamorous people," says Mrs. Ellis, the niece. "I like to think of the age of tycoons, when they were all friends."

After a lifetime of avoiding personal publicity (he paid a press agent to keep his name *out* of the papers and was for years the "anonymous donor" who financed practically every civic cause in Georgia), Mr. Woodruff has suddenly decided he doesn't mind a little credit for his deeds.

When he took over the company in 1923, he recalls, "It was largely a soda-fountain business heavily in debt. I took the company and spread it around the world—with the help of a lot of fine people." Recalling his favorite decision, made during World War II, he says, "I didn't ask anybody about it. I just told Ike every man in uniform would have a Coke for a nickel regardless of how much it cost the company." That decision made "Coke" possibly the most recognized word on earth.

Of even more interest than Mr. Woodruff's sudden decision to talk to outsiders is his surprising insistence that Joe Jones open up and talk about his years with "the boss." Mr. Jones paints an affectionate portrait of Mr. Woodruff, but it is one of eccentricity.

Mr. Woodruff dropped out of college after less than a year, citing boredom. He never read a book, or even a letter longer than two paragraphs. He never made a public speech. He took a nap every day after lunch. He flew on a commercial airliner only once, from Birmingham to Memphis, and didn't like it. And despite his reputation as a great endower of the arts, he never listened to music. He took parties to the theater and left them there, and the only paintings he liked were of wildlife.

"He considered himself an excellent salesman—that's all," says Mr. Jones. "That's all I've ever heard him say: 'I was a damned good salesman.'" The man and the company were interchangeable, Mr. Jones says. "You couldn't separate them. He was the company, and the company was him."

Even so, Mr. Jones says Mr. Woodruff "was strictly big picture. He always had plenty of people to take care of the details, and he played as hard as he worked. He'd take five people to Gleneagles, Scotland, to play golf for two weeks, but he always had a [business] reason for it, other than just playing golf." (His interest in golf, however, was serious; he and Bobby Jones founded the Augusta National Golf Club and the Masters tournament.)

What Mr. Woodruff didn't learn from books he picked up with an insatiable thirst for travel and conversation. "When he was facing a big decision, he discussed it with everybody," Mr. Jones says. "I remember once when he was contemplating a management change I asked Lawrence Calhoun—his chauffeur—if the boss had talked to him about it. Lawrence said: 'No sir. But he will.'"

When he became curious about how the world sugar market

worked, Mr. Woodruff went off to Cuba on extended trips with his friend Milton Hershey, of candy-bar fame.

But even when traveling, the boss displayed none of the typical interests. "He doesn't care anything about history," says Mr. Jones. "We were in Rome on one trip, and he agreed to take an automobile ride one Sunday morning. We'd been riding about 15 minutes when our cab driver said, 'Two blocks down this way is St. Peter's Square.' Mr. Woodruff said, 'This is close enough. Drive on.'"

As Mr. Jones says of his own life: "I hope someday to have the opportunity to go back and see all the places I've been." In the meantime, Mr. Jones will spend his days beside the boss, screening his phone calls, reading his mail, reviewing his various trusts—and deflecting his occasional worries about money.

"He says to me, 'Joe, how much am I worth?'" Mr. Jones chuckles. "I say I don't know, and he says, 'Well, if you don't, who does?' Then he'll say: 'Well, I guess maybe I can make it.'"

On this particular day, though, the boss isn't troubled about money; he wants to ride to the hunt. After a brief nap in his enormous bed carved with horse and dog figures from spruce knees, he appears—decked out in chartreuse jacket, green shirt and turquoise-stone string tie from his Wyoming ranch—and the plantation staff bolts into action.

Richard, the dog handler, selects ten fine pointers from the multitude in the kennels and loads them into the cages on the back of the wagon. Ben, the mule driver, selects a huge team from among the dozen in the stable (here the boss notes: "Mules are very expensive now"). The hunters climb into the French army saddles on their horses.

Attendants help the boss up onto the wagon and into his soft leather bench, where he dons a lap robe, lights a cigar and whistles for Bobo, his pet Labrador, to join him. The wagon, with its four-foot red-spoked wheels, two-way radio, water tank and Coca-Cola cooler, leads the way, followed by the hunters and two station wagons.

"I used to be a very good shot," the old man says. "Go several days without missing a shot. Now I can't shoot at all because of my eyes. Ninety-one years old don't sound like much, but it's a hell of an old man."

The hunt doesn't go particularly well because of the dry weather, but the boss insists that someone shoot some birds so he can see Bobo work. Finally, Bill Adkins, the Ichauway superintendent, brings down two quail, one of which is still fluttering when Bobo delivers it into Mr. Woodruff's gnarled hands.

"How many'd you kill?" he asks Mr. Adkins.

"Two, boss."

"How many times'd you shoot?" he presses.

"Twice, boss."

"Hmmph," the boss says. "One wasn't dead."

Then the old man climbs off the wagon, gets into one of the station wagons and heads for home. When he arrives, a servant hands him an ice-cold Coke.

—JOHN HUEY, January 1981

31. *Fishing with His Nose*

NEW YORK—Who knows what evil lurks in the hearts of mackerel? Albert Weber's nose knows.

For while a nose is a nose is a nose in most cases, Mr. Weber's proboscis stands between this country and one heck of a stomachache. Mr. Weber is the recognized dean of organoleptic analysts—food sniffers. He is one of some two dozen Food and Drug Administration chemists around the country who use their beaks instead of their beakers to check the healthfulness of suspect foods for which there aren't any convenient chemical tests. Mostly, that's rotten fish. Mr. Weber is the only one who does this nose work full-time.

His snout has been compared to Namath's arm, Heifetz's hands and Einstein's brain. Its judgments are accepted almost as law in court cases involving hundreds of thousands of dollars in rejected foodstuffs.

Though he is over 70 (he won't say how much over), the FDA considers him so valuable that it has been postponing his retirement year to year while, with his help, it is trying to train four men to replace him.

None of these men thinks he can quite do the job. Of course, none of them wants to. Neither, for that matter, did Mr. Weber back in 1943 when fate tapped him. A graduate chemist with a master's degree, he was testing food with his tubes and microscopes in the FDA laboratory in Brooklyn as he had for years when a call came in from the Boston office: A shipment of suspicious perch was on its way. There was (and is) no acceptable chemical test for fish; they have to be smelled. And that day the three fish smellers in the office were out of town. The boss looked for a fill-in.

"I knew I could smell fish," Mr. Weber recalls, "but I tried to keep it secret. Nobody would volunteer for this kind of work." Nevertheless, Mr. Weber was fingered for the assignment, while an expert was rushed out of retirement to check his work.

"There was a lot of rotten stuff in there," Mr. Weber reported, and when the expert saw how the rotten had been separated from the not-so-rotten, he announced to one and all, "Hell, this guy's a fish smeller." And ever since, Mr. Weber has been.

The drawbacks to the trade became apparent immediately. Mr. Weber recalls the subway ride home that afternoon. "Somebody would sit down next to me, and less than a minute later they'd get up and leave. I didn't know why they kept getting up."

Then he arrived home. "My wife took one sniff and said, 'My God, what were you doing today? Get those clothes off and take a shower.'"

In the 32 years since then, Mr. Weber hasn't grown to like his work any better. "How can you when you have to smell that stink all day?"

he asks. But he has made adjustments. He will not allow friends to see him at work. He drives home alone. His wife stays out until after he has had a chance to shower and change. But the FDA needs him, and he says loyalty keeps him on the job.

He smells about 4,000 fish or shrimp in a day and rates them Class I (good commercial), Class II (slightly decomposed) or Class III (advanced decomposed—or, as popularly known, "Phee-yew!"). Some samples, he says, are "beyond Class III—you have to smell those at arm's length." Often in such cases he says he can tell by looking from across the room that a sample is bad. But visual opinions won't stand up in court if a food dealer challenges the FDA's rejection. Mr. Weber has to smell everything that comes his way.

Usually he breaks the skin of the fish or shrimp with his thumbnails and quickly sticks his nose into the crevice for a sniff. "As a rule, one sniff will do, but on the borderline, maybe four. If you can't make up your mind by four sniffs, you shouldn't be doing this work," he says.

But if seafood lovers can rest secure in Mr. Weber's nasal abilities, they might be disturbed by the FDA rules that govern his decisions. The boxes of food that he samples are chosen at random from shipments selected for testing by FDA investigators. How many shipments are selected for testing depends on how good the recent experience has been with similar items from the same packer or the same country. Mr. Weber must rule a shipment acceptable if the portion he samples contains no more than 20 percent Class II or 5 percent Class III.

Thus some fish or shrimp of the "Phee-yew!" variety are regularly passed with the FDA's blessing, and Mr. Weber says he suspects that some companies, mostly overseas, may knowingly take decomposed food and add it to good food in acceptable proportions to obtain the higher prices available in the United States.

"I have a hard time buying fresh fish," the sensitive Mr. Weber says, adding that he often shuns fish in stores even though he would have approved the same fish at the laboratory.

While such foods offend him aesthetically, Mr. Weber says the health hazard they present is small. "Chances are if you took it home and ate it, nothing would happen," he says.

Though Mr. Weber's sniffing skill helps him avoid the stomachaches of the less perceptive, it leads to ailments peculiarly his own. "I've developed an allergy to the smell of decomposed frog legs," he says. "They give me headaches. I have to take a couple of antihistamines before I can smell them."

As a standard GS13, step five, Mr. Weber earns $24,724 a year. He does reserve the right to walk off the job, however. "If you get a lot of stink, you can't do as many because your nose gets tired," he says. "You have to go out of here and rest your nose." How does one rest one's nose? Find fresh air and "try to breathe normally," the expert says. He also refuses to work beyond the end of the normal day if his nose starts to give out. "I'm not a mechanical instrument that you can turn off and on," he reminds his superiors.

The work has its rewards, though—like the thrill of finding "an odor I didn't expect." Such discoveries can be important, because odors must be identified scientifically with decomposition before they can be used as a basis for rejecting food. "Our policy is that if you can't prove it's decomposed, the product gets the benefit of the doubt," Mr. Weber says.

For example, Mr. Weber long had been suspicious of a fruity odor he sometimes found in rock-lobster tails, but he couldn't identify it so he couldn't reject the tails, then, recently, he intentionally left some tails out to decompose as part of a teaching exercise for his trainees. "That same odor developed, so we knew from then on it was decomposition," he says.

Mr. Weber also is rewarded by the admiration of his colleagues. One is Sidney Kahn, director of Fitelson Labs Inc., a private service sometimes hired by food merchants who want scientific evidence with which to challenge the FDA's rejection of their products. Mr. Kahn says that "people don't fight back too often" against Mr. Weber because "there's no objective evidence, like chemicals, that you can turn to. You have to rely solely on noses, and his nose has been declared the international expert."

Mr. Weber is flattered but not pleased by the importers who switch their questionable shipments to other ports from New York to avoid Mr. Weber's nose. Earlier this year the FDA noticed a sudden switch in questionable fish cargoes to Philadelphia. Mr. Weber was dispatched immediately and, with the help of two chemists whom he trained there, managed to foil the diversionary tactic.

Colds slow him down but don't stop him, he says, and, besides, he doesn't get them very often. He absolutely forbids his trainees to use colognes, lotions, shampoos, tonics or soaps with an odor. Nor may they smoke.

Scientists are working to relieve professional sniffers of at least part of their agony. The government is sponsoring a project to develop a chemical index of the decomposition of canned tuna. But Paul Girace, 27, one of the chemists Mr. Weber is training to take over, is skeptical that such technological progress will rescue him. "Al (Mr. Weber) can examine organoleptically 24 cases of tuna fish in two hours," Mr. Girace observes grimly. "To do it with chemicals would take a couple of days."

—JONATHAN KWITNEY, October 1975

32. *Blowing Up on the Job*

PINEHURST, Idaho—Knee-deep in toxic water, Mike Knodel flinches and claws at the cloud of gnats blocking Lookout Mountain Mine. "Gee, I didn't hear about these," he says, stepping past a broken timber toward darkness.

Mr. Knodel doesn't like surprises on the job. The known quantities of Lookout Mountain Mine are trouble enough. Among them: 3,280 feet of shaft, with loose rock and rotted beams, bear spoor and rats' nests. Somewhere inside, seven cases of old dynamite have broken down into a pile of stuff that includes nitroglycerin.

The explosives rank low on his list of perils. Mr. Knodel is the Northern Region Blaster Examiner for the U.S. Forest Service, a member of an unusual fraternity of government explosives-experts trying to make nature more user-friendly by blowing things up. His blasts have smoothed hiking trails, deepened fish ponds, prevented avalanches and stopped forest fires. He sometimes blows to smithereens the carcasses of large animals, which left lying around attract bears and distress tourists.

Blowing shut some of the country's deadliest old mines is a big part of his $22-an-hour job. For the most part, Mr. Knodel enjoys his outdoor work. But he doesn't like to be in the mines. "I don't handle tight spaces very well," Mr. Knodel says, grimacing as his hard hat brushes against moss. "I can't imagine how people made a living in these mines."

There are thousands of abandoned mines in the United States, particularly on the vast public lands of the West. The government calls them "attractive nuisances," because they draw explorers who occasionally wind up getting trapped or killed.

"We try putting up signs, and people ignore them," says James Robbins, a mining engineer for the U.S. Bureau of Land Management, who accompanies Mr. Knodel into Lookout Mountain. "We put up bars, and they get torn down."

The government has stepped up a years-long campaign to plug the mines, and Mr. Knodel, who closes about two of them a month, has knowing hands. One sign of his skill is that his hands remain unscarred, unlike those of many who spend years with bombs. The soft-spoken 52-year-old also has sidestepped bear traps set a century ago by gold miners and fought through spider webs a foot thick. Rattlesnakes like mines, despite levels of zinc, arsenic and lead that kill off fish.

At Lookout Mountain, the gnats add to the challenge. They thin out as the men push forward, single file over a jumble of collapsed support timbers, which are now as soggy as old breakfast cereal. Mr. Knodel points out a pink paper tube stuck into a hole in the ceiling, dangling a rat's tail of burned-out fuse. "Definitely a charge," he says. Nearby is an empty crate of Vulcan ("a kick in every stick") dynamite.

It would be easier to just close mines without inspecting them, but that would be bad for the bats. All mines must first be closely checked for moth wings, guano and other signs that bats have moved in. Some species, such as Townsend's big-eared bat, are in sharp decline. If bats are found that need protecting, the Forest Service will close a mine using bars or dirt, always providing egress for the bats.

Lookout Mountain has no bats, and no rattlers, but like other mines dug between 50 and 150 years ago, it has a history. When a mine is found, people like Mr. Robbins interested in the lore of the West want to retrieve any unusual equipment for museums. The Vulcan dynamite box is a collectible—but it has stains on it that may well be nitroglycerin. Nitro, which doesn't decay, remains dangerously volatile even after many years. The box stays put and the men keep moving, past graffiti from 1941 of a flower and a skull.

Several hundred feet along, amid old coffee cans and blasting-cap boxes, the murky walls suddenly turn neon blue. Copper seepage, says Mr. Robbins, a mine lover who spent many of his student days at the Colorado School of Mines under the mountains near Aspen, while his friends were skiing. Mr. Knodel, a vigorous outdoorsman who first learned how to handle explosives while clearing land on an Oregon ranch, doesn't share Mr. Robbins's enthusiasm for the mines, but he is warily curious. "What's that black ooze coming out of the walls, Jim?" he asks.

"Black ooze," Mr. Robbins explains. The tunnel narrows to the width of an ample coffin at the mine's end. To show how hard navigation is even in this well-defined space, they turn off their headlamps. The absence of light is a color beyond darkness.

Mr. Knodel breaks the silence with a rock tossed down a nearby shaft. Fifteen seconds later, there is a splash. He heads back to the mound of old explosive, eager to finish his work. "Man, I'd much rather blow up a horse than be in a mine," he says.

As it happens, Mr. Knodel is also co-author of Agriculture Department document 9523-2315-MTDC, "Obliterating Animal Carcasses With Explosives." It recommends using up to 55 pounds of water-gel explosive for an adult horse, after horseshoes have been removed to prevent dangerous debris. Charge placement is critical; doubters may see Mr. Knodel's video of an unsuccessful whale demolition, which wrecked a car and rained pungent hunks on onlookers a quarter-mile away. "It's the kind of thing you want to get right the first time," he says. "That way, there's just a little pink haze to worry about."

At the nitro pile—a mix of wood, paper and dynamite in pink, orange and gray—Mr. Knodel inventories the ground for blasting caps, powder and any sticks of dynamite that rats may have dragged from the main pile. "Very decomposed, very unstable," he says, crouching 18 inches from the mound. Out in the open, he says, detonating the explosives would make a crater 40 feet deep.

For a moment, he seems uncertain. "I can't guarantee the road on top of this mine is going to be there when I'm done," he says. Gingerly, he places four charges—festive-looking bright-red cones—in the nitro heap. An intact dynamite box collapses under the weight of one of the two-pound charges, and after some consideration, he adds a fifth cone.

"Cheap insurance," Mr. Knodel says.

He rips a paper tag from a spool of shock tube, a flexible pipe laced with gunpowder that serves as a fuse, and pockets the tag so as not to litter. Mr. Knodel backs out of the mine and takes position on a hill beside the mine where a battery-powered igniter waits. "We're ready to rock and roll," he says, pressing the button. "Fire in the hole!"

The blast lights up the entrance to the mine. The explosion shakes the mountain, and trees press upward, their roots tested. After a moment's silence, the boom returns from across the valley, a louder crack that echoes for several seconds. The Lookout Mountain Mine has become a mess of rubble and noxious gas. Birds begin to chatter madly.

Mr. Knodel won't know the full extent of his success for two weeks, until the gas has dissipated and inspectors can take a close look. But from just outside the mine, it appears to have been closed, the mountain hasn't collapsed, and Mr. Knodel is relieved to be back in the great outdoors.

"Twenty-nine years, and every shot is different," he says.

—QUENTIN HARDY, December 1997

33.   *"Bear Hunting Is Hard on Wives"*

OKANOGAN FOREST, Wash.—Bernard Paque seldom smiles. But a wide grin creases his features now as he shuffles through a foot of fresh snow and four baying hounds to chuck a snowball at a snarling mountain lion perched in a short pine one leap away.

For 23 years, almost all his working life, Mr. Paque (pronounced puh-KAY) has made his living behind his pack of hounds, primarily running down and killing black bears to minimize timber damage. As the sole remaining professional hunter for a timber-company group, he has a lifestyle as primitive as the old frontier, and often as violent.

Benefits abound. The 52-year-old Mr. Paque goes to work along old trails that are often shrouded in the bewitching beauty of silent dark pines heavy with fresh snow. The air is fresh. Deer, grouse and other wildlife abound. The job is exciting and Mr. Paque loves it. He also is good at it. By his own count, he has bagged 2,300 bears, 550 bobcats and 73 mountain lions, or cougars, over the years.

But "Bernie's days as a professional hunter are numbered," says his boss, Ralph Flowers. For one thing, black bears, his main quarry, aren't in surplus in the Northwest anymore, so are no longer hunted year-round without limits. Also, instead of killing bears to curtail springtime tree damage, Washington timber companies are more and more using an experimental feeding program. And to hunt down those bears that nevertheless remain destructive, the authorities are increasingly giving special permits to sport hunters, leaving less work for professional hunters like Mr. Paque.

The thought of abandoning his work depresses Mr. Paque. "I've had a lot of fun," he says. To bridge the change, he is trying to build a livelihood out of guiding sport hunters; that mountain lion he just chucked a snowball at is "reserved" for a client. But there is no certainty that Mr. Paque can convert an obsolescent occupation into a modern means of support.

When Mr. Paque first became a professional hunter at the age of 28, bears were so numerous near his home in Clallam Bay, Wash., that "if you fell down and your gun went off, chances are you'd hit a bear," he says in a rare overstatement.

He didn't plan a career of running hounds. He had "picked brush" for florists and taken two years of wildlife biology in college before dropping out to work in a flour mill. He had trained a few hounds and was hunting bears solely for sport when he was hired for his present job in 1964 by the timber-company group, the Washington Forest Protection Association.

His success in the '60s as a bear hunter because of his skill with dogs became a Northwest legend. "Those dogs were like a machine," recalls his boss, Mr. Flowers. "When they hit a bear track, that bear was dead." Mr. Flowers is supervisor of animal-damage control for the protection association.

Mr. Paque made $275 a month and $15 a bear tail at first and enough later to support a wife and two sons. In his best year, including some money made guiding, he made $20,000, taking as many as nine bears in one day. But it was grueling work, especially before he had telemetry collars to find lost or injured dogs. "Bear hunting is hard on wives," says Karen Sanderlin, his present mother-in-law. "A man stays out all night and comes home and says, 'I slept in the woods waiting for my dogs.' She says, 'Sure.'"

And the job, or perhaps his enthusiasm for it, did partly cost him his marriage of nine years. His present marriage to Robin, a lively woman of 33, is obviously a happy one, but his work worries her. "It used to be that when he came in covered with blood, I'd insist on knowing what happened," she says. "Then I'd find out he was crawling through the brush and shot a bear at three feet." She shudders and adds, "I don't ask anymore."

Mr. Paque, who carries only a revolver, defends such tactics. "When my dogs corner a mean, rank-smelling boar bear, they've got to know I'm going to back them up. And sometimes that means crawling into the bushes to shake hands with that bear." Once, he recalls, as he raised his .44-caliber revolver, a bear crunched down on the gun—and on his hand, immobilizing it. He had to wrestle free to pull the trigger.

His transition to guiding hunters hasn't gone smoothly. "Bernie worries about clients not getting game—he works hard for them," observes Frank Sanderlin, Mrs. Paque's stepfather, a 235-pound lumberjack.

Mr. Paque collects his $1,750 fee for a six-day mountain-lion hunt whether the hunter gets anything or not. The seven-foot, 135-pound mountain lion in that short pine has been treed for 28 hours waiting for the client, who is overdue from Alaska. Finally, the client arrives and, before moving on to other game, shoots the cougar.

Some hunters, Mr. Paque concedes, would reject such a setup as unsporting. "It depends on the client," he says, "but few hunters would pass up a full-grown tom like this one."

Probably Mr. Paque's biggest hurdle to success at guiding is his lack of business instinct. "Bernie's totally honest, and that's fine," Mr. Flowers says, "but he's too easygoing. Some clients take advantage of him."

Bears are more numerous than mountain lions, and Mr. Paque guarantees a bear hunter a bear for a $600 fee. But sometimes, after the dogs have cornered a bear some distance away, the client will say the guarantee isn't fulfilled because he is physically unable to climb the rough terrain to shoot the animal. In one case, Mr. Paque says, he treed three bears for a client over three days, providing food and a room—and didn't collect a fee. "It's disappointing," he says.

While mountain lions are magnificent animals with powerful bodies, long claws and awesome teeth, Mr. Paque considers them "sissies." His real love is chasing black bears. "You get in a tree with a bear and he's liable to climb down and whip you," he says. "Their personalities vary so much you can't tell what one will do."

That is dramatically demonstrated on a recent fall morning as he guides a bear hunt with this reporter as his client. It is an hour before dawn and Mr. Paque's pickup is chugging slowly along an old timber road. Atop the truck, chained to the hood on a rug, two "strike dogs"—whose job is to find the first track of the quarry—sniff the air for a whiff of a bear that has crossed the path. Four more hounds—the "chase pack"—whine with excitement in a cage in the truck bed.

A couple of miles away, Mr. Sanderlin drives along another timber road in his truck, which also carries strike dogs and a chase pack. Intermittently, the two compare notes by CB radio.

Suddenly, the two strike hounds on Mr. Paque's truck begin baying wildly and he unchains them. When they race off squalling on a hot trail, he flips open the cage door and the four hounds leap from the truck in full cry.

But this bear is a "runner," and the five-mile chase leads into an Indian reservation, off-limits to whites. Mr. Paque spends the rest of the day following the faint beep of his telemetry wand to recover the scattered hounds.

But his spirits are high. "Tomorrow we hunt the A-team. We've even got the fabulous four," he says, referring to his fastest and most fearless hounds, which have been resting. As it turns out, their talents are needed. Shortly after dawn, two strike dogs, trying to work out a cold track, cross the fresh trail of another bear and catch up with it after a short chase.

Listening intently to the wild baying of the two dogs, Mr. Paque concludes: "We've got a mean one. He prefers to fight it out with the dogs rather than climb a tree." He releases four more hounds, which quickly join the battle.

As the hunters approach, the 200-pound male bear slips away unseen in the thick underbrush. The six hounds, squalling and snapping, bring it to bay again a half-mile away in a heavily timbered valley, but it moves as the running men near.

Finally, the bear errs, turning to charge the dogs 50 yards from the hunting party. Two quick slugs from a rifle and the hunt is over.

"Hunting with friends, two rigs and CB radios is fun," Mr. Paque says. "But when I'm chasing through the woods, just me and the bear and the dogs, now that's a bear hunt."

—KEN SLOCUM, February 1987

34. *Charles Atlas, Grandpa*

NEW YORK—He is a 76-year-old grandfather now and his hair is gray, but boys who dream of routing bullies at the beach do not know that, so they put their dreams on coupons and mail them to him. For them, as for their fathers, Charles Atlas is still the high priest of manly power, the patron saint of sunken-chested farm boys and fat, pimply-faced city kids straining for virility.

Mr. Atlas—"It's my real name, I had it legally changed over 50 years ago"—sits behind his desk in a poorly lighted gray room on the seventh floor of one of the city's vintage office buildings. The wooden desk is old and uncluttered. The chair creaks and leans ominously to one side.

That famous photo of Charles Atlas in a bathing suit, feet spread apart as if straddling the world, fists clenched, and mouth radiating

Apollo-like confidence, hangs close by. It was taken in the mid-'30s, more than a decade after he won the title of World's Most Perfectly Developed Man, and it is slightly faded now. He was, as he puts it, "in shape then."

He still is. Charles Atlas, once a scrawny kid who really did have sand kicked in his face by a bully, gets up and clenches his fist again, politely asking a visitor to feel the bicep, which bulges. So does the forearm. He opens his tailored silk suit, good-naturedly boasts that his stomach is still hard and pounds it repeatedly as proof.

"That's enough, Charles. Stop it," says Mr. Atlas's friend and business partner of 41 years, Charles P. Roman. Mr. Roman engineered their company from its beginnings, and he now sits in an adjoining office whose desk is piled with papers. Charles Atlas Ltd. grossed a little more than $1 million last year, says Mr. Roman.

Mr. Atlas estimates that six million to seven million body builders—or would-be body builders—have taken his mail-order course since it started in 1923, including a Peruvian defense minister, members of the British royal family, theatrical people and sports stars, such as Max Baer. About 12,000 are taking it at any given time. The lessons go out of offices in New York and London in English, Spanish, French, Portuguese, Italian, German and Dutch. For $35, subscribers get 12 lessons—one a week—followed by a 13th "perpetual lesson." They also may buy vitamins if they wish.

The Atlas system, called Dynamic Tension, consists of exercises that work muscles against one another. There is no equipment to buy. Exercise four of lesson one, for example, says: "Grip fingers of both hands and pull out powerfully upwards, over and back of head. Splendid for chest, shoulders and hollows in neck. Repeat till tired."

If the would-be superman has spent $35 to gain power for evil ends, he is set straight in the first lesson, because the Atlas system is a total plan for *health*, not just muscle-building. Proper diet, breathing, posture, persistence and general mental attitude are stressed throughout. "Avoid all dissipations and injurious habits that you know to be wrong," warns lesson one. And, "Think high and beautiful thoughts. You will be honored, respected and looked up to. Others will see, by your bearing, that you have PERSONALITY, RESERVE POWER and MAGNETISM. Kindly read that again."

Mr. Atlas, a sensitive man, deeply believes what he preaches— "It's a religion with me," he says. His followers are mostly rural youths whose average age is 16, although they come as young as 11. "We also get some real old ones," says Mr. Roman, "but we don't send them the course until we get a note from their doctor."

The World's Most Perfectly Developed Man has changed only a little since he won his title. His chest has gone from 47½ inches to 43 inches, and he has lost "seven or eight pounds." He weighs 178 pounds now. At 5 feet, 10 inches, he is about an inch shorter than when he won the title. ("As you grow older, I think you shrink.") But his neck is still 17 inches, biceps 16½, waist 32 and forearm 14. He attributes this to exercising half an hour every morning and night, eating properly and leading a clean life. He doesn't drink or smoke, but he does occasionally chew gum, which, he says, is good exercise for the face.

"We are what we eat," Mr. Atlas explains. "You can eat for happiness or sadness. Food is life, and people should have a balanced diet." What's ruining people's bodies is pastries and sweets, he adds, looking disapprovingly at his overweight visitor. "You can exercise for 1,000 years, and if you don't eat the right food, it doesn't mean a thing," he says.

"I've taken good care of myself," adds Charles Atlas. "I can swim four miles, and when I get my second wind, I can run or swim all day. But a sound body and sound mind go together. They always will."

Mr. Atlas was born Charles Siciliano in Italy and was brought to Brooklyn in 1903 at the age of 11. His father, a farmer in Italy, became a foreman in a candy factory here and died at 96. Charles, an only child, weighed less than 100 pounds when he was 16.

"One day I went to Coney Island, and I had a very pretty girl with me," he says, recalling the incident that inspired a classic ad. "We were sitting on the sand. A big, husky lifeguard—maybe there were two of them—kicked sand in my face. I couldn't do anything, and the girl felt funny. I told her that someday, if I meet this guy, I will lick him." The girl did not wait around for the confrontation.

His life changed soon afterward when, one morning, he carefully studied his pets as they exercised.

"I got the idea from my own cat and dog. My dog would stretch this way and that. The cat would do the same thing. They were both in good shape. I decided to go to the Bronx Zoo and watch the animals there. The lion came out, stretched, shook himself, and in the next cage the tiger was doing the same thing. The gorilla was chinning himself. I asked, 'Why can't this apply to the human body?'" He decided it could, and he began exercising. Within a couple of years, he began to resemble the Charles Atlas that now hangs on the wall of his office.

Mr. Atlas' adopted name came before his transformed body. He and some friends stopped at a Coney Island hotel that had a wooden statue of Atlas. His friends started calling him "Atlas," perhaps facetiously, and it stuck.

"I liked that name because it's nice and short. It's proven to be a fine name. It's easy to remember and shows strength. The only problem is that some people think I'm Greek."

Mr. Atlas won the World's Most Perfectly Developed Man title in 1921 and again in 1922, picking up a $1,000 check each time, before the contest was discontinued. He then borrowed $3,000 from his mother, which, added to his winnings, was used to launch his mail-order body-building business. Mr. Roman, whom Mr. Atlas describes as "a college graduate with six months' experience in advertising," appeared soon after that. They have been working together ever since. "He handles the business and I take care of the physical culture," adds Mr. Atlas, who has an eighth-grade education and some night school credits.

At first, the company advertised in Western and detective pulp magazines. In the '40s, it switched to science and men's adventure magazines, and now it advertises in automobile magazines. It has been in comic books all along. The London office also takes out radio spots during soccer matches.

Letters come to Mr. Atlas by the hundreds each year, and they are sources of pleasure for him.

"Dear Mr. Atlas, When I sent you my money, I was a little skeptical about the results guaranteed. Well, after one year of faithfully following all your directions, my entire life has changed. Before the course, I had one of the worst inferiority complexes of anyone I had ever heard of. Besides this, my grades in school were average. Well, the change in me has been phenomenal. . . ." The New York State high school student who wrote that letter attributed gaining 53 pounds, winning a position on his school's track team, and getting a State Regents scholarship to Charles Atlas.

He added this postscript: "No bully would ever dare kick sand in my face."

—WILLIAM E. BURROWS, June 1969

35. *One Writer's Novel Problem*

SAN JOSE DOS CAMPOS, Brazil—Ryoki Inoue, the world's most prolific novelist, has a problem you wouldn't expect: Almost nobody knows who he is. You won't see him hobnobbing with the literati, or signing movie deals. A rare autograph seeker mistook Mr. Inoue for another Brazilian record-holder, the fellow who bounced a soccer ball off his head for 19 hours straight.

Yet Mr. Inoue can claim a truly astonishing oeuvre. Some authors aspire to produce a trilogy of books, the more ambitious a whole shelf. Mr. Inoue measures his output in entire walls of novels. "Here they are—or at least some of them," he says, pointing to two walls of his study that are covered with shelves full of his works. Production on such a grand scale doesn't leave Mr. Inoue much time for literary appreciation. "Truthfully, I haven't even read all the books I've written."

For the pulp-fiction king, that's a perfectly understandable oversight. Mr. Inoue, known to millions of Brazilian readers by such pseudonyms as Tex Taylor, K. Luger and Billy Smart, has turned out 1,039 books since abandoning a medical career to start writing a decade ago. Most of his works—which are usually between 100 and 200 pages—are easy-to-read Westerns with titles such as *Oh, Those Texans* and *Priest or Bandit?*

Mr. Inoue, who writes exclusively in Portuguese, won't make anybody's shortlist of Nobel candidates, but he lays claim to the title of fastest literary gun in the West: He has churned out complete chapters during trips to the bathroom; a whole book while having his truck worked on in a garage; a novel and its sequel in an afternoon on the beach—where he also wrote the entire 14-page newspaper for the coastal village in which he was then residing. (He moved a couple of years ago to San Jose, a quiet town near Sao Paulo, partly to be unburdened of daily journalism.)

When the *Guinness Book of World Records* recently affirmed Mr. Inoue's No. 1 ranking in titles published, the award certificate was already 15 books out-of-date by the time it arrived from England.

In the peculiar literary milieu inhabited by Mr. Inoue, tennis elbow is more of a threat than writer's block. Burnout is a problem only insofar as it affects his computer keyboard, which must be replaced every five months. An exclusive contract with a publisher is impractical, since Mr. Inoue writes books faster than ten Brazilian pulp presses combined are able to publish them. "Brazil hasn't yet developed the capacity to absorb me," says the pipe-smoking 49-year-old author, whose father was Japanese and mother was Portuguese.

Some Brazilian critics aren't impressed with Mr. Inoue's style. "Inoue's speed is directly proportional to his disinterest in punctuation and adjectives," writer Anabela Paiva says. But as he has branched out into slightly higher-grade schlock, primarily detective and adventure tales, he has also attracted admirers. "Some of his books wouldn't be put to shame next to certain foreign books that occupy the best-seller lists," writes Okky de Souza, of Brazil's largest magazine, *Veja.*

What's the secret of his prodigious output? Mr. Inoue gets asked the question so often that he did what you might expect: He set aside an afternoon and wrote a guide for aspiring hack writers.

"The plot has to be dictated by the taste of the readers and by the necessity of the market," he writes, eschewing all pretense to producing art. Mr. Inoue generally shies away from political novels: "The reality of the scandals always far surpasses fiction." He also shuns crusading works about the oppressed. "Nobody likes to identify with misery."

Pulp tenderfoots are advised to begin by setting down their first inspiration, be it a dialogue, a description or an action scene. The writer can worry later whether the passage fits in Chapter 1 or Chapter 10. "The important thing is to abandon inertia—even if it means walking sideways like a crab," Mr. Inoue writes.

The author also recommends alternating between several projects at the same time. Say that Jay Windy, a nom de plume Mr. Inoue reserves for his most flamboyant Western dramas, is stuck for inspiration. Mr. Inoue might then try tapping the imagination of Charles Hardwood, the pseudonym he uses for his laconic World War II fictions.

Before he had adopted any of his 39 literary alter egos, Mr. Inoue worked for a decade as a surgeon in a public hospital. Even in the operating room, though, he was a frustrated cowboy, known for wearing boots and Western jeans under his white operating gown.

In 1986, Mr. Inoue took a shot at writing about the American West—even though he himself had never traveled farther west than Newark, N.J. In ten days, he tapped out the 128 pages of *MacLee's Colts,* the saga of an aging pistolero. Two weeks after he sent the manuscript to a publisher, an envelope came back with a check for the equivalent of $30 and a terse note: "Write some more."

He did. To support a wife and two children—comfortably, but not lavishly—on the meager pulp paychecks, Mr. Inoue developed a system allowing him to write up to three books a day. The formula covers everything from the maximum number of characters (20), to the minimum number of killings (five), to the obligatory number of romantic scenes (two, and tame ones at that). Woe to the unfortunate characters who happen to be on the page when Mr. Inoue runs into a snag with the plot. "Dynamite," he says, "resolves a lot of narrative complications."

By 1991, Mr. Inoue entered the literary record books, passing a Spanish romance novelist who had written 700 books.

As he has moved beyond Western settings, Mr. Inoue has tried adopting what is, by his lights, a more painstaking literary approach. "I like doing one book in three days, rather than three books in one day," he says. A milestone in this new phase was *And Now, President?* a tale of a U.S. president whose conniving counselors slip him a slow-acting poison that mimics the effects of AIDS. Besides selling an impressive 35,000 copies, the 1992 work was also the first book Mr. Inoue ever wrote under his own name.

The author also spends time coaching his 22-year-old son, who already has written a score of pulp novels. "He's beginning young enough to be really productive," Mr. Inoue says.

The old man himself isn't washed up yet, though. One night at around 10, with several bills stacked next to his computer as motivation, Mr. Inoue starts to type.

The yarn begins in an airport, where Mr. Inoue's fictional hero, adventure novelist Roy Hamilton, is accosted by a gorgeous, mysterious female passenger. Against his better judgment, Roy is lured away by this femme fatale. Soon he is peering down the business end of her .45, the start of the adventure that will embroil him in a high-speed chase with corrupt cops and a firefight with drug traffickers. By the end of the story, Roy has acquired a wife, a fortune in stolen drug money and a new identity.

Mr. Inoue finishes writing the 195-page book at 5:30 a.m., having consumed most of a packet of pipe tobacco and half a pot of coffee. Stumbling, bleary-eyed, outside to get some breakfast, he is stopped by a newsboy hawking the morning paper. The world-champion wordsmith demurs. "Who has time to read anymore?" he asks.

—MATT MOFFETT, February 1996

CHAPTER FIVE

OBSESSIONS

───────────

36. *The Longest Replay*

MERIDIAN, Idaho—The Spring Valley Bible Church congregation finishes singing "We Are Standing on Holy Ground" and its pastor, Mark Stewart, ascends to the podium and begins his sermon, titled "How to Enjoy the Rest of Your Life."

Bill Buckner, seated among the worshipers, has given the subject much thought. "All I have to do is live with myself. I have to like myself," he says, his signature auburn mustache graying at the edges. "If I can do that, whatever they do or say, I can laugh it off."

In game six of the 1986 World Series, a slowly hit baseball trickled through Mr. Buckner's legs. The error cost the Red Sox the game, helped prolong their 68-year championship drought and forever changed William Joseph Buckner's life.

"Buckner Boots Big Grounder" trumpeted a *Boston Herald* headline the next morning. Tom Brokaw phoned early for an interview.

And after the Red Sox squandered a three-run lead in game seven and lost the series to the New York Mets, it was settled: Posterity would anoint Mr. Buckner poster child of the choke.

Twelve years later, his remains one of the most famous miscues in professional sports. And his notoriety has metastasized. Actor Charlie Sheen paid $93,500 at auction for the "Buckner ball." A sorry softball team in Washington, D.C., named itself the Bill Buckner Emulation Society. The Boston rock group Slide christened its debut album *Forgiving Buckner*. And Mr. Buckner's name has become a colloquialism for goat or gaffe. The *San Francisco Chronicle* recently branded a failed bond proposal "the political equivalent of the grounder that dribbled through Bill Buckner's legs."

"I'll be seeing clips of this thing till the day I die. I accept that," says Mr. Buckner, a few months shy of 50. "On the other hand, I'll never understand why."

After his error, Mr. Buckner lingered in baseball for ten years as a player and a coach, hearing weekly incendiary comments about the play. But he skirted the spotlight and moved here in 1993—even as he continued to coach in the pros. This summer is his first in 29 years out of professional baseball.

Rolling plains of alfalfa and barley blanket the Buckner spread in this small suburb of Boise. Watching his wife, Jody, ride horseback, Mr. Buckner tucks a pinch of tobacco into his cheek and says, contrary to speculation, he didn't run away from Boston. "I was coming out here even if I was the hero of the World Series," says the California native who bought an Idaho ranch in 1974 after falling in love with the place on a visit. Still, he doesn't miss the obloquy. Earlier this month, Red Sox pitcher Pedro Martinez told a group of reporters: "I know why Bill Buckner can't come back. They hate him forever."

Immediately after the error, Mr. Buckner didn't foresee baseball ignominy. "The first thing that went through my mind was, 'God, I should've caught the ball, but I get to play in the seventh game of the World Series,'" he says.

But in the flash of a camera, the world had its goat. "Oh, what the [players'] wives said," recalls Mrs. Buckner, who retreated to her childhood home on New York's Long Island after the game while Bill went out for a drink. "I remember grabbing my little Christen out of her crib and crying."

Rain postponed game seven and a stab at salvation. It never came. Instead, Mr. Buckner joined a fraternity of men forever held liable for sins committed afield. Men like Ralph Branca of the Brooklyn Dodgers and Mitch Williams of the Philadelphia Phillies who served up epochal home runs. And Fred Merkle, the New York Giant whose base-running error was blamed for costing the Giants the pennant in 1908.

In the fall of 1986, Mr. Buckner was in the twilight of a 22-year career that saw him collect 2,715 hits (48th all-time) and a batting title. But the next spring, only the error remained. "Through your legs!" heckled spectators home and away. The abuse spilled off the field, too. A traffic contretemps turned ugly when a motorist recognized Mr. Buckner and baited him about the slip-up.

So maybe it was a blessing in July 1987 when Boston released its quiet first baseman. The Buckners left for the sanctuary of Martha's Vineyard. And when a fan there approached Bill and Jody to say that Bill was his hero, they cried.

It pained Mr. Buckner that he needed a public pardon. "When I looked at myself in the mirror, I perceived it differently," he says. "It's like getting accused of stealing something you didn't steal." Indeed, his wasn't the lone blown play. Boston pitcher Bob Stanley, just before the Buckner error, threw a wild pitch that allowed the Mets to tie the game. But Mr. Stanley's gaffe didn't stick.

A week after Boston cut Mr. Buckner, the California Angels signed him. He played there a year, then was traded to Kansas City, where he spent the 1989 season. It was in Anaheim that he became teammates with Donnie Moore, an Angels pitcher who had become that city's fall guy. Mr. Moore had served up a wrenching home run in the 1986 playoffs that had allowed Boston to beat California and go on to the World Series. "He'd make a joke about it and I'd just say, 'Hey, it's part of the game,'" recalls Mr. Buckner.

A year later, though, it was no joking matter: Mr. Moore killed himself, an act that some sports writers blamed on the constant heckling. Mr. Buckner says that immediately after the death, a reporter for the Associated Press called him, asking if he had considered suicide. "What they did to my husband," says Mrs. Buckner, her eyes and voice trailing off. "Everything short of crucifying him."

Craving absolution, Mr. Buckner returned to Boston in 1990, at age 41, before requesting an invitation to try out for the team. He made it, and soon after, on hobbled ankles, legged out the only inside-the-park home run of his career. "I remember driving home that night and seeing all these visions; hitting the game-winning home run of the World Series." But three weeks and a shoulder injury later, his playing career was over.

Mr. Buckner is driving his Chevrolet Silverado along Route 84 when a promotion for Boise comes on the radio: "Wide open spaces. Great schools. And a great place to raise kids." He ponders this for a moment, then says, "I'm really glad I got my kids out of Boston. I'm happy with the direction they're going in."

The Buckners moved with their three children to Meridian in the summer of 1993, even as Mr. Buckner worked out of Knoxville, Tenn., and Syracuse, N.Y., as a hitting coach for the Toronto Blue Jays organization. Today he goes largely unrecognized—and likes it that way.

"This isn't a professional-sports town," says Mrs. Buckner, adding that those who do recognize her husband are courteous. "Nobody in this town would talk about Willie in a derogatory way."

Indeed, Meridianites seem protective of Mr. Buckner, who has immersed himself in business and civic affairs here, recently buying a General Motors dealership and working on some real-estate projects. "Everybody makes errors or stumbles," says Will Berg, the city clerk. "You can't dwell on it."

Mr. Buckner's friend Jerry Iverson says, "People could care less."

And Mr. Stewart, his pastor, affirms, "The Lord helps him out on this thing."

Still, even in this pocket of the American West, the blunder intrudes. In the run up to last year's World Series, the error appeared in a promotion on a local television network affiliate. "We both saw it and didn't say anything. I froze," says Mrs. Buckner.

And kids can still be cruel. "You always meet that one kid who has something stupid to say," says Mr. Buckner's 14-year-old daughter, Christen.

But Mr. Buckner says he is inured to all the flak: "I can honestly say it doesn't bother me anymore."

His children don't let it bother them, either. Christen and her 16-year-old sister Brittany both play on softball teams wearing No. 22, their dad's number from his early playing days. And his son, Bobby, nine, sleeps beneath a poster of his father at bat for the Red Sox.

Maybe the surest indicator that Mr. Buckner is over the error is his continued dedication to baseball, albeit at a much more relaxed level, and his sense of humor. He runs local hitting clinics (without pay) and coaches Bobby's Little League team. And when he developed his first real-estate project here, a subdivision of starter homes, he couldn't resist naming it for a place you would think he might rather forget:

He named it Fenway Park.

—JOSHUA HARRIS PRAGER, July 1998

37. *The Bean of His Existence*

GIRTON, England—Build a better mousetrap and the world will beat a path to your doorstep. Breed a better bean and it's another story altogether.

Over the past two decades, Colin Leakey has succeeded in developing a low-flatulence bean, an achievement that long has eluded many scientists.

Dr. Leakey, a past winner of the Meritorious Service Award from the Bean Improvement Cooperative for other work in the field, has duly noted his research in such papers as "Progress in Breeding Non-Flatulent Phaseolus Beans," published in the *Journal of Grain Legumes,* and "Beans: Fibre, Health & Gas," presented to the Processed Agri-Food Quality Conference.

He founded Peas & Beans Ltd. to capitalize financially on his breakthrough, but also, as with many scientists, to see some broader good come of his discovery.

Neither has happened, yet, to his great frustration. Peas & Beans's annual sales, about $16,000 a year, hardly amount to a hill of, well, you know what. Seed companies and bean canners in the United States and Europe largely have disdained his new variety. Efforts to get funding for further research and development have been rejected by the British government and the European Union.

This doesn't make sense, he says. "Beans are good food value, high in protein and dietary fiber at a low price," explains Dr. Leakey, whose field of beans is a 1½-acre rented plot behind his red brick house in this village just outside Cambridge. "I want to improve the consumption of beans as a way of improving nutrition."

The only obstacle to the world eating more beans, he maintains, is the obvious one: Because beans aren't the most digestible food, eating them can be uncomfortable. And his Prim bean—yes, as in prim and proper—is the solution because it would make them more palatable and popular.

Not everyone, of course, thinks the world needs a better bean. "Whilst we are interested to understand more about this development," notes Steve Marinker, a spokesman for the British unit of H.J. Heinz Co., the big purveyor of baked beans, "the reality is that beans as a high-fiber product have an effect on the digestive system that is no greater or no less than any other high-fiber product."

But Heinz is in a minority. Indeed, why Dr. Leakey's low-gas beans haven't caught on is puzzling to others. His beans not only are less filling, they taste great, attests Raymond Blanc. The chef and owner of Le Manoir aux Quat' Saisons, a highly regarded French restaurant near Oxford, says: "That man has spent his whole life on nonflatulent beans. He has succeeded. The quality of his beans is quite brilliant. I cannot understand why the market has not taken it."

Mr. Blanc exaggerates. Dr. Leakey, son of anthropologist Louis Leakey and half-brother of conservationist Richard Leakey, hasn't spent all his life on the low-gas bean, but it is the culmination of a distinguished career in bean science. "If life is worth living, it's because there are continuing challenges," he explains. "Whether it was my father finding the evolution of man or my brother saving East African elephants or me finding a new and better bean . . . If one is not finding new challenges one might as well be a vegetable."

The Bean Improvement Cooperative, in honoring Dr. Leakey in 1989, noted that "his expertise encompasses a wide range of areas," including "the establishment of a list of descriptors for Phaseolus vulgaris genetic resources." (Phaseolus vulgaris is Latin for the common bean, the "vulgaris" not meant to imply that there's anything wrong with it.)

A rumpled gray-haired man, Dr. Leakey, 63 years old, can be a bit absentminded. Arriving at a train station to pick up a reporter, he opens the door and lets in the wrong person and then drives and talks for a mile and a half before realizing his mistake.

"He's as eccentric as hell," says John A. McGill Jr., executive vice president and treasurer of the Michigan Bean Shippers Association, who nonetheless praises Dr. Leakey and pays him the highest of compliments: "He's a bona-fide beaner."

A graduate of Cambridge University who studied biochemistry, botany and physiology, Dr. Leakey began specializing in beans while working in Uganda in 1961. His work eventually took him to Chile, where he visited a village marketplace in 1979. When he asked why some beans cost more than others, peasant women modestly managed to get across the notion that the "rich man's bean" had certain properties that were easier on one's stomach.

It was the beginning of Dr. Leakey's quest.

Back home, he excitedly went to work to breed out the bad and breed in the good. "This got me into a sideline of becoming an expert on flatulence, going to libraries and reading everything ever written on it," he notes. "I have come to the conclusion that flatulence is a very good thing. It's a normal mechanism for ridding oneself of chemicals that can be carcinogenic."

Then why not breed a bean that produces more gas? "That's an extremely good and sensible question," Dr. Leakey replies. But the answer lies more with human nature than science: People are more likely to eat beans, which are healthy, if they produce less gas.

Exactly why beans cause gas is a matter of some debate among experts, Dr. Leakey not being the only scientist to plow this ground. "I've been in this business for three decades, and the amount of money spent in research on flatulence in beans is enormous," Mr. McGill explains.

The National Aeronautics and Space Administration once financed studies on gas, which "may present a problem in the closed environment of space flight," as one scientific paper at the time noted. Researchers in Idaho and Michigan—big bean-producers—have studied how to reduce bean gas. DuPont Co. says it is developing a low-gas soybean using traditional breeding techniques. "It's a serious business issue," a spokesman adds.

Conventional wisdom is that beans cause flatulence because they have lots of oligosaccharides, sugars that are hard to digest. These sugars end up in the lower intestines, where they are fermented by naturally occurring bacteria and produce gas. Reduce the oligosaccharides and you lower the gas.

Dr. Leakey disagrees. He thinks bean skins contain chemicals that inhibit enzymes that normally disperse gas into the bloodstream; instead, the gas exits elsewhere. So he has breeded out these enzyme inhibitors. "We're talking about more than ten years' work," he notes. "You crossbreed the right parents, then work through six or seven generations, selecting what you want and discarding what you don't." His first low-flatulence bean was harvested in small quantities in 1990.

One reason for Prim's sales problems: "Big bean companies are worried about marketing low-gas beans because it implies their other beans are high-gas, so it'd be negative marketing," grumbles Peter Dealtrey, a plant-breeding consultant and unpaid director for Peas & Beans Ltd.

Now, Peas & Beans has a new strategy. Rather than focusing on selling seed beans, it hopes to find partners to grow and process the Prim (and other regular-gas varieties Dr. Leakey has developed) and market them as ready-to-eat beans in jars, using recipes whipped up by his wife, Susan.

The smell of beans wafts from the kitchen at the Leakey household at lunchtime on a recent afternoon. Mrs. Leakey has cooked up batches of chile sin carne and porotos granados (beans with sweet corn and zucchini squash). Dr. Leakey tucks into his beans. "Good, aren't they?" he says. "I like chile sin carne best."

So, how often do the Leakeys dine on beans? Actually, only about once a week, Mrs. Leakey confides. "Colin likes them more than I do."

—LAWRENCE INGRASSIA, April 1997

38. *Y2K Alert! (But It's 1980)*

STELLE, Ill.—The neat frame houses that line the spotless streets here seem pulled from the pages of *Our Town*. Behind unlocked doors, mothers raise children, while fathers provide for them.

Yet with one foot apparently frozen in time, the other races against it. The 120 traditional people who live here hold a not-so-traditional belief: On May 5, in the year 2000, they believe violent volcanic eruptions and earthquakes will destroy most of the earth.

Their plan is to build lighter-than-air vehicles, in which they will float above the tumult. Later, when things have settled down, they will too, many of them heading for a new city in the Pacific.

They will call it "Philadelphia."

By that time, they expect to have hundreds of thousands in their ranks. For now, though, the town rises out of the Illinois cornfields like a misplaced movie set. It is the stereotypical American small town—except for the countdown toward doomsday.

"There are two purposes to Stelle," explains Mary Anne Bastean, a 31-year-old former Californian who came to Stelle last year. "We want to make a safe place for higher beings to incarnate in our community and join us in the Pacific, as well as create the technology that will allow us to survive the turn of the century."

The aim, however, isn't necessarily to create a totally new society. "We want to go back to the values that middle-class America came from," Ms. Bastean says, "rather than the shells that they've become."

These kinds of beliefs set Stelle apart from other groups that are prophesying a turn-of-the-century cataclysm, says John White of Cheshire, Conn., who has written a book about such prophecies. "It is values, not events, that the people of Stelle are living for," he says. "There have been so many end-of-the-world predictions that didn't come true, and Stelle is aware of that."

Mr. White considers the Stelle residents cultists, although they try to dissociate themselves from the word *cult,* especially since the Jonestown catastrophe. But Mr. White notes that "Stelle is attempting to use high technology of a sophisticated sort; it isn't just a flower-power, back-to-nature type, as most of these groups are."

Members of the group agree, and they insist they are making progress, although turnover has been high. About 800 people have lived in Stelle for varying periods since it was established on 240 acres of farmland in 1973. They have come here, typically in their

20s or 30s, from all over the country, from many professions and religions. And they haven't been recruited. They come simply because of one book—"The Ultimate Frontier," by the group's spiritual leader, Richard Kieninger.

"When I read the book, it rang bells and hit home," says 29-year-old Tim Wilhelm, a former Ohio teacher who came here five years ago. "It answered all my questions, like what is the purpose of life. I wanted to help carry civilization through the turmoil at the turn of the century."

In the book, published in 1963, Mr. Kieninger recounts how a secret, ancient organization chose him to establish a community in Illinois and lead its members to the Kingdom of God in the Pacific. As a not-so-gentle reminder of his mission, representatives of the organization carved a name in his thigh at the age of 12, he says. He adds that the name *Eklal Kueshana* is in a secret ancient language and means, in part, "the Harbinger of Aquarius." Mr. Kieninger, who says it would be in bad taste to show a reporter his carved thigh, uses "Eklal Kueshana" as his spiritual and pen name.

If Mr. Kieninger is to lead mankind into a new era, however, just about everybody here agrees it won't be through charisma. Short, slightly round-shouldered and plain-looking, Mr. Kieninger speaks colorlessly of his dreams for Stelle. He says he is still in contact with the secret organization, and he is confident that the group will reach its final goals. But he admits that there is plenty to accomplish in a short time.

For one thing, Stelle still looks more like a section of town than an entire community. Seven years have brought 34 wooden homes, two school buildings, and a water and sewage-treatment plant, all built by Stelle residents. There are four small businesses, which along with the town itself, employ about half of the working residents. The rest work in nearby towns, such as Kankakee and Chebanse.

That isn't nearly as self-sufficient as Stelle wants to be. The town is racing against its prediction that there will be an economic upheaval in the United States within the next few years. If Stelle doesn't survive that crisis, it won't even get a crack at the cataclysm.

So Stelle is pouring much of its $450,000 annual budget into the town's office of technology, headed by Mr. Wilhelm. An experimental "envelope house," which has two separate insulated walls, is being built to conserve fuel. The technology office also is constructing a still, which it hopes will eventually satisfy all of the town's fuel needs by converting corn into alcohol.

It also isn't forgetting May 5, 2000. "I could go for days into the different possibilities we've discussed," Mr. Wilhelm says, "like high winds, earthquakes and so on." He has built a greenhouse, for instance, "in anticipation of the fact that standard farming practices will be useless, and we will have to go to a controlled environment."

Meanwhile, he continues to gather information on the lighter-than-air technology that is to save the group 20 years hence. But no work has been started on building a vessel.

The lofty plans, however, are above most of the people here. They believe in the efforts and support them by giving a tenth of their income to the community. For them, the technology is only part of survival. "If we can't grow as people," one member says, "we won't deserve to live in Philadelphia."

In Stelle, "an individual is learning to be responsible for each phase of his life, as well as for the whole," says Malcolm Carnahan, president of the Stelle Group, which functions as a sort of mayor's office. "It's the way people mature."

In the political arena, for instance, members must vote or they will be expelled. Similarly, Stelle encourages entrepreneurial spirit, and many of its residents are partners in Stelle businesses—a woodworking shop, a metalworking shop, a construction company and a plastic-moldings plant. "They don't just go to work for someone," Mr. Carnahan says. "They also have to learn to run it, to take responsibility for it."

"But most important is the emphasis on the nuclear family, with the women as mothers and fathers as breadwinners. Motherhood and family have much more importance than society gives them today," says Mr. Carnahan's wife, Joanna. "The mother here is a professional mother."

Mrs. Carnahan, who has two young children, says, for instance, that she is constantly researching early-infancy education and taking part in Stelle workshops that help mothers raise children. "Mothers are expected to teach kids how to read by age three and write by age four," she says.

They are also expected to screen out negative influences, such as the violence that typically appears on television. The Carnahans have a TV set, but now it stays in the closet. "We hooked it up to a video game a few years ago," Mrs. Carnahan recalls. "It was good for teaching eye-hand coordination."

Despite Stelle's ability to tune out the problems of the outside world, the town has had plenty of problems of its own. In 1975, for example, Mr. Kieninger was expelled by the town on charges of womanizing. He has since returned to visit the group as its spiritual leader, but he spends most of his time setting up another community, near Dallas.

Even more serious was a prophecy, uttered a number of years ago by Mr. Kieninger, that America would see its 200th birthday, but not its 201st. When 1977 came and went, a lot of Stelle residents also went.

Still, many have rationalized the failures. "Looking at history, the U.S. really wasn't formed in 1776," Mr. Wilhelm said. "My tendency is to believe that the 200th birthday is on the anniversary of ratification of the Articles of Confederation—1981."

Some Stelle members see Mr. Kieninger's failings, and the group's ability to survive, as proof that Stelle isn't merely a cult but has a validity of its own.

"In seven years it has established itself as an economic and social entity that has survived a lot of crises," says Curran Jeffrey, who left Stelle a few years ago to pursue a career as a writer. "So even if the world doesn't turn topsy-turvy, even if it doesn't collapse, it still is a tremendously meaningful way to live."

—LAWRENCE ROUT, February 1980

39. Claim That Tune!

John Mason, former chairman of Nevada's Republican Party, came to Washington in May to lobby for an ambassadorship. For small talk, he recounted how he had been the teenage guitar slinger on "Wipe Out," the seminal 1960s surf-rock instrumental by the Surfaris.

Mr. Mason has told the story for years. References have appeared in newspaper profiles since he ran unsuccessfully for lieutenant governor in 1994. "The life of the song is far greater than I thought the recording would be," he told a reporter in May.

Drum roll, please: Mr. Mason didn't play on "Wipe Out." The closest he came to being a Surfari was in 1963, when he was in a group that impersonated the band for several weeks. A fellow impostor says a club owner who discovered the ruse chased them out of Calgary, Alberta.

Nearly 40 years later, a puzzling trend continues. People with no role in "Wipe Out" keep trying to claim a piece of one of rock's most magical spontaneous moments—a frenzied, two-minute, 37-second, drum-and-guitar rave-up by four teenagers that became every wannabe rocker's dashboard-banging standard.

"Since the day it started, there have been people claiming to have been there," says Robert Berryhill, the real Surfaris' rhythm guitarist. "It's too numerous to count—probably hundreds."

Last year, a man tried passing himself off to newspapers in San Diego, Calif., as the Surfaris' lead guitarist. In March, obituaries for Morton Downey Jr., best known for a loud U.S. talk show, said he wrote the song—a canard he floated years ago. Then there was the gas-company repairman who noticed a Surfaris' album in Mr. Berryhill's home one day in 1967. "I was in that band," he told Mr. Berryhill's wife. "I was on rhythm guitar." Pointing to the rhythm guitarist on the back-cover photo, Gene Berryhill replied, "See this person right here, this is my husband."

Counterfeit oldies acts tour regularly, but the surfeit of fake Surfaris is part of another phenomenon—bogus minor celebrities seeking renown, not remuneration. People surface occasionally pretending to be one of the 30 kids who appeared over the years in the *Little Rascals* movie shorts. Old bands are vulnerable because many used stand-ins. The Surfaris are especially so because, unlike the Rolling Stones or the Beatles, few ever knew what they looked like. "There really isn't enough limelight to go around, so people are looking for reflective glory," says Fred Wilhelms, a Nashville, Tenn., lawyer for Artists & Others Against Impostors.

The Surfaris formed in September 1962 near Los Angeles. The five teenagers liked surfing and emulated the reverb-heavy, staccato instrumentals of surf music's patriarch, Dick Dale. After a few months playing dances, they recorded their first song, "Surfer Joe," at a $12.50-an-hour studio in Cucamonga, Calif., that December.

They needed a B-side, so they made one up on the spot. Lead guitarist Jim Fuller, then 15, plucked a melody. Drummer Ron Wilson, 18, speeded up a cadence from his high-school marching band. Mr. Berryhill, 15, strummed his guitar and recommended drum-solo breaks. Pat Connolly, 15, played bass. Saxophonist Jim Pash, 13, had to work that night, so there's no horn on the record.

Mr. Fuller suggested opening with a switchblade click and calling the song "Stiletto," but they opted for breaking a shingle to simulate a surfboard cracking. The band's manager, Dale Smallen, added a mocking cackle he did for laughs at parties and the immortal words "Wipe Out!"

Mr. Smallen had 2,000 copies pressed to sell at gigs. A few months later, Mr. Smallen sold the master tapes for a $200 advance and a royalty of four cents per single. The two producers who ended up in control of the songs, Richard Delvy and John Marascalco, in turn sold shortened, remastered versions to Dot Records for a bigger royalty. Then, after "Wipe Out" started selling big in Fresno, Calif., the band sold its four-cent royalty for $2,000—chump change for a single that would sell 500,000 copies by year's end.

Fake Surfaris started popping up almost immediately, the first after Dot requested a whole album. One of the documents that Mr. Delvy, himself a drummer, signed with the label listed members of his own band, the Challengers, as the Surfaris. The substitute Surfaris recorded the album's other ten songs. According to affidavits filed later in a court suit, Dot released the album as the Surfaris' "Wipe Out" without knowing that none of the real Surfaris were on those ten songs.

The real Surfaris say they recorded ten songs, too, "but when we finally heard the album, everything but 'Surfer Joe' and 'Wipe Out' was somebody else," says Mr. Pash, whose sax wasn't even on those two songs.

By now, the Surfaris—and their parents—were wise. They fired Mr. Smallen, demanded that the album's credits be corrected, joined Decca Records, hired a lawyer and sued everybody involved. In June 1964, the four boys on "Wipe Out" secured a $47,000 settlement (equivalent to $270,000 today) and got back the future royalties they had sold. Mr. Pash, whose only complaint was having his image inappropriately used on the album cover, got $3,000 and the unique distinction of being formally disassociated from "Wipe Out." Lawyers got 20 percent of the boys' settlement and future royalties. Messrs. Delvy and Marascalco also retained shares.

After "Wipe Out" hit, a lesser-known group that had called itself the Surfaris first asserted a legal claim on the name. They lost and became the Original Surfaris—and then added "Wipe Out" to their repertoire.

Creating more confusion, a band called the Impacts released an instrumental called "Wipe Out" just before the Surfaris' song took off. "The chord progression is exactly the same," insists Merrell Fankhauser, the Impacts' guitarist and songwriter. "I still can't believe that it was a coincidence." He considered suing, but to untrained ears, the songs have nothing in common beyond an opening "Wipe Out" yell. His case is further hurt by a tape recording made some years ago in which he is heard introducing "Wipe Out" as "the tune that really got it started for me," and then starting his own song before shifting into something that sounds like the Surfaris tune. "The fantasy becomes the reality," quips the Surfaris' Mr. Pash, who supplied the tape. Mr. Fankhauser says he was playing a version of his own song.

Last year, a man named Jim Agnew told reporters in San Diego that he played lead guitar for the Surfaris. At the time, he ran a non-profit program called "Blues in the Schools," which sponsored performances to expose students to that genre. Mr. Agnew told the *San Diego Reader* that he was the real Surfaris' Jim Fuller—his stage name, he said—and even identified himself as Mr. Fuller on old publicity photos. After the *Reader* located Mr. Fuller, Mr. Agnew confessed. Contacted recently, Mr. Agnew initially declined to be interviewed and apologized, in a voice mail, "on behalf of the Surfaris." Reached later, he says, "I only played with them three or four times." Mr. Pash insists that "there was never anybody in my band by that name."

Mr. Mason, the would-be ambassador, began his career as a fake Surfari in 1963, after concert promoter Donnie Brooks tried to book the real band on a Canadian tour. The band members' parents wouldn't let them skip school. So Mr. Brooks hired the Vulcanes, a band that included Mr. Mason—now an entertainment lawyer who was Nevada's GOP chairman from 1995 to 2000—to tour as the Surfaris, people involved say. (Mr. Brooks says he doesn't remember doing that, but allows that "it could have happened.")

To avoid detection, the Vulcanes drew mustaches and beards on Surfaris albums shown to radio interviewers, recalls Vulcanes saxophonist Don Roberts. After the tour's last gig, a Calgary club owner "accused us of being impostors, which we were," Mr. Roberts adds. "He chased us over 100 miles."

Over the years, Mr. Mason has told a former law partner, reporters and others that he was in the Surfaris, and he discussed the matter with several people while in Washington this spring. Nevada Rep. Jim Gibbons, a novice guitarist himself, was completely fooled: "I knew of John Mason when he was a rock star," he says. "But I didn't put it together until he or somebody else said, 'This is the John Mason that is the guitarist with the Surfaris.'"

Asked to explain, Mr. Mason initially insists that he recalls recording "Wipe Out." But then he says he was honestly mistaken, explaining that he'd recorded with other bands. "I'm going to confess to confusion," he says. "I thought it was the real group." He later deleted Surfaris references from his law practice's promotional autobiography, calling them "perhaps misleading and inaccurate." As for an ambassadorship, Mr. Mason says the White House has told him there won't be any openings for a while.

Today, Mr. Smallen, the ex-manager with the laugh, lives in a hotel and complains that he made only $220 off the single. The real Surfaris continue profiting from "Wipe Out," which twice hit *Billboard*'s Hot 100 chart, reaching No. 2 in 1963 and No. 16 in 1966. The band broke up in 1967, but the song has been licensed to numerous movies and commercials. Last year alone, "Wipe Out" generated about $225,000 for the band and its attorneys, says Lawrence Parke Watkin, the band's main lawyer.

In 1989, a brain aneurysm killed Mr. Wilson, the group's drummer, at age 44. Mr. Connolly, the bassist, has long been out of touch with the others. Messrs. Fuller and Pash still tour as Surfaris. Mr. Berryhill, a devout Christian, says he uses "'Wipe Out' as a draw to tell people about the Lord" in another band with his wife and two sons.

Both groups legitimately call themselves the Surfaris and maintain Web sites with the latest news, including this March 18 press release from Mr. Berryhill: "'Wipe Out' Was Not Written By Morton Downey Jr."

—PHIL KUNTZ, August 2001

40. *This Cup Must Not Be Runneth Over*

WINNIPEG, Manitoba—Cold beer flows and rock music blares while, in a corner of the backyard, partygoers have their pictures taken with tonight's guest of honor: the Stanley Cup.

A few are plotting a bit of mischief: Will the National Hockey League's championship trophy get tossed into the pool?

Not if Scott North can help it. The slight 30-year-old fidgets at poolside while giddy revelers gulp beer from the cup's sterling silver bowl. Two have underwater cameras at the ready. "The cup does not go into the pool," Mr. North keeps repeating. "Please."

Like the brawlers who protect star scorers from rough stuff in the NHL, Mr. North has to keep bad things from happening to the Stanley Cup, symbol of hockey supremacy for 103 years. He and two of his co-workers at the Hockey Hall of Fame in Toronto take turns escorting the trophy on a postseason tour unlike anything in sports. Each member of the championship team gets the cup, wherever he likes, for a day or two. With it comes Mr. North or one of his colleagues, pro hockey's cup-sitters.

Escorts have long accompanied the cup on publicity trips, but it was generally unsupervised on player visits until midsummer 1994. That year, members of the New York Rangers took it bar hopping, used it as a horse's feedbag, let it drop out of a car trunk and banged it up badly enough to require cosmetic surgery.

Two years earlier, the cup got stuck on a drain in the backyard pool of Pittsburgh Penguin Mario Lemieux. Last summer, a New Jersey Devil ran his boat aground in Lake Superior while ferrying the cup home after a night at the bar. It has also been lost, stolen, booted into a canal, and used as a flowerpot and a peanut dish.

Lord Stanley, the sixth governor general of Canada, didn't have such hijinks in mind when he established the cup in 1893. But NHL officials say the summer odyssey gives players a rare chance to share their achievement with the people closest to them. "It's what you grow up dreaming about," says Mike Keane, the Colorado Avalanche player hosting the cup in Winnipeg.

At 35 pounds and just under 3 feet tall, the cup bears the engraved names of close to 1,000 players, coaches and owners whose teams have won the NHL title. Its look changed frequently in the early part of the century, evolving to its current barrel shape in 1959. Originally purchased for about $50, the cup today is insured for $100,000.

This summer the cup has traveled from Vaudreuil, Quebec, where goalie Patrick Roy used it to raise money at a charity golf tournament, to Warren, Mich., where defenseman Craig Wolanin lugged it to his cousin's high-school graduation party. Chris Simon took it fishing with his grandfather in northern Ontario. Stephane Yelle posed for photos and signed autographs at his elementary school in tiny Bourget, Ontario. The cup made its first overseas-player visit, to star-scorer Peter Forsberg's boyhood home in Örnsköldsvik, Sweden.

All along, a cup-sitter has strived to keep the precious chalice safe and in sight. On duty for the mid-August trip to Winnipeg is Mr. North, officially the Hall of Fame's manager of special events and facility sales. He has ushered the cup to many NHL events and donned white gloves to carry it onto the ice when the Avalanche completed its sweep of the Florida Panthers in June.

Today's journey begins in Denver. The cup spent the night with Mr. North at a Ramada Inn, secure in its blue, foam-padded chest. He removes it for a quick polishing before heading to the airport, where ticket agents have been alerted. Mr. North obliges one who pleads for a photo, unlocking the chest while waiting travelers crane their necks for a look. "Isn't it amazing?" one says.

"They just eat it up," Mr. North says.

He plays down the security part of his job, calling himself an "ambassador" and "facilitator."

"The players have too much respect to mess with the cup," he says. Never mind that Mr. Keane, a scrappy, 29-year-old winger with shaggy red hair and a goatee, was a member of the 1993 Montreal

Canadiens team that dunked the trophy in a player's pool. Mr. North expects nothing but "a lot of fun."

He gets an inkling that Mr. Keane might have a different idea of "fun" shortly after the player collects him and the cup at the airport. Mr. North is outlining a few rules—for example, only players and their immediate families should hoist or drink from the cup—when Mr. Keane hints that it could take a swim.

No way, Mr. North insists. Water and chlorine could corrode the silver and cause who-knows-what other damage, he says, adding, "My butt is on the line." Mr. Keane dubs him "the bloodhound." Mr. North sighs. "This is going to be an interesting night," he says.

First stop is Mr. Keane's modest home. His wife, Tammy; their dog, Molson; and a dozen or so family members eat Kentucky Fried Chicken and pose for photos in Avalanche T-shirts and caps. They laugh when Mr. Keane's brother sits his infant son in the cup. Mr. Keane's 97-year-old grandmother arrives. "Hey, Sparky," he calls out affectionately, "there's somebody here who's even older than you."

The family reassembles that evening in the backyard of friends Paul and Cathy Cholakis, who have known Mr. Keane since he played youth hockey with one of their three sons. The cup is set on a table beneath a white canopy. Mr. North asks for a sturdier table, lest the cup take a spill.

Waiters in striped referee shirts serve more than 90 guests amid Stanley Cup–shaped ice sculptures and a cake resembling the Avalanche logo. A banner stretched behind the in-ground pool reads, "Way to go, Mike!" with a caricature of Mr. Keane smoking an enormous victory cigar. Winnipeggers are especially appreciative; they just lost their pro team, the Jets, to Phoenix.

Flashbulbs pop as guests clamor for pictures with the cup. They peer and point at the trophy's engravings, searching for names of favorite players and distant relatives. The ban on hoisting is roundly ignored; one guest dons a hockey jersey and gloves and cavorts with the trophy aloft for the cameras.

Soon lime wedges are floating in the beer slopping over the cup's brim. A dozen whooping young men quaff from the cup, two at a time. Two police officers who show up to quiet the party wind up posing with the cup. "We don't care about the noise," one says. "Have a good time."

Mr. North dares not move from his spot near the pool. A number of guests have informed him that, rule or no, the cup is going for a dip. Finally, he warns Mr. Keane that if the trophy goes into the pool, it won't be available for a charity golf outing the next day. Nor will it make a party hosted later in the week by one of Mr. Keane's teammates.

"Sometimes you've got to say whatever it takes to make them not do whatever you don't want them to do," Mr. North explains. He brushes off the supposedly prohibited drinking and hoisting. "I'm just worried about the pool," he says.

Mr. Keane, who is known in the NHL as a team leader and was the Canadiens' captain last year, tells his pals to leave the cup alone. Mr. North relaxes enough to enjoy a beer. But he still isn't out of trouble. One guest tries to take Mr. North into the pool. He sidesteps the lunge and the attacker winds up drenched.

Mr. North packs up the cup, undamaged and undunked, around 1 a.m.—not a moment too soon. Mr. Keane begins roaming the yard for dry people to toss in the drink. A number of wrestling matches break out, including one that leaves the Cholakises' fence minus a few slats.

Still, Mr. Keane's buddies insist they never meant to harm hockey's Holy Grail. "Hey, we don't want to wreck the Stanley Cup," says Dean Court, a radio ad salesman who skates with Mr. Keane in a local summer league. "The boys are rambunctious, but they're not stupid."

—BRYAN GRULEY, September 1996

CHAPTER SIX

WHAT WE WROTE HOME ABOUT

41. A Navy and Its Demons (and Dragons)

VIENTIANE, Laos—"We are not rich like the American Navy," says Prince Sinthanarong Kindarong, as he fords a mud-puddle and then carefully picks his way past several weed-camouflaged mounds of water buffalo dung. He's on his way across Royal Navy headquarters to show a visitor one of the ships under his command.

The gunboat, minus guns and engine, is resting on the riverbank, awaiting repairs. "It has been here for some time," says the prince, referring either to the boat or to a chicken, which has laid three eggs under the rusted hull.

Prince Sinthanarong—like most prominent Laotians, a cousin of this country's king—is commander of the Royal Laotian Navy, one of the smallest, poorest and least combative naval forces in the world. This is not inappropriate, for Laos would surely be one of the world's least noteworthy nations were it not for the North Vietnamese and Americans. Their conflicting goals in Indochina have long since turned supposedly neutral Laos into a battlefield and many of the nation's decidedly unmilitaristic and apolitical people into war refugees.

The Laotian Army gradually has been drawn into the Indochina war. Thousands of mountain tribesmen, paid and directed by the CIA, serve as intelligence and guerrilla operatives. The Army has increasingly—though not always very willingly—been called upon to defend towns and roads, or at least its own primitive outposts, from Communist attack.

The 700-man Royal Laotian Navy, in its wisdom and perhaps to its credit, has managed to remain largely irrelevant to the war. Unadvised, unequipped and unaggressive, it is the quintessential Asian nonfighting force. It has never been Americanized, which at least means it will never need to be Laotianized.

Information on the Royal Navy is not easily come by. French officials here believe that Americans advise the fleet. Some Americans believe it has French advisers. In fact, the Americans have no naval officers at all in Laos. The French used to have one, but he left the kingdom last year. "He has not been replaced; the French economy is in very bad shape you know," says French-educated Prince Sinthanarong.

There is an American Navy captain in Bangkok who is accredited as naval attache to the royal fleet. But he declines to answer any questions because all his information is "classified." Discussing the Royal Navy would be of "direct benefit to the enemy," he says. The captain also refuses to discuss American aid to the Royal Navy. It appears to be far from munificent, however.

According to Prince Sinthanarong, the Royal Navy has 28 vessels: Two 52-foot gunboats called vedettes, a dozen 36-foot vedettes, seven U.S. Navy surplus landing craft and seven transport craft "of local construction in material of wood." The prince notes, however, that the fleet is not entirely operational. According to *Jane's Fighting*

Ships, in which Laos rates an even more cursory mention than Gabon or Guatemala, the Royal Navy has 34 ships, of which 11 are "in commission" and 23 are "in reserve."

All these statistics may be somewhat deceptive. Here at naval headquarters there are only five boats afloat. Four are wooden transport vessels, all lacking engines. The fifth is by far the largest ship in the Royal Navy—an 80-foot, iron-hulled monster with a towering black smokestack. The ship is powered by a wood-burning furnace. It was built in 1904. On shore, awaiting repairs, are six vedettes and a landing craft. The prince explains that it will take some time to clear this backlog: "We can repair only two ships a year," he says.

If Vientiane naval headquarters is a somewhat placid place, the Royal Navy's base at Pak Se, in southern Laos, is a naval graveyard. Of nine vessels on display one recent morning, six were resting ashore in rusted "reserve"; two others were afloat but engineless. The ninth boat was operational and bristled with four mounted machine guns. A young sailor aboard the gunboat was asked if the guns were ever fired. "Yes," he replied, "but only in practice."

What the Royal Navy largely lacks, aside from boats, is water. Laos is nothing if not landlocked. The Navy thus is limited to river operations, mostly along the Mekong, which enters northern Laos from China and Burma and flows out of southern Laos into Cambodia, Vietnam and the South China Sea.

The Mekong is a generally benevolent waterway—wide, muddy and meandering. But there are some hazards, including rocks, rapids, sandbars, ten-foot catfish and—according to most Laotians—river dragons. Prince Sinthanarong, who admits to literary talents, describes some of the dangers in the Royal Navy manual:

"The Mekong, by its hazardous and tumultuous course, its shifting riverbed strewn with sandbars and menacing rocks, the violence of its currents and whirlpools, the dangers presented by its many rapids and by the great seasonal fluctuations of its level, demands, as much from men as from boats, great skill to confront the vicissitudes of navigation which, at all times, constitute a great part of adventure."

The vicissitudes of navigation are not eased much by the Royal

Navy's intricate, hand-painted navigation charts. Unfortunately, many of these works of art date back to the 1950s, which means they do not precisely correspond to the realities of the Mekong's constantly shifting riverbed.

The second largest river in Laos is the Sekong, an increasingly important route for North Vietnamese supplies moving from the Ho Chi Minh trail area of eastern Laos down into northern Cambodia. The Royal Navy, however, doesn't operate on the Sekong. This is partly because the United States is said to be airdropping mines into the river. These mines are set to explode upon the approach of any metal object—which would include Royal Navy gunboats. The North Vietnamese, of course, use mostly wooden sampans and bamboo rafts. And, when the North Vietnamese want to ship metal cargo down the Sekong, they generally float empty oil drums down the river first to detonate the mines.

But the Royal Navy would be likely to stay off the Sekong in any case, since confronting the North Vietnamese is not one of its missions. These are listed in the Royal Navy manual as reconnaissance, liaison, transport, fire-support and unloading. Loading is not listed, though perhaps it's assumed.

In reality, the Navy—when it has ships in commission—mostly seems to carry military supplies and, occasionally, troops. Also, it sometimes escorts convoys of civilian vessels past riverbanks controlled by the Pathet Lao (Laotian Communists). The Pathet Lao have no known Navy, except for some rafts and sampans. This rules out classic naval warfare, Prince Sinthanarong explains.

But the Royal Navy has seen combat. Its major engagement of recent years was the 1968 battle of Pak Beng, in northern Laos, when five sailors were killed and 12 wounded. Asked to describe the battle, the prince simply replies: "ambuscade" (ambush). Casualties have since been significantly reduced. Last year only three men were wounded. This year one man was killed in another "ambuscade."

The Navy's most dramatic engagement, however, took place during one of several coups d'etat in 1960. Naval forces sailed up the

Mekong and shelled Vientiane. "I don't think they hit anything," recalls Gen. Boun Theing, who emerged as a winner in that particular coup. The Navy, however, was on the losing side. As a result, it went into "reserve" for several years until a naval rearmament program began in 1964.

—PETER R. KANN, November 1970

42. A Fence Without End

WOMPAH GATE, Australia—The Great Wall of China is about 1,500 miles long. What's so great about that? The Dingo Fence runs for 6,000 miles.

Heads of state who visit Australia don't usually come out to walk along the Dingo Fence. It isn't a whole lot to look at. But it's impressive enough to get Pilot Kerry Provis to put down the novel he's reading and circle his Piper Cherokee around for a better view.

From a few thousand feet, the land looks like brown bread overgrown with pale green mold. It also looks as though someone has taken a knife edge and drawn a sharp line across it. That's the fence.

It starts way down south near the Great Australian Bight, works its way across the Great Victorian Desert, turns north through the Great Artesian Basin, then swings south again along the Great Dividing Range and ends up in the South Pacific near a place called Surfers' Paradise. It should be called the Great Dingo Fence, but Australians are modest.

Dingoes are wild dogs that kill sheep. The fence cordons off the southeastern third of the continent for the sheep. The dingoes get the rest.

Kerry Provis puts the Cherokee down with a crunch and rolls up to Wompah Gate. That's all it is. Just a gate in the Dingo Fence. A sign says anybody who leaves it open will wind up in the clink. On the ground is an empty bottle of Duke's Own Very Fine Scotch Whiskey. The gate is conveniently located just under a thousand miles from most of Australia's major cities, in the middle of nowhere. From horizon to horizon, the land is silent and empty, except for a mob of kangaroos relaxing under a lone shade tree.

A wisp of dust rising in the distance heralds Geoff Smith in his land cruiser. Geoff is an overseer for something called the Wild Dog Destruction Board, which was good enough to send a telegram through the Royal Flying Doctor Service alerting him to our visit. With nine "boundary riders" Geoff tends a 217-mile stretch of fence here on the border between the states of New South Wales and Queensland. The riders and their families live in cottages along the fence, spaced 25 miles apart. Their assignment: Watch for holes.

Geoff rolls a cigaret and clamps it firmly in his front teeth. He pushes the cowboy hat off his forehead, rubs the back of his neck and explains the fence: "It's six foot high, on the average, and a foot in the ground. You got a plastic netting one foot in the ground and one out. Then two foot of rabbit netting and three foot of marsupial netting. You got a top running wire, a belly wire and two down below, gauge 1.6 mils . . ."

A horn honks. There's a truck trying to get through the gate, and Geoff's car is blocking it. "Sit here for a week and nobody passes," Geoff says. "Just get here today and we got a traffic jam."

He moves his car and the truck rumbles through with a dog howling in the back. "G'day mate," Geoff yells to the man in the truck, and he secures the gate.

A few feet on the other side of the Dingo Fence is a line of cracked, sun-bleached posts with a few rusty wires clinging to them. That is (or was) the Rabbit Fence. Back in the 1880s, when Australia was first fencing itself off, the menace was rabbits. Millions of them would swoop down and eat every blade of grass in sight. So thousands of miles of rabbit fence were strung. But that didn't bother the rabbits. "There's nothing you can do to stop a rabbit," Geoff says.

"They just hop over it or dig under it." So the government gave up on the Rabbit Fence and converted it to the Dingo Fence.

The Dingo Fence works fine against dingoes, as long as there aren't any holes in it. That's a problem. The fence is forever under assault. Kangaroos go walloping into it at full tilt, punching big gaps. Emus—goofy-looking birds with long legs and no wings—do the same. "They'll hit the fence at 30 miles an hour, bounce off, pick themselves up and away they'll go again," Geoff says. Wild pigs are worse. "They just tear up the bloody fence. You know what pigs are like, I guess. Nothing's pigproof."

Something there is that doesn't love this fence. In the desert, where it undulates over high dunes, a big blow will bury the fence in sand. Or the wind will burrow underneath and the fence will fall down. Here, in what they call "stony clay country," bush fires during droughts burn through the fence, leaving it charred and weak. When there aren't any droughts, there are floods. In 1974 heavy rains brought the usually trickling Bulloo River raging into the normally dry Bullagree Swamp. Wompah Gate was inundated. Geoff Smith's house, with Geoff and his family on the roof, was washed away. The fence was mangled for miles.

Almost four years later, the water, starting just east of here, is still 20 miles across. Geoff drives toward it and stops when the earth goes doughy. This is where the boundary riders have to get out, load fencing on their backs, and trek through the muck to rebuild the fence as it emerges from the receding swamp. If they didn't, this would be dingo country.

That would mean more work for Geoff Gash, the "dogger" on this stretch of fence. He hunts dingoes for a regular salary plus $10 a "scalp." In 1976, he came in with only 17 dogs; the fence must be doing its job. It would be nice to meet Mr. Gash, who is 64 years old and has been hunting dingoes all his life, but nobody knows where he is. "He pretty much lives in his car," Geoff Smith says. "Wherever there's dogs, he camps. You can't keep track of him."

There used to be two doggers here. The other one, Billy Baldwin, called it a day a couple of years ago at age 72. After Geoff Gash, there isn't likely to be anybody. Finding boundary riders isn't as hard, but it's hard enough. Not everyone is suited to the life; people go crazy out here. "The odd ones never go anyplace for months on end," Geoff Smith says, driving along the fence to Laurie Murphy's house. "We've had 'em shoot 'emselves and do all sorts of things. They stay at it too long. They're usually mad as hatters."

Laurie Murphy, who is in his 60s, has been riding the fence for 16 years. He has a beer belly, a cracked, sweat-stained leather hat, a fine white stubble on his chin, and all his marbles. In the early days, boundary riders were presented with two tents and two camels and sent on their way. Today they have all the amenities: radios, electric generators, windmills that pump water, trucked-in food. "Oh, no, we're not isolated or anything like that," Laurie says.

When the thirst moves him, Laurie goes to Tibooburra, a town an hour and a half's drive from here on bush tracks. Tibooburra is so small it is completely invisible from the air, but it has two bars. "I like a beer," Laurie says.

Most of the time, he and his wife, May, are happy to stay at home, a little place with a corrugated iron roof and an accumulation of sheds, gas cans and old tires around it. Inside, the floors are covered by several kinds of linoleum. There are folding tables and chairs in the living room. On the walls are pictures of race horses and cows, a picture postcard of Elvis Presley and one of the Queen. In the freezer is a whole pig.

"I love the bush," May says.

Laurie nods. "We never worry about getting around much," he says.

Driving back to the airplane at Wompah Gate, Geoff Smith and Kerry Provis, the pilot, get into a discussion. There is a difference of opinion in Australia about the dingo. To some, it's savage. To others, it's sort of cuddly. Sheep farmers say dingoes eat sheep, but scientists wonder if they aren't partial to wombats and wallabies. In the big cities, there are a few people who want to breed dingoes and keep them around the house.

"Come across any pups lately?" Kerry asks.

"Oh yeah," Geoff says.

"I want a couple. Pay good money."

"Not allowed to keep 'em, you know," Geoff says. "A dingo is a wild animal. Some will go through 30 or 40 sheep at a time. Just tear 'em to pieces."

Kerry sighs, "Ah, well. . . ."

Geoff drives on in silence. He has been on the fence nine years, keeping the dingo out. It's a good fence. And, when you come to think about it, maybe the dingoes have been pretty good neighbors. At the gate, Geoff watches Kerry climb into the cockpit. He waves goodbye and starts to drive off.

Then he stops again and calls out, "How big you want those pups?"

—BARRY NEWMAN, May 1978

43. *The Last Word*

SAPINTA, Romania—As parting shots go, this was a doozy:

"During my life, I liked many men. I loved to drink and have a good time with handsome men by my side. But you, Darvai, my husband, as long as you live you should think only of me, because you'll never find another wife like me."

So reads the grave marker of the village good-time girl, who lies near the village butcher:

"I slaughtered many pigs and ate much meat," says his epitaph. "Maybe it was the meat that killed me. I wanted to grow old, but death put me in the ground at 43."

Who lies near the village bartender:

"During my life I had two wives. One was my lover, the other my maid. As a bartender, I always served big glasses filled to the top. I leave you with a mug of beer and say goodbye."

Who lies near the village lumberjack:

"I was drunk and walked into the woods and had an accident. The logs fell on top of me. To you who still live, be careful and don't do what I did."

Together they all are buried in Sapinta's "merry cemetery," where the dearly departed truly get the last word, and often the last laugh, in a country where daily life above ground is as drab as an old Communist documentary. Some 600 ornate wooden crosses awash in blues, reds and yellows display carved caricatures of the deceased and bear several first-person lines of verse in a bawdy peasant dialect. Even Nicolae Ceausescu, the dour dictator who was executed during the 1989 revolution, is said to have chuckled during a visit to the Sapinta graveyard.

"I am deeply impressed with the artistry," he scribbled in the guest book.

Stan Ion Patras, the cross maker at the time, felt obliged to carve a portrait of his powerful visitor. He chiseled "Nicolae Ceausescu, may he live many years" and personally presented it to the Communist leader. Afterward, the cemetery flourished as a rare patch of free expression and the cross maker was allowed to entertain all manner of visiting foreign dignitaries, a special treat in a country where Ceausescu had outlawed contact with foreigners.

Sapinta is a hard-luck village of 5,000 people folded away in the rolling hills of Romania's far north, a stone's throw from the Ukraine border. They are poor people; among them they possess five tractors and no indoor toilets. They are industrious people; most every house has beautiful, hand-woven wool rugs hung out for sale in the front yard. They are feisty people; two years ago, when a neo-Communist mayor took over the town's administration, they blocked roads in protest and stared down the national army.

"Independent. Stubborn," says Grigore Lutai, the priest at the Sapinta Orthodox Church, which is surrounded by the cemetery. "They always want to do what others don't."

In 1932, for instance, Mr. Patras started carving the crosses, the caricatures and the rhymes for no other reason than, as far as he could tell, no one else was doing it. Indeed, the cemetery is designated as a United Nations cultural landmark because it is the only one of its kind.

Beyond the cemetery's wooden portal, where ducks and chickens trundle over the graves, this mortal world meets the afterworld. Often with a bad hangover.

"Since my wife left me, I withdrew to a vile bar," says Stefan Gheorghei, whose grave marker shows him sitting at a table holding a drink. "I drank and was happy with my friends. You who still live, be happy as I was, enjoy life as I did."

Dumitru Holdis, though, has another story. "Schnapps is pure poison that brings pain and tears. Death came and stepped on me. To you who love schnapps as I did, it will also happen to you."

Mr. Patras, who often was paid in brandy, preferred that people compose their own verses before going to the grave. But for those who didn't have time, he consulted with the relatives before beginning to carve. Since most of the people of Sapinta were illiterate then, he delighted in taking some literary license.

"None of the relatives would complain because they couldn't read what he wrote," says Dumitru Pop, the current cross carver who took over after Mr. Patras died in 1977. "Now most everyone can read, but still I am honest. I carve what I see. I am an observer of the world."

And in this part of the world, strange things happen; dead men do tell tales:

"Here I lie without my head," says Ian Sauliuc. "I was a simple shepherd. A bad Hungarian came and shot me in the head and severed it from my body. May he be damned for all eternity."

"Cursed be the taxi that came from Sibiu," says Marie Turda. "In all of Romania it could find no place to park except in front of our house, where it ran over me."

"Lying in bed I was struck by lightning," reports Grigore Tite. "My mother was grief-stricken. She had only one son who went to earth so young. Oh, you treacherous death."

Communists from the Ceausescu era are buried here and there, praising the party and hailing the hammer and sickle. And since the 1989 revolution, crosses have appeared commenting on life in political prisons.

But most of the graveyard chatter is filled with loves and regrets.

"I loved horses and women. I loved to sit at the dinner tables with women of other men. I'm sorry I died so young," laments one.

"When I was a young lad in the village, I loved to dance to the sound of the violin. But after I got married, my wife wouldn't let me. And I died in sorrow," wails another.

Some of the deceased scold their children: "Remember, I raised you and did everything for you."

Some boss around their spouses: "You, wife, come over here now and bring me my lunch."

And some talk to their sheep: "Come on, you sheep, come on. You love life, not like me, poor me. For I had to leave you."

In Sapinta's here and now, the church roof leaks when its rains. The colors on the cemetery's old crosses are fading. New paint is scarce and expensive. Money is tight. Still, the living of Sapinta go about their farming and weaving, their drinking and singing, composing their epitaphs and envisioning their crosses in their heads.

"I have told my congregation, it is your moral duty to be buried in this cemetery and have a cross made when you die in order to carry on the tradition," says Father Lutai, the parish priest. "For the poorer people, the church will pay—somehow we scrape together the money for the paint and the wood. We must do it. This cemetery, it is a record of our lives."

Dumitru Bodnar, a 65-year-old tractor mechanic, reckoned his was about over when soldiers surrounded the town in 1992 and dragged him away from an anti-Communist protest. Then and there, in the clutch of the soldiers, he settled on his everlasting message:

The portrait will show him riding a tractor, with a key in one hand and a hammer in the other. "Here lies Dumitru Bodnar," he will say for eternity. "I was a mechanic. I always worked hard. As long as I lived, I hated the Communists. And I loved the schnapps. Drink one on me."

—ROGER THUROW, June 1994

44. *Touring God's Country*

THE GARDEN OF EDEN, Syria—You drive a few miles north from Damascus on the road to Aleppo, turn left, cross the railroad tracks, pass the pencil factory and the orange-juice bottling plant, bump past some tents inhabited by Palestinian refugees, wave to two somnolent Syrian soldiers and pull to a stop at the pink-painted trees.

And there you are—whence it all began: Eden.

It isn't precisely as God describes it. No cherubim, for instance. No flaming swords. The vegetation is a bit sparser than the Lord leads you to expect in the book of Genesis when He refers to "every tree that is pleasant to the sight." The flora consists mainly of leafless birch trees whose trunks have been painted pink or blue in a dubious attempt at beautification. The river that God says watered Eden and then parted to form four great rivers seems to have narrowed into a single muddy stream. Altogether, it might be your average urban American park in winter.

To be truthful, this isn't everybody's Eden. Syria's historical and bitter rival, Iraq, claims that Eden lies south of Baghdad, somewhere near the Persian Gulf. And some Russians claim that Paradise lies in sunny Soviet Georgia.

Still, any paradise is hard to find and one at hand is well worth two afar. Besides, Syrians cite "proof" for their claim: Not far from here is a crypt on a mountaintop that Syrians say contains the remains of Abel, the slain son of Adam and Eve. (Of course, in a part of the world where almost everything is contested, the Egyptians allege that Abel is entombed in Cairo.)

To be fair, one also must acknowledge that Paradise is a relative sort of thing. For Arabs, accustomed to a topography of endless sand and stone, any paltry patch of grass or other greenery seems positively paradisiacal. So, to many Arab minds, is any place patronized by beautiful women not draped in black.

In the summer months this particular Eden is said to be lush with both greenery and femininity. But at this time of year here there are only bare trees, some wilting roses, some Royal Crown Cola umbrellas shading empty pink picnic tables, and a paunchy and balding old man who is smoking his water pipe.

"You have come to the right place. Absolutely. This is Eden," says Abu Hisham Ayub al-Hindi. "And this is tobacco and this is Hubbly Bubbly," he adds, pointing to his pipe.

Mr. al-Hindi, it turns out, is the proprietor of this little piece of Paradise and of "Modern Ghouta," the very best restaurant in Eden.

Mr. al-Hindi is adamant that Adam and Eve once cavorted on this very spot. "For sure," he says. "For sure." In summer, he says, beautiful women walk among his painted trees picking peaches, bananas, figs—and apples. "Just like Eve."

Among the sundry things that seem to be lacking in the garden of Eden are serpents. Perhaps they have all taken to their winter lairs, but there isn't a snake to be seen—though Mr. al-Hindi promises there are plenty when spring comes to Eden.

The Bible, of course, tells us that Adam and Eve were cast out of Eden for tasting forbidden fruit at the invitation of the serpent. Mr. al-Hindi, however, offers another explanation: They ate corn, he says, which gave them diarrhea; rather than despoil Paradise, they departed.

It is an interesting thesis; and it turns out to be a controversial one, at least to Mr. al-Hindi's Syrian Christian assistant. "No, no, no, no," says the young man, who until now has been sitting silently, nodding assent to every word uttered by the proprietor of Paradise. "There was no corn. No corn. Eve ate an apple. She listened to the devil, not to her husband. There is the proof that women aren't trustworthy."

A few hundred yards farther into Eden, Mohamed and Salah, two Syrian youths, are herding sheep. Both boys are convinced they are in Paradise because "it's green and there's water."

Many millenniums ago, two other youths tended sheep here and the elder, Cain, slew the younger, Abel. Mohamed and Salah are aware of the ancient sibling rivalry, but Mohamed says he has no problems with his younger brother. He adds: "The youngest always obeys the eldest."

—KAREN ELLIOTT HOUSE, January 1984

45. *Smoke Got in Their Eyes*

NEW YORK—Some 200 books have been written over the past 14 years in one room here.

Betty Friedan worked on *The Feminine Mystique* in the room more than a decade ago. More recently Nancy Milford wrote *Zelda* there and Robert K. Massie turned out *Nicholas and Alexandra*. Theodore H. White worked there on his *The Making of the President* books.

This incubator for best-sellers is the Frederick Lewis Allen Memorial Room, tucked away on the first floor of the huge New York Public Library at Fifth Avenue and 42nd Street. It is a place where authors come to do research and write, and to smoke if they wish.

The room is named for the editor of Harper's who wrote *Only Yesterday*, an account of the 1920s, and other books on American life, and who liked to smoke, which is why there's an Allen Room today.

The Allen Room has 11 carpeted open cubicles. With space for so few writers at a time, it isn't the easiest place to gain admission to. A writer must have proof of a signed contract with a known publisher, and even then he may have to wait several months to get a cubicle assignment from the Research Libraries Administration Office on the second floor. The current waiting list has about a dozen names.

Because of the demand for space, a writer isn't allowed to use the room more than nine months at a time. "It's like a pregnancy," says Mrs. Friedan. But when she was working on *The Feminine Mystique*, she recalls, the library let her overstay her time briefly "when they saw how hard I was working."

Writers like the room because of the cubicles, which have bookshelves, a chair and a desk (you bring your own typewriter); because they don't have to clear their books away at night; and because of the privacy. "I go in there to write secure from interruptions, not to look at the books," says Arnold Gingrich, publisher of *Esquire*. "There are no phones or visitors."

For a place that's a second home to so many well-known writers, the Allen Room is remarkably modest-looking. Although refurbished last year at a cost of $2,500, the 17½-by-32-foot room still has a threadbare look, literally: The carpeting is worn. The cubicles, while convenient, are barely large enough to work in, and the chairs aren't especially comfortable. Furthermore, there's no view. Facing an inside courtyard, the Allen Room is noted for its gloom.

Though silence is the rule, there are occasional disturbances. For one thing, some of New York's mounted police are permitted to tether their horses in the courtyard and, as Mrs. Milford soon discovered, "You'll be in the middle of a phrase and there'll be neighing."

Other disturbances include the sound of writers thinking out loud, pacing and, on occasion, chatting. "The only person nobody could stand was Betty Friedan," says Mr. Gingrich. "She drove everybody mad with her noise."

"But generally," says Ferdinand Lundberg, who wrote *The Rich and the Super-Rich* in the Allen Room, "if you start talking, someone'll shush you." Most of the writers are there to work, he says, "and a few come in, do their stuff and leave without ever saying a word to anyone." One such is Mr. White of *The Making, etc.*, who says:

"I happen to be one of the most surly people in the world, and when I'm writing I want to be left alone. I don't think I talked to anyone while I was there."

Most of the writers save their conversation till midafternoon when they descend in groups of two or three to the employees' cafeteria on the ground floor for a coffee break. "Then," says Mr. Lundberg, "they all start talking at once. I guess it's because they've been pent up so long." Anyway, noise doesn't disturb Mr. Lundberg. "I started out as a newspaperman in Chicago," he says, "and I can work while the building falls down around me."

The writers generally go out of their way to get along with their colleagues, but sometimes there are disputes over such things as opening a window. And Mrs. Milford has noticed that "a few writers try to establish territorial rights and pick their own cubicles, despite the fact that they're assigned."

The main complaint these days is the smoking in the room, the only place in the library where smoking is permitted. Yet that's precisely why the room was founded. Mrs. Allen recalls that her husband, who before his death in 1954 was also a trustee of the Ford Foundation, loved to work in the Public Library. "But whenever he wanted a cigaret, which was often enough," she says, "he had to stop whatever he was doing and step outside."

After his death the Ford Foundation set up a $25,000 fund in his memory and Mrs. Allen suggested that it be put to use to create a place in the library where writers could smoke. The recent cost of refurbishing the room was paid for by the remainder of that fund.

"If you find smoking relaxing, as I do," Mr. Lundberg says, "you work in the Allen Room." But even he says that on occasion "the place fills up with smoke." To avoid the fumes, a few writers have even moved to the Typing Room or the Wertheim Study, two other rooms set aside by the library for writing and research.

Most of the authors, however, wouldn't think of deserting the Allen Room. Besides the convenience and privacy, there is a certain status. The Typing Room is mainly for writers of magazine articles. And it isn't air-conditioned. The Wertheim Study is largely used by graduate students doing research. Typing isn't permitted there.

Among the Typing Room's adherents is David Kahn, who wrote much of *The Codebreakers* there. Because the Typing Room is on the second floor and thus closer to the Main Reading Room on the third, "we get faster delivery of our books" for research, he says. He also likes the fact that the Typing Room is large and airy with windows that face south and get the sun. And Mr. Kahn doesn't like air-conditioning anyway.

"I chose substance over status," he says.

Other advantages of the Typing Room include more space to work in. The room is about twice the size of the Allen Room and has four long tables at which the writers work. "If you're a spreader outer," Mr. Lundberg says, "you use the Typing Room." While users of the Typing Room must clear away their books at night, few of them find this a disadvantage. Lockers are provided for $1 a month.

A frequent user of the third-floor Wertheim Study is Barbara Tuchman, the writer of historical works, who put up the money to create the room in 1964 in memory of her father, Maurice Wertheim, former publisher of *The Nation* and a founder of The Theatre Guild.

"I like to get my research down on cards," says Mrs. Tuchman. "It's my way of crystallizing my thinking as I go along." She does her actual writing at home.

One advantage all three rooms share is that the keys that open them up—all the writers are supplied with one—also open up the employees' washrooms. "That's a big plus," says Mr. Kahn. "The public ones aren't always so clean."

—STEPHEN GROVER, July 1972

46. *Yes, We Have No Bananas*

ATHENS—Are there no bananas in Olympia?

Yes.

Are there no bananas in Thebes? Yes. In Corinth? Yes. In Sparta, Marathon, Delphi? Yes, yes, yes.

Are there no bananas on Crete?

That depends on your definition of banana. Little green pods do grow on that Greek island, on scorched, drooping plants that look as though they want to be banana trees. They are called bananas (the Greek word for banana is pronounced banana), but they don't taste much like bananas—or, at least, that's what people say. A foreigner can't easily get a taste of a ripe Cretan banana. They are all sold secretly, on the black market. To buy a banana anywhere in Greece, you need a connection.

All over the world, people take bananas for granted. A bunch of bananas off the boat from Panama isn't exactly what dreams are made of, right? Well, in this country, dreams *are* made of bananas.

Alien bananas are contraband in Greece. For Greeks, a sweet, yellow, pulpy Panamanian banana is the forbidden fruit.

"Greece no banana," says the taxi driver at the Athens airport, ecstatically accepting an exotic beauty as a tip. A traveler has just slipped through customs with a bunch in a brown paper bag, defying a five-pound limit. The driver tenderly places his in the glove compartment. "I show it to my grandson," he says.

It has been 12 years now since the last banana boat sailed away from Piraeus. There are children in Greece today who don't even know what a banana is. Greece was a dictatorship in 1971, and dictatorships sometimes do strange things. The one in Greece outlawed the traffic in foreign bananas.

The head of internal security, Col. Stelios Pattakos, gave the order. He was born on Crete, a bone-dry island, and was friendly toward some farmers there who had it in their heads to try growing a fruit native to equatorial jungles. The colonel got rid of the competition. Still, the Cretan crop was so puny it couldn't satisfy a 50th of the Greek passion for bananas. The price went up. The government imposed controls. And then the banana peddlers went underground.

When the dictatorship collapsed in 1974, Col. Pattakos was sentenced to life imprisonment for non-banana-related offenses. Democracy returned—but bananas didn't. Bureaucrats do strange things, too.

A banana avalanche, they determined, would hurt the Greek apple business. Everybody would suddenly stop eating apples and start eating bananas. It didn't do any good to argue that comparing apples and bananas was like comparing apples and oranges. So Col. Pattakos got life, and the Greek people got life without bananas.

One man, on his own, has borne the greatest burden of bananalessness. His name is Myron Mauricides. He has short gray hair and a thick neck that cranes forward when he walks. He stoops. He wears crushed cord jackets. He looks like Jack Lemmon in one of his more exasperated roles.

Mr. Mauricides is the head of the Association of Greek Banana Importers.

When he is presented with a banana during lunch at an Athens cafe, Mr. Mauricides's eyes go limpid with nostalgia. "Ah, smell," he says, taking a whiff and hiding the thing under his napkin. "You know, after the war, people used to bring nylons. Then it was Scotch. Now they bring bananas."

For 23 years, until 1962, Mr. Mauricides was a middleman on 42nd Street in New York. He fixed up American companies with Greek distributors. Then he thought, "If I can get accounts for other people, why not get one for myself?" So he got the Bristol-Myers account and moved back to Greece.

Mr. Mauricides did well, so well that Bristol-Myers moved to Greece, too, and put him out of business. "I snooped around for something else," he says. "Bananas looked good."

Thus, Myron Mauricides became the first person to sell boxed bananas to the Hellenes. "We had a boat coming in once a week, like clockwork," he says. Then the junta struck and bananas were finished. "There isn't much more to talk about," Mr. Mauricides says, "except 12 years of frustration."

Only once since the onset of prohibition have Greeks plumbed the joys of the true banana. For three wild months in 1978, while a free-thinking minister looked the other way, they ate through an entire year's supply—50,000 tons. That is 300 million bananas, 33 for every man, woman and child. Nobody knew if he would ever see a banana again.

After the binge, some truckers began to smuggle bananas in from Germany. One was caught and thrown into jail, and that was the end of that. For a time, Yugoslavian tourists took to sneaking into the country with bags full of bananas. They made a killing and went home loaded with blue jeans. Then Greece imposed the five-pound limit. Yugoslavian tourists were forced to surrender their bananas at the border, or else eat them on the spot.

"Can you imagine the scene?" says Mr. Mauricides. "Somebody should make a Broadway musical out of this!"

Intent on breaking the apple lobby, Mr. Mauricides proposed that the government allow bananas into the country and then impose a banana tax. "They tax liquor. Why not bananas?" he asks. "Listen, the government could take in $120,000 a day on this. Why not turn the banana to your advantage? Why not squeeze the banana for all it's worth?"

The government won't bite. (It won't comment, either.)

Now Mr. Mauricides is in court. He requested an import permit. The government denied it. He sued. A judge found for bananas. But the case is sensitive. So it has been sent up to the Council of State, the highest administrative court in the land.

Greek banana policy is at issue in the Common Market, too. Greece is a member, but it won't let in Common Market bananas. Where do bananas grow in the Common Market? In Martinique and Guadeloupe; those are Caribbean islands, but in France they are considered as French as Champagne. The Common Market banana case appears destined for the European Court of Justice.

Myron Mauricides has finished his fish. For dessert he orders fruit salad: a dish of sliced apples and oranges. Mr. Mauricides takes a bite. His lips curl as if it were a mouthful of quicklime. Stealthily, he slips his smuggled gift from under his napkin and cuts it into the salad. He tastes, and smiles. "An apple," he says, "is no substitute for a banana."

But can a Cretan banana stand in for a Chiquita? The way to find out is to eat one. An exhaustive search of Athens fails to turn up a clandestine banana pusher. The alternative is a voyage to Crete and a long drive to the village of Arvi, on the island's south coast, where the Cretan banana was born.

The road to Arvi, corrugated by a grader, would probably puree a truckload of Chiquitas. It winds down to the sea out of a desiccated mountain, past patches of stunted banana trees toasting in the summer sun.

Arvi has a street, a hotel, a cafe. It has a store that sells seeds and bug killer. Dimitrias Hatzakis and Yiorgos Spanakis are in there one morning, drinking coffee. Mr. Spanakis runs the store. Mr. Hatzakis grows bananas.

"Let me tell you about the climate here," says Mr. Hatzakis, who is fat and bald and who used to be in construction. "This is the only place in Greece that the sparrows don't leave in winter."

"We have the smallest rainfall in the country, though, unfortunately for the bananas," says Mr. Spanakis, stroking his mustache. He has decorated his shop with cactus plants.

"Bananas need humidity," Mr. Hatzakis says. "It's our only problem."

Neither the corrugated road nor perpetual drought has prevented prosperity from making its way here. The banana growers of Arvi, Mr. Hatzakis boasts, are the richest farmers in Greece.

"When a smuggler offers four times the official price," he says, "you have to look at the practical side of bananas." But you don't want to be caught selling at four times the official price, so "we write out false receipts," says Mr. Spanakis.

"If they start importing, that will be the end of us here," Mr. Hatzakis says. He has a better idea: government money to build greenhouses. Production would shoot up, prices would come down, and the Greeks would be in banana heaven. Mr. Hatzakis has a few greenhouses already, and he offers a tour of them.

Set up on the mountainside, they are covered with soft plastic and fed by black rubber hoses that look like errant sea snakes. Inside, the heat is equatorial, and the air is thick with moisture and the sweet smell of mulch. The trees are tall and full; water beads on their leaves. The fruit, though small, appears to have true banana potential.

"We could compete with imports," Mr. Hatzakis says. "Just give us ten more years."

Would it be possible to taste one of his hothouse bananas?

"Oh, you won't find any here," he says, emerging into the sunlight. "We ship them green. We don't have ripe bananas in Arvi."

Yes.

—BARRY NEWMAN, July 1983

47. Of Counterculture, Counter Cultures and Pig Rights

BERKELEY, Calif.—It's business as usual at Jerome Morrison's sidewalk rock crystal stand on Telegraph Avenue here. He patiently listens to a customer's psychic and energy needs and suggests she would benefit from "the self-love transmitting properties" of a nice polished piece of rose quartz.

"Take it into the bathtub with you," says Mr. Morrison, who also proffers, without prompting, a lecture on the dark side of crystal energy. "Atlantis, you know, was destroyed" when power-hungry Atlanteans misused the energy of huge red-crystal "generators."

Just up the street at Shambhala Booksellers, the metaphysical lunch crowd shuffles in to peruse titles on Tibetan healing arts, soul travel and the sensual secrets of ancient Indian sex-breathing methods. One customer leafs through *The New Man,* a book whose thesis is that a race of mutant New Age Homo sapiens, emerging from genetic seeds planted by enlightened ancients 3,500 years ago, will soon flourish and save the world from greed.

Outside, on the sidewalk, a man with long hair, yellowing teeth and a battered guitar is delivering stand-up comedy to an audience more interested in shopping for tie-dyed baby underwear.

"If you have no money, they call you a bum. If you have money in a bank, they call you politically incorrect. I don't get it," he says.

Oh, Berkeley, Berkeley, Berkeley. If it's true that the eccentrics of earth moved to America and the eccentrics of America to California, then the eccentrics of California have a special place in their heart for this funkily scenic haven on the east shore of San Francisco Bay.

Berkeley, population 105,000, earned its reputation in the turbulent '60s as a crossroads of the counterculture and a kiln of the free-speech movement. While much of America has spent the decades since then growing conservative and homogeneous in front of television sets, Berkeley has continued to march, organize, protest, meditate and stir its yogurt (organic, of course) to a different drummer.

Not that it can't enjoy itself the while. These days, the town is a curious and seemingly contradictory blend of the radical and the chic. Its streets are full of speechifiers and New Age peddlers, and its politicians spend as much effort assailing U.S. foreign policy as mending streets; yet revolutionaries of a different kind have added a decidedly upscale patina to Berkeley's fringe cast. So many first-class (and expensive) restaurants, bakeries, gourmet food shops and wine stores have opened here in recent years that some say the counterculture is being challenged by a counter culture.

"This is a town in which half the people are seeking to overthrow the federal government while the other half are seeking the perfect croissant," says R. Howard Bloch, head of the University of California-Berkeley French department, who after 15 years here has satirized the town in a novel called *Moses in the Promised Land*. His protagonist is an environmentally conscious termite eradicator specializing in "sensitive rehabilitation of unwanted insect species."

Mr. Bloch marvels how Berkeleyites can simultaneously indulge leftist politics and bourgeois tastes. Shopping at a chic French bakery not long ago, he found a $16 tart that bore, in elegant whipped-cream script, the slogan "Victory to the Sandinistas." He's also fond of recalling the time an advocate of Berkeley's strict rent controls declared, in full earnestness, that it was the redistribution of cash freed up by rent control that permitted the epicurean enterprises to flourish.

Skeptics like Mr. Bloch aside, Berkeley tends to see itself not as far-out or sold-out but as far ahead, an incubator of ideas that, though seemingly radical at first, often prove durable and even exportable. The mayor, Loni Hancock, ticks off a few: Berkeley gave birth to the disabled-rights movement, she says. It was the first American city to shun investments in companies with holdings in South Africa. It was in the vanguard of U.S. communities declaring themselves sanctuaries for Central Americans seeking political asylum. It pioneered the idea of phasing out Styrofoam fast-food packaging for environmental reasons.

All of these proposals have since taken root elsewhere, some vigorously. But other sparks spun off from the Berkeley maelstrom have produced effects beyond their goal: The town's embrace of civil rights for the homeless has attracted a large transient population, and now complaints of drug dealing and related crimes are growing. And Berkeley's once-proficient elementary-school system now is, by any objective measure, a mess. Parents of some 35 percent of eligible children send them to private schools, often complaining of a zealous busing system dedicated to pinpoint racial balance, and of budget cuts and mismanagement that have lopped off teachers and gutted enrichment programs.

Mayor Hancock, who would be a radical in Cleveland but is a middle-of-the-roader here, is determined to fight Berkeley's flaky image without forsaking a larger role in the universe. She is determined not to turn the town—coveted by developers for its scenic hills and proximity to San Francisco—into an upper-class BMW ghetto.

Her flamboyant predecessor, Gus Newport, made headlines by galloping off on official visits to Cuba and taking mortar fire while on sympathy visits to El Salvador's Marxist guerrillas. Ms. Hancock is known as a workaholic and conciliator who has kept an eye on the international political horizon but her feet firmly on Berkeley's sidewalks.

One day, she spends the afternoon on the phone to U.S. Embassy officials in El Salvador helping arrange the release of the mayor of a Salvadoran village—a Berkeley "sister city"—apparently kidnapped by rightists. On another, she surveys one of the first fruits of a drive for "socially responsible" businesses: the redevelopment of a long-mothballed spice-plant site.

The project passes moral muster in Berkeley: It preserves historic buildings; it includes low-income housing and subsidized space for craftsmen; and a biotechnology company for which it provides space promises to give locals first crack at any new jobs.

This isn't to say, of course, that a nuclear-waste processor or munitions maker would have a place in Berkeley's happy eclecticism, or that Berkeley is in any way going mainstream. Even hard-core Berkeleyites winced last summer when—after one waterfront commissioner murdered another in gruesome fashion—the city offered free group psychiatric counseling for residents traumatized by the crime.

Then there's that whole array of uniquely Berkeleyian pursuits: classes in "non-violent jujitsu"; the Church for the Transformation of Depression; seminars for "recovering Catholics"; vegetarian potluck dinners dedicated to the rights of performing animals. They help explain why the place is often ridiculed as "the People's Republic of Berkeley" or—the currently preferred term of derision—as "Berserkeley."

In the tradition of constant street theater that best describes Berkeley politics, some 400 residents clashed last March in a rancorous debate over whether to adopt a Palestinian refugee camp as a sister city. The measure failed 6–3 following a rally by a typically Berkeley-esque coalition: fervid supporters of Israel in league with homeless people carrying placards reading ADOPT US!

And last week Berkeley turned its attention to a new municipal cause. The Citizens Humane Commission was the setting for a spirited debate on whether to exempt Chinese potbelly pigs—miniatures sold as household pets—from an ordinance that effectively bans regular barnyard pigs from town. The issue wasn't, as one might suppose, whether potbelly pigs are sufficiently domesticated, or whether they smell; instead, explains a commission spokeswoman, it was "whether it is humane to impose domesticity on yet another animal," given the onerous conditions under which many already live.

The commission has just forwarded a lukewarm pro-pig recommendation to the zoning department. But one commissioner vows to fight on, contending that domestication of any animal "deprives that animal of living its own life."

"Be assured," says the university's Prof. Bloch, "that Berkeley is crazier than ever."

—KEN WELLS, January 1989

48. *A Night Among the Snipers*

SARAJEVO, Bosnia-Herzegovina—At a Serbian sniper post in a charred mountain restaurant, the afternoon poker game is just under way when Muslim gunners open fire.

Bullets fly past with a faint, high-pitched whine. Machine-gun fire rakes the pine trees, showering needles around the Serbian post. The card players scramble for their guns. Then, huddled behind log barricades, they wait as a gray-bearded man peers through opera glasses.

"Maybe they are over there," he says, gesturing vaguely at a bullet-ridden house. One man shrugs and fires wildly. Another curses as his hunting rifle jams.

"Dammit, where are my socks?" shouts another soldier, irritable from being awakened from his nap inside a crude lean-to of burst sandbags and chipped cinder blocks.

After a few minutes, the Muslims cease firing and the Serbs return to their cards. "Let's hope that keeps Ali Baba quiet until dark," says the gray-bearded man, using Serbian shorthand for Alija Izetbegovic, the leader of the Bosnian Muslims.

Since spring, the Serbs of Bosnia—supported by Serbs from the rest of the former Yugoslavia—have clashed with their predominantly Muslim neighbors, who control much of this city and who have declared an independent Bosnian state. Occupying the hills that encircle Sarajevo, the Serbian gunners have for months been viewed as global outlaws, ruthless and regimented killers who rain death and destruction on a helpless city.

But the view from front-line posts—visited at random and without military escort—isn't always so intimidating. Here, the self-styled army of the Serbian Republic of Bosnia-Herzegovina seems at times a loose corps of ill-equipped, ill-trained and even underfed troops enduring what looks like a wretched camping trip. At one post, the latest recruit is a young female secretary and the newest arms shipment is a pair of Tommy guns, straight out of a James Cagney gangster film. Serbian irregulars—whose numbers are roughly equal to the army's 35,000 men—are even more ragtag, appearing more like bikers than fighters, with ponytails, running shoes and black patches bearing skulls and crossbones stuck on their mix-and-match fatigues.

Beneath a thick crust of bravado, often stoked with plum brandy, many Serb army units appear driven not by dreams of a greater Serbia, but by fear of a foe they regard as fanatical and better-armed than themselves—dubious notions fostered daily by Serbian propaganda.

"The Muslims have the best weapons from rich Arab sheiks, and Khomeini warriors leading them into battle," says Mirko Orevehsek, a music teacher who cradles his machine gun as if it were a guitar.

Mr. Orevehsek's army post, in the parking lot of the gutted restaurant just above downtown Sarajevo, is near the bobsled run in the 1984 Winter Olympics. In August, Muslims tried to take this perch in a bloody offensive that stalled 50 yards from the restaurant's balcony. Since then, the two sides have been holding their ground, exchanging daily volleys across 150 yards of pockmarked rooftops and trees pruned by machine-gun fire.

The two sides also exchange jokes and insults over shared radio frequencies. Muslim snipers invite their Serb counterparts over for coffee—"Only Turkish coffee," they quip—and even poke fun at their own propaganda. In one recent broadcast, a phony newscaster reported that Muslims had been attacked by both Serbian and United Nations forces with grenades, tanks and tactical nuclear weapons—but managed to repel the attack with only one soldier injured.

Such ironies abound in a war that pits neighbor against neighbor. At the restaurant post, most of the soldiers pass the day studying pornographic magazines from Zagreb, the capital of another enemy, Croatia. A soldier named Jelko says he often came to the restaurant before the war with Croat and Muslim girlfriends. As head of a small export-import firm in Sarajevo, he had 12 employees, only two of them Serbian.

"I don't fight for ideology, or religion, or nationalism," says the bearded, gap-toothed 30-year-old. Pointing toward his home, which he fled three months ago, he adds: "I fight because I want to be back down there with my books and my CD player and my Gitanes cigarets."

These days, he subsists on cheap Macedonian tobacco and daily rations of bread and gruel. He dozes, when he can, a few feet from his machine gun, on a wooden pallet made from one of the restaurant's doors. His unit's toilet is a chair with its cane bottom missing, which soldiers carry into the woods behind the restaurant. Water is scarce, as Muslims control the electricity that powers Sarajevo's water pumps, which are in Serb hands.

The Serbian soldiers fight for 48 hours, then rest for 24 behind the lines. Paid only $60 a month, they can do little with their free time except search for scarce cigarets in towns behind the lines. At the front, while his comrades pore over comic books and pornography, Jelko huddles in his lean-to, reading the stories of Isaac Bashevis Singer. He reads this and other Jewish fiction for clues about his own nation's unraveling. "In Poland and Russia, an ancient Jewish life vanished just like that," he says. "Now, maybe Yugoslavia dies the same way, for nothing."

A month ago, Jelko's best friend in the unit poked his head above the barricades, then fell back, muttered "Mother, Mother," and died from a bullet in his neck. "He was an only child," Jelko says. On Monday, a rocket-propelled grenade hit the woods just behind the restaurant and blew off the legs of a soldier strolling up the hill to bum a cigaret at the next post. His blood still stains the lush, needle-strewn path through the pines.

None of the eight men in Jelko's unit, or neighboring units, have helmets or flak jackets. They have no night-vision equipment, no ammunition for their bazooka. One man carries a World War II rifle. There are no formal ranks. The nominal commander, a 24-year-old, has vanished for the day, the soldiers say, to sleep with a girlfriend.

A short walk up the hill, through trees strung with cable for radio phones, Diana Stoyanovic sits surrounded by men from nearby units. The 31-year-old secretary has a submachine gun swung over her drab olive uniform. She joined 15 days ago and is nervously awaiting her first taste of combat. "I do not shoot so well," she says, "but from what I see here I will be no worse than the men."

The Serbs claim they aren't snipers, because they fire only at fighters and only when fired upon. But Sarajevo, strung along the valley floor just below, is an easy and tempting target. Through telescopic sights of the Serbs' best guns, it is possible to peer in downtown windows and see the faces of the few pedestrians sprinting from building to building. The city's shattered skyline shows just how much damage artillery has done, most of it the work of the Serbs' vastly superior guns.

For some Serbs, enraged at the loss of their homes, there is little remorse about shooting at former neighbors. At a well-fortified mortar and machine-gun post on the eastern edge of Sarajevo, Mirko Mihalovic has a commanding view of Muslim positions. "It is just like killing rabbits," the 62-year-old civil engineer says as flares light the night skies and guns open fire. "I feel nothing," he says.

But at the hillside restaurant, the atmosphere is different. As night falls, Jelko breaks an ammunition box with his boots and feeds it as kindling for the fire. Another man pours coffee into plastic grenade casings that double as mugs. A newcomer passes around yet another dirty magazine. "Military reading," he jokes.

The first snow has already fallen on peaks higher up, and Jelko isn't looking forward to long months of stamping his feet and huddling by the fire. He goes on 24-hour leave at dawn and will head for the library for a new writer he wants to read, and a particular title. In halting English he says, "For who it is the bell tolls?"

—TONY HORWITZ, September 1992

49. *Things Are Hopping in New York*

Julien Bronson of Bronson Tropical Birds in New York refuses to discuss the matter, but his five wallabies have escaped.

Mr. Bronson's loss is science's gain, however. As a result of the mass escape, hitherto unknown scientific data on the Australian marsupial's habits have come to light, and it now is possible to update the Encyclopaedia Britannica section (volume 23, VASE to ZYGO) on wallabies. Make it read: The wallaby can outrun a policeman, is afraid of nine-year-old boys and is found wild in Westchester County, N.Y.

The wallabies, which look like scale models of kangaroos, escaped from Mr. Bronson's backyard in suburban Bedford, N.Y., last August. Mr. Bronson, who is in the wallaby export-import game, apparently kept the breakout quiet, perhaps because it may be illegal to run a house of wallabies in Westchester County. (Westchester's officials aren't really sure what the county's wallaby laws are, but the building inspector in Bedford says he thinks it's illegal to wilfully keep wallabies there. Would offenders be taken to kangaroo court?)

It isn't known who made the first wild-wallaby sighting in the county. The shy animals generally do their hopping about at night, and they probably were seen by several natives who figured it would be best just to keep quiet—and quit drinking. A few weeks ago, though, a wallaby was hit by a car, and the word now is spreading that there really are wallabies in Westchester.

One man who has made two wallaby sightings is Allan Crisfield, a 27-year-old patrolman in Bedford. The first time was several weeks ago. He says a wallaby hopped right across the road in front of his patrol car at three in the morning. "I didn't tell anybody about that one," he says. "When you're on routine patrol and you see a kangaroo, you start to wonder," he adds.

Then one night a couple of weeks ago, he says, "three men came running into headquarters and said a kangaroo just went over the hill.

They looked like they were in shock." Armed with a dog-catching net, Mr. Crisfield gave chase. "But he'd run, stop, look at me—then zang!—off he'd go again," he says. "He was faster than the devil."

Was it the same wallaby each time? "I don't know, they all look alike to me," he says. Did the wallaby look hungry? "I wouldn't know what a hungry one looked like." Did the wallaby look scared? "I couldn't tell if *he* was scared."

One reason Mr. Crisfield didn't get his wallaby might be that he used the wrong equipment. Mr. Bronson's wallabies came from New Zealand, according to Mrs. Bronson (she didn't know her husband didn't want to discuss the matter), so this newspaper, trying to be helpful, went to a lady who works at the New Zealand consulate and who is wise in the ways of wallabies. She was asked how to catch a New Zealand wallaby. "Boomerangs," she says, "that's what the aborigines use."

Wallabies come in various sizes, and—since Mr. Bronson isn't talking—no one really knows how big the Westchester wallabies are. Patrolman Crisfield says the one he chased was about a foot and a half high. But Scott Peer, a nine-year-old who saw one in Chappaqua last Thursday, says it was about three feet tall, according to his mother. But Mrs. Peer adds, "It doubtless looked bigger to a young boy."

Scott Peer got within 10 or 12 feet of the wallaby, he told his mother, and perhaps it's just as well he didn't get any closer. David Nellis, a mammalogist at the Bronx Zoo, says wallabies "have a pretty bad kick." He says they have another major weapon, too: "Big toenails." But Mr. Nellis notes that wallabies are vegetarians and "aren't going to attack you like a lion."

Mr. Nellis doubts that the wallabies can last the winter in Westchester. "It's possible they could survive until it gets very cold, down around zero," he says. But then, he says, they'll probably die of exposure or pneumonia or starvation—"just like if a man gets lost in the North Woods."

Mr. Nellis also doubts that anybody can catch a wallaby, but nevertheless Mr. Bronson is said to be offering a $50 reward for the capture and return of a wallaby. (But a captor probably could hold out for more. Mrs. Bronson says the animals, which were to be shipped to the zoo in Rome, are worth $250 each.)

Any captor will also get a plaque from the "Mt. Kisco Patent Trader," a semi-weekly paper serving upper Westchester and Putnam counties. The "Patent Trader," which broke the kangaroo story, has started a Katch-a-Kanga-Kontest. The contest is open to all area people except employees of the "Patent Trader" or the Bronx Zoo. The contest, the paper says, is "void where prohibited by law."

—MICHAEL GARTNER, August 1967

50. *The Struggles of Otter 76*

VALDEZ, Alaska—It is 9:32 last Thursday morning, and Otter 76 is fighting for her life. She is pinned to a makeshift operating table in a clammy elementary school gym, lungs scored by petroleum poisons. She rattles and gasps, slow spasms rolling up in waves from her hind flippers to her bewhiskered snout. She foams at the mouth and she excretes crude oil. It takes four men to hold her down.

"Come on babes, hang on," exhorts Jeanie Clarke, a volunteer otter attendant from England. Veterinarian Riley Wilson, also a volunteer, frantically pumps drugs into the animal. "Live, damn it," he mutters, and implausibly, Otter 76 does live. The seizure subsides. At 9:43, Otter 76 goes back into her pen, and Mr. Wilson shakes his head and tells a colleague: "I didn't think she'd win that battle."

There will be more battles for her a few hours later. Otter 76 is one of hundreds of otters plucked from Prince William Sound since Exxon Corp.'s tanker, the *Exxon Valdez*, ran aground March 24 and smeared the sound's emerald waters with ten million gallons of oil. Of those otters, only 134 made it alive into the improvised otter rescue center set up here in a gym by a patchwork crew of top marine mammal experts, volunteer animal lovers and hired hands. Their struggles to keep dying otters alive are desperate, touching, occasionally maybe even heroic. Sixty-eight of their otters have died so far.

The otter slaughter has become the most striking symbol of the nation's worst oil spill; the animal's mortality rate here has shocked even otter experts. It is far above anything ever seen in previous oil spills, even though otter rescue may be the only post-spill operation in which about everything that can be done is being done. Otters that make it to the rescue center are swiftly scrubbed clean, pampered and spoon-fed, given oxygen, antitoxins and antibiotics and tender love and tears and prayers.

And still, they die. In a pen ten yards away from where Otter 76 lies exhausted and trembling, a lactating mother otter, its newborn gone, sprawls listlessly. A young pup, its mother gone, rests fitfully in another pen nearby. The pup begins to whimper and cry, the mother answers, and a great keening chorus of otters swells up. Someone suggests maybe bringing mother and pup together, but it can't be done: Mother's milk is probably poisoned. So the motherless child and the childless mother sing their strange song, off and on, for hours.

A day later, they die within two hours of one another.

As of yesterday, there were 46 otters checked in at the otter hospital, just a small piece of an environmental picture that seems to darken daily. Scientists now say that as many as 4,000 otters—more than a third of the sound's pre-spill population—are presumed dead.

Some 5,000,000 gallons of oil remain on the water. On many miles of shoreline, oil has seeped through the gravelly beaches into subterranean cavities. Tides will leach that oil back into the waters where the otters swim, probably for years.

All of which means they will be busy down at the otter rescue center for a long, long time.

The center was thrown together in the first frantic days following the spill by a ragtag team of animal lovers and volunteer veterinarians under the loose direction of the Sea World Research Center of San Diego, which is affiliated with the same Sea World that runs the killer whale and porpoise shows. Exxon is footing the bill, and Sea World's marine mammal experts say they have a blank check.

In three sleepless weeks, the center has gone from tiny, suffocating quarters in a junior college administration building to the less tiny but still suffocating quarters at the elementary school gym. Six rows of wooden pens, 96 pens in all, stretch from beneath one basketball goal to the other. A mixmaster of copper and plastic pipes snakes underfoot and overhead. The place is wet and the temperature is 47 degrees and it reeks of marine life. And marine death.

Early in the disaster, as many as 50 boats were retrieving otters and bringing them in for treatment. That's down to five boats now, all manned by professional registered otter rescuers. The U.S. Fish & Wildlife Service last week ordered amateur otter rescuers to cease and desist because "otters are mean and they bite," a spokesman explains. Five boats on the vastness of Prince William Sound are like five ants on a parking lot, and a lot of people here find this an incomprehensible step that will only mean fewer otters saved.

In any event, capturing the otters and getting them back to land can indeed be tricky work. Until they become too sick to mount any defense, even oiled otters will scramble and dive to get away from human hands. Mike Lewis, a biologist with the state's Department of Environmental Conservation, displays a jagged gash that loops around the whole circumference of his thumb.

"Tried to catch an otter with bare hands and duct tape," Mr. Lewis says. "For the first and last time."

He opens the cargo hatch of his helicopter; the otter, which was finally captured and stuffed in there, chewed through a six-inch section of steel sheeting. Helicopter pilots say one chopper came within a split second and a few feet of crashing into the sound when a 100-pound otter the pilot thought was dead revived and rampaged through the cockpit before being subdued.

Otter 76 presented no such difficulties. She was snared on April 5 while lying in the snow 30 feet from the water's edge on Knight Island, where some of the heaviest concentrations of oil hit. She didn't look too bad then. Her coat, golden brown with veils of silver and gray along her neck and snout, was only lightly oiled.

Once caught, otters are brought to a small scrubbing station in the junior college building. This is stage one of otter triage and it can be wild. One day last week four otters arrived, yowling in cages like the ones people use to take their dogs on airplanes. Jeremy Fitz-Gibbon, a barrel-chested mammal expert from the Vancouver Public Aquarium, inspects the otters as otter nurses load syringes and pass out rain gear. "This guy's got oil on him," Mr. Fitz-Gibbon announces.

Neil Utkov, a vet from Memphis who came here as a volunteer, pumps two shots of anesthetic into the struggling otter. What about an injection of antibiotics, someone asks. "Wait until he's out," the vet replies. "I don't want this guy to feel any more hurt than he has to."

In 15 minutes the animal is unconscious and laid out on webbing suspended over a basin. A load of Toxiban, a black slurry of activated charcoal meant to absorb oil poisons and pass through the body, is pumped through a tube down the otter's gullet. Then, using Dawn dishwashing liquid and hoses with garden spraying attachments, otter attendants painstakingly knead the animal's fur. Greasy, gray-black stew bubbles up between their fingers. Oil.

It takes about an hour and a half to scrub and dry each otter— almost too long for this animal. Midway into the process, he pops up as if on a spring and begins snapping at his handlers. "Easy boy," Mr. Utkov coaxes. He injects another blast of Valium into the animal, but the otter continues to fidget and writhe for the remainder of the operation.

The otters brought in on this day wear relatively little oil, an encouraging sign, but no guarantee of survival. R.V. Chalam, a toxicologist and pathologist from San Diego, says one of the things that has shocked scientists here most is the number of different ways in which oil is killing otters. Otters were always known to be particularly vulnerable to oil because they have no blubber and can't float or stay warm for long once oil mats their fur. Most of the missing and presumed dead otters in the sound just sank.

At the rescue center, however, Mr. Chalam's autopsies show that "these animals have livers that are totally destroyed, that crumble in your hand like dust." Additionally, "their immune systems are completely defused, making them extremely susceptible to secondary infection. There is emphysema not only in the lungs but throughout the body."

Mr. Chalam says this means that otters are being violently poisoned by the benzene, toluene, xylene and numerous other toxins in oil, which apparently can invade their bodies through inhalation, ingestion or simple penetration of the pores. In other words, it means "incredible pain."

A few hours after her seizure on April 13, Otter 76 seems to stabilize somewhat. She even tugs at a towel; otters, it turns out, like towels and like to curl up and hide their heads in them. Henry Iverson, an Athabascan Indian who is tending Otter 76, uses tongs to dangle a shrimp in front of her snout and she takes it, a good sign. "Man, I'd like to see her kicking back on a beach with her shades on and a can of beer in her paw," he says. "This girl's been through too much." Otter 76 spends the rest of that day and night resting, trembling some but eating a bit. "Maybe she'll make it," Mr. Iverson says. "At least she's holding her own."

Other otters are not. Outside the gym, ten mesh-covered pens have been set up. The otter doctors have found that moving outside sometimes perks an otter up; some otter attendants have even taken to calling the dimly lit gym the "Death House." But even outside, Otter 81, nicknamed Otto, lies shuddering in a blue cage. Jake Matulka, a volunteer from Anchorage, kneels motionless in front of the cage, resting his head against it. He watches silently for several minutes. "I think he's going down," Jake says finally, to no one in particular. "Come on bud, play with your towel. Come on."

Otter 81 lingers for about an hour more. He dies at 5:18 p.m. on April 13.

Not all the news at the center is so grim. On Friday, April 14, a handwritten sign near the center's entrance proclaims that six otters treated here and shipped out to Point Defiance Zoo near Tacoma, Wash., earlier in the week are still alive and doing well. YEAH!! the sign reads. It is a moment of accomplishment and of progress. The center shipped six otters out to Sea World two weeks ago, but only one survived.

Eventually, all the otters the center manages to save will have to be sent somewhere—and it probably won't be back into the wild. "They can't go home again," says Mr. Fitz-Gibbon. "They're better off in aquariums than in oil." Scientists say they may try transplanting some otters to other regions, but they fear the otters will swim back to their home waters, no matter how distant.

Those who work with the otters stow away the small victories to help them cope. Many of the otter handlers came as volunteers and stayed on as Exxon shifted to a paid staff. Some have been here for weeks, and they've seen a lot of melancholy things. Jeanie Clarke, the English volunteer, was vacationing in Anchorage when the oil spilled. She hitched the six-hour ride to Valdez to help otters; one day two weeks ago, she spent 17 straight hours nursing a pup. "I was sitting in the cage with it, holding it in my arms when it died," Ms. Clarke says. "Even after the tears, that stays in your gut."

Carolyn McCollum, a writer from Cary, N.C., also came to help the animals. "I drive a car, I use oil," says Mrs. McCollum, who is 30 years old and pregnant with her first child. "In a sense, I share in the blame for this. I had to do something." She has lost three otters, the most recent one on Friday night.

"She was moaning and crying, like a little girl on a Ferris wheel," Mrs. McCollum recounts. "It got to where I knew she was brain dead, but she was still breathing. You can't just put her in a bag and forget about her." So Mrs. McCollum cradled the otter in her arms until it stopped breathing, some time around 10 p.m.

At about the time Mrs. McCollum's otter died, one of the veterinarians checks up on Otter 76. She has been showing some signs of improvement, eating four shrimp and three pollack earlier that evening. The vet looks her over and scribbles two notations rapidly on Otter 76's chart.

The first is "Possible eyesight loss." The second is "Pregnant." Otter 76, it has been discovered, is fighting not for one life, but for two.

The scientists at the center say they're learning as they go. "We know a lot more than we did about the logistics of trying to save animals," says Terrie Williams, a research physiologist from Sea World who is running the day-to-day operations of the center. "We know it's a nightmare."

But no breakthroughs on how to actually save otters from oil—what drugs, if any, might limit the corrosive damage, for example—have been made. The scientists are talking with Exxon about establishing a permanent research facility here to keep searching for more effective treatments.

"That's the only good that could ever come out of this disaster—some knowledge that might help us save animals when this happens again," Ms. Williams says.

Ms. Williams stands near the pen where, just a few hours before, Otter 76 began heaving for breath again. The otter was given Regalan to reduce inflammation and more Toxiban, the poison absorber. She was force fed, too, but soon she fell once more into short, jerky convulsions.

At 3:15 a.m. Saturday morning, Otter 76 shuddered one last time and died.

—CHARLES McCOY, April 1989

CHAPTER SEVEN

PLAY'S THE THING

51. *Fish Story*

TALLAHATCHIE RIVER, Miss.—"Snaaaaaaaaaaaaaake!!!"

The voices from the three aluminum boats are loud enough to make 35-year-old Murrah Hardy wheel around in neck-deep water. But the four-foot water moccasin a few feet away is only a distraction.

Fully clothed, he plunges back into the swift and muddy current. Mr. Hardy has come here in hopes of doing what he does often: catching a really big catfish. His method might charitably be called unusual. After several dives, he surfaces, only to utter the single worst word from a fisherman's mouth: "Nothing." Undeterred, he moves on to another spot.

In early summer in the Mississippi Delta, when the corn and beans are waist high, an odd lot of fishermen set out looking for what amounts to an underwater wrestling match: to catch big cats without rods, reels or bait—no gear except their bare hands.

Known here and in other pockets of the South as hand-fishers, they wade or dive in rivers and "oxbow" lakes. Their favored quarry is the prehistoric looking flathead catfish. Squinty-eyed and yellowish, a really big flathead could swallow a basketball. Catches of 40-pounders are common, and a few have tipped the scales at over 90 pounds.

Some think the grabber method is all madness. In spawning season, hand-fishers find a catfish bed, typically a hollow log, where females have just laid their eggs. More often than not a touchy male stands watch, like a guard dog. The grabber reaches in and the fish bites the hand that feels him—locking its sandpapery jaws around his arm. The fisherman then tries to hang on as he drags the fish to the surface.

"It's like sticking your hand inside a mad bulldog's house," says 39-year-old Ronnie Davis, a fellow farmer and regular fishing mate of Mr. Hardy's.

Hand-fishing, also known as grabbing or grappling, is no sport for the meek. "One time," says a stoic Mr. Davis, "I put my foot at the hole of a big blue cat, and the fish bit the tennis shoe off my foot. I went back down and snatched it out of his mouth." His personal best: a 75-pound flathead.

It probably isn't surprising that regular grabbers get knocked around a lot—scars, abrasions, even broken bones are common. Herman Green, a 72-year-old Louisianian who learned the sport from a blind hand-fisherman, still has a reminder from the struggle with his record 65-pound catfish years ago—a crooked middle finger broken when the fish went crazy.

Mr. Green says he has even had some 60-pounders use their powerful tail to "roll me over and over underwater." Sometimes a day of grabbing ends even more tragically: A few years ago, a 28-year-old man died in Lake Eufala in Oklahoma while hand-grabbing; his arm became caught between pieces of concrete.

Smaller blue catfish proliferate around here. But the flathead catfish, known to academics as *Pylodictis olivaris* and to locals as the flathead, yellow cat or mudcat, is generally the largest and among the tastiest. One allure of grabbing is that a good trip can fill an entire freezer with catfish, a Southern delicacy best fried in a cornmeal coating. The U.S. catfish record is 109 pounds, 4 ounces. The fish was taken by rod and reel; there is no category for hand-grabbers.

Big catfish are quite aggressive and "they'll certainly come up and take ducks and muskrats," says Don Jackson, a professor at Mississippi State University's wildlife and fisheries department. There are stories—probably apocryphal—"of pioneering women in these parts losing small children," he says.

Mr. Jackson is now studying grabbing as part of a broader effort to get Delta natives to view the Delta's rivers, including the Tallahatchie, as regional treasures instead of merely conduits for the flood waters that sometimes hit this area. The Tallahatchie is already enshrined in popular culture as the inspiration for Bobbie Gentry's 1960s hit song, "Ode to Billie Joe," a mournful ballad of teen suicide.

And at least for now, there is no danger of overfishing by grabbers. That was the conclusion of Jay Francis, a Mississippi State University graduate who wrote his master's thesis on the sport. Mr. Francis witnessed 1,362 grabs—including two fish over 60 pounds—as part of a three-year study on the Tallahatchie River and the Big Black River.

His research, "Recreational Hand-grabbing as a Factor Influencing Flathead Characteristics in Two Mississippi Streams," indicates that it takes just a few successful spawns to repopulate a length of river. At the same time, the number of hand-grabbers—given the eccentricities of the sport—is likely to remain small.

Out here on the Tallahatchie, a muddy river about 50 yards across in northern Mississippi, Messrs. Hardy and Davis and friends find their "holes" with uncanny precision. They use broken limbs or rocks as reference points. "Right past that stick," Mr. Hardy shouts to the boat's driver as he points to a limb overhanging a bend in the river.

With the boat in place, he dives down and feels the river bottom with his hands for the hole where the catfish is nesting. All the while, he must attend to heavy currents, not to mention alligators, snakes and snapping turtles. The latter "can snap a boat paddle like a toothpick," notes Ronnie Thomas, wildlife biologist for the U.S. Department of Agriculture's Natural Resources Conservation Service.

During the season in Mississippi, from mid-May to the first week in July, hand-grabbers are allowed to capture fish from natural cavities such as logs or holes in stream banks, as well as man-made structures. Some use discarded hot-water heaters, submerged wooden boxes and, for this crew on the Tallahatchie, modified metal containers to create artificial nests.

Techniques vary. Some grabbers don't actually grab, but instead use big hooks, tied to ropes, that go through the catfish's jaw. Some grabbers hold their breath, while other prefer full scuba gear. In Lake St. John, an oxbow lake near the Mississippi River on the Louisiana side, Tony Mozingo and Robert Storey fish using a "third lung"—an air compressor floating on a truck inner tube with plastic hoses attached to two mouthpieces.

In this lake, the men search hollow cypress stumps. Mr. Storey, after a long, hot and thus far futile day, vanishes in a cloud of tiny bubbles and emerges a few minutes later smiling. He has a fish—but unfortunately not a keeper. Under hand-grabbing rules, catfish less than 24 inches long have to be thrown back.

Still, Mr. Storey, whose personal best is a 32-pound flathead, is hooked. Says the stocky young Mississippi farmer whose grandfather and great-grandfather were hand-grabbers, "You catch one, and you can't wait to come back. It's addictive."

—MARK ROBICHAUX, July 1996

52. *Golfing in the Spring: One Hole, Par 70*

KODIAK, Alaska—Silver-dollar-sized snowflakes come tumbling out of the mist, delighting Andy Lundquist. "With any luck," he says, "it'll even get worse."

Luck just pours down on Mr. Lundquist, the chairman of the third annual Pillar Mountain Classic—a two-day, one-hole, par-70 golf tournament recently completed here. It is played over a course so perverse and in weather traditionally so bad that merely finishing is a feat. Indeed, by the time a half-dozen four-wheel-drive pickup trucks groan up the side of Pillar Mountain for the final day of this year's event, flakes are pelting horizontally through an enveloping fog.

"It's a lovely day for golf, gentlemen," says Glenn Yngve (pro- nounced ENG-vay), another tournament official. Emerging from his truck, Mr. Yngve leads a gaggle of players, clutching golf bags and pulling their parkas tightly around them, in a ten-minute trudge to a level spot of snowy ground. He bids play to begin with an admoni- tion: "Remember: Keep one foot on the ground and no stabbing above the elbow."

Warren "Pogo" Good ignores Mr. Yngve's advice, steps up to his ball and wallops an eight-iron. The ball—painted Day-Glo orange to improve its visibility—slices off into the billowing snow and disap- pears (forever, it turns out) into the murky gloom. Mr. Good, like Mr. Yngve a commercial fisherman, won this very tournament two years ago; this time, he forfeits a stroke and says: "I got a bad feeling about this."

Small wonder, considering the course. It is a four-mile, 1,400-foot vertical climb roughly following a rocky, abandoned four-wheel- drive road. A steep ravine and ball-swallowing alder thickets define the rough on the lower course.

Above the tree line, icy winds, freezing temperatures, blowing snow, thigh-deep drifts and impenetrable fog alternate to keep things interesting. The hole—a green plastic five-gallon bucket—sits in a bowl of snow at Pillar Mountain's peak.

Professional Golfers' Association tournament rules apply, with exceptions for local conditions. Golfers must play balls where they lie or forfeit a stroke. But players are allowed to carry hatchets and handsaws to clear away thickets and can tote snow shovels to probe for lost shots and topple shot-blocking snow banks.

Bending the rules seems to be rampant and is generally tolerated if cleverly executed. An example: Last year, a player whose shot landed in his caddie's backpack 50 yards downrange was allowed to retrieve his ball from the backpack—technically a violation—and play it from the top of a bottle sticking up from the pack.

But the shenanigans come to a halt during the playoff round, when the top seven golfers from the tournament's first day are stalked by scorekeepers.

It was during a dark, cold lull in the fishing season three years ago that the Pillar Mountain Classic crawled out from beneath a wager at Tony's Bar and became a golf tournament. A bored Mr. Yngve laid down $100 and bet fellow fisherman Steve "Scrimshaw" Mathieu that he could golf to the peak of Pillar Mountain, looming right above town, in fewer strokes. Kodiak, a town of 5,000 and hub of a huge salmon-fishing industry, lacked a real golf course but had no lack of would-be golfers, or bettors either. Soon there were 21 other challengers.

Mr. Good, who won the first event, couldn't participate last year when a volcano blew up near Anchorage and grounded his flight from that city to Kodiak. Mr. Mathieu prevailed, shooting a course-record 43 despite icy 80-mile-an-hour winds. So this year's tournament, which attracts 43 entrants, nine of them women, is billed as a showdown of the former champions.

Most participants are locals, but the challengers include Dwight Mahoney, a fisherman from Camden, Maine, and Shailer Cummings, a Miami scientist who has entered himself and his caddie as a team known as the "Miami Slice." The winner will get $746.14—what's left after giving half of the entry fees to Kodiak charities and deducting expenses associated with stocking the tournament's liquor supply.

With his opening swing in the tournament's qualifying round, Mr. Mathieu proves that playing good golf here doesn't always count for much. He lofts a straight-arrow 100-yard shot—only to lose it in an alder thicket.

The same fate awaits his next effort; and Mr. Mathieu, an affable but competitive spirit, caucuses with his caddie, Clifford Truman, and his spotter, a man who goes by the name "Coyote," whose jobs are to stand downrange and track his shots. Mr. Mathieu's advice—not printable in this newspaper—seems not to make much difference. Yet a third shot falls unfindable into the rough.

John "Buddha" Ure, a competitor in Mr. Mathieu's foursome, tells Mr. Truman: "Scrimshaw's going to have to replace you with an ugly dog, partner." Mr. Truman, looking mournful in a red floppy wool hat, says: "I'm not sure, but I think he's already fired me."

Coyote, who won't confess to having a last name, is clearly having a poor day. Usually considered an eagle-eyed tracker of golf balls, he gained tournament immortality last year for tracking down an inebriated golfer who had wandered off for what could have been an eternal nap in the snow.

On Mr. Mathieu's fourth shot, Coyote finds redemption by spotting a ball buried in a tangle of alders and spruce. He sizes up the effort required to clear a swath for a shot and declares it impossible, saying: "I don't have enough alcohol to tackle a job like that."

That makes it a considerable job, since Coyote is carrying a pint of brandy in one pocket, a pint of mystery liquor in another and a jar of white lightning tucked inside his buckskin jacket. Less daunted by the task at hand, Mr. Mathieu begins a logging operation. His 30 minutes of sawing proves pivotal: His next shot lands in a clearing 150 yards beyond, and he ends up with a 39 to enter the final round.

Just up the trail, Toby Sullivan, clinging like a mountain goat to a ravine wall, manages to get a seven-iron on his ball, perched halfway up the steep, grassy face. The ball spurts up optimistically, but gravity quickly intervenes. The ball thumps down, rolls between his feet and skitters into a creek 30 feet below. Mr. Sullivan, who seems to end up in the ravine a lot, won't win the tournament but does win the best nickname: Lee Ravino.

At the top of the course, in thick, swirling fog, Maria Minkoff takes her 160th shot of the day and says, "I can't believe I'm doing this." Neither can a lot of people. Ms. Minkoff has waddled all the way up the course dressed in a Daisy Duck costume. She waddles off into the fog and ends up with a 172.

Meanwhile, Mr. Good, whose amateur golfing credits include two holes in one, easily makes the finals by blazing to a record-setting 30. Later, at Tony's Bar, the official tournament headquarters, he explains his strategy. "I bought a lot of drinks for my competitors last night. I left early myself. I suspect I created a lot of hangovers."

In the final round on Day Two, the seven finalists start from scratch at the midway point on the course. The swirling snow and soupy fog give Mr. Good the hangover he has given to others. He loses ball after ball and finishes dead last with a 24. Mr. Mathieu gets a literal case of cold feet when he forgets to wear plastic bags over his tennis socks. It seems to chill his game, and he finishes in a three-way tie for third with a 20.

Meantime, Rick Lindholm, a Kodiak building contractor and tournament newcomer, has made it to the brink of the green with only 13 strokes. He chips his ball off a rock. It skitters into a deep footprint near the cup and pops out—right into the bucket. Mr. Lindholm is the new champion with a 14.

Unheralded Tony Durr, the editor of the Kodiak newspaper, sneaks into second with a 19 and says, in retrospect, it was easy: "When I quit trying to play golf, I did all right."

—KEN WELLS, April 1987

53. *Having a Fling or Two*

ACTON ROUND, England—With surprising grace, the grand piano sails through the sky a hundred feet above a pasture here, finally returning to earth in a fortissimo explosion of wood chunks, ivory keys and piano wire.

Nor is the piano the strangest thing to startle the grazing sheep this Sunday morning. A few minutes later, a car soars by—a 1975 blue two-door Hillman, to be exact—following the same flight path and meeting the same loud fate. Pigs fly here, too. In recent months, many dead 500-pound sows (two of them wearing parachutes) have passed overhead, as has the occasional dead horse.

It's the work of Hew Kennedy's medieval siege engine, a four-story tall, 30-ton behemoth that's the talk of bucolic Shropshire, 140 miles northwest of London. In ancient times, such war machines were dreaded implements of destruction, flinging huge missiles, including plague-ridden horses, over the walls of besieged castles. Only one full-sized one exists today, designed and built by Mr. Kennedy, a wealthy landowner, inventor, military historian and—need it be said?—full-blown eccentric.

At Acton Round Hall, Mr. Kennedy's handsome Georgian manor house here, one enters the bizarre world of a P. G. Wodehouse novel. A stuffed baboon hangs from the dining room chandelier ("Shot it in Africa. Nowhere else to put it," Mr. Kennedy explains). Lining the walls are dozens of halberds and suits of armor. A full suit of Indian elephant armor, rebuilt by Mr. Kennedy, shimmers resplendently on an elephant-sized frame. In the garden outside stands a 50-foot-high Chinese pagoda.

Capping this scene, atop a hill on the other side of the 620-acre Kennedy estate, is the siege engine, punctuating the skyline like an oil derrick. Known by its 14th-century French name, trebuchet (pronounced tray-boo-shay), it's not to be confused with a catapult, a much smaller device that throws rocks with a spoonlike arm propelled by twisted ropes or animal gut.

Mr. Kennedy, a stout, energetic 52-year-old, and Richard Barr, his 46-year-old neighbor and partner, have spent a year and £10,000 ($17,000) assembling the trebuchet. They have worked from ancient texts, some in Latin, and crude wood-block engravings of siege weaponry.

The big question is why.

Mr. Kennedy looks puzzled, as if the thought hadn't occurred to him before. "Well, why not? It's bloody good fun!" he finally exclaims. When pressed, he adds that for several hundred years military technicians have been trying fruitlessly to reconstruct a working trebuchet. Cortez built one for the siege of Mexico City. On its first shot, it flung a huge boulder straight up—and then straight down, demolishing the machine. In 1851, Napoleon III had a go at it, as an academic exercise. His trebuchet was poorly balanced and barely managed to hurl the missiles backward. "Ours works a hell of a lot better than the Frogs', which is a satisfaction," Mr. Kennedy says with relish.

How it works seems simple enough. The heart of the siege engine is a three-ton, 60-foot tapered beam made from laminated wood. It's pivoted near the heavy end, to which is attached a weight box filled with 5½ tons of steel bar. Two huge A-frames made from lashed-together tree trunks support a steel axle, around which the beam pivots. When the machine is at rest, the beam is vertical—slender end at the top and weight box just clearing the ground.

When launch time comes, a farm tractor cocks the trebuchet, slowly hauling the slender end of the beam down and the weighted end up. Several dozen nervous sheep, hearing the tractor and knowing what comes next, make a break for the far side of the pasture. A crowd of 60 friends and neighbors buzzes with anticipation as a 30-foot, steel-cable sling is attached—one end to the slender end of the beam and the other to the projectile, in this case a grand piano (purchased by the truckload from a junk dealer).

"If you see the missile coming toward you, simply step aside," Mr. Kennedy shouts to the onlookers.

Then, with a great groaning, the beam is let go. As the counter-weight plummets, the piano in its sling whips through an enormous arc, up and over the top of the trebuchet and down the pasture, a flight of 125 yards. The record for pianos is 151 yards (an upright model, with less wind resistance). A 112-pound iron weight made it 235 yards. Dead hogs go for about 175 yards, and horses 100 yards; the field is cratered with the graves of the beasts, buried by a backhoe where they landed.

Mr. Kennedy has been studying and writing about ancient engines of war since his days at Sandhurst, Britain's military academy, some 30 years ago. But what spurred him to build one was, as he puts it, "my nutter cousin" in Northumberland, who put together a pint-sized trebuchet for a county fair. The device hurled porcelain toilets soaked in gasoline and set afire. A local paper described the event under the headline "Those Magnificent Men and Their Flaming Latrines."

Building a full-sized siege engine is a more daunting task. Mr. Kennedy believes that dead horses are the key. That's because en-gravings usually depict the trebuchets hurling boulders, and there is no way to determine what the rocks weigh, or the counterweight nec-essary to fling them. But a few drawings show dead horses being loaded onto trebuchets, putrid animals being an early form of biolog-ical warfare. Since horses weigh now what they did in the 1300s, the engineering calculations followed easily.

One thing has frustrated Mr. Kennedy and his partner: They haven't found any commercial value for the trebuchet. Says a neigh-bor helping to carry the piano to the trebuchet, "Too bad Hew can't make the transition between building this marvelous machine and making any money out of it."

It's not for lack of trying. Last year Mr. Kennedy walked onto the English set of the Kevin Costner Robin Hood movie, volunteering his trebuchet for the scene where Robin and his sidekick are cata-pulted over a wall. "The directors insisted on something made out of plastic and cardboard," he recalls with distaste. "Nobody cares about correctness these days."

More recently, he has been approached by an entrepreneur who wants to bus tourists up from London to see cars and pigs fly through the air. So far, that's come to naught.

Mr. Kennedy looks to the United States as his best chance of getting part of his investment back: A theme park could commission him to build an even bigger trebuchet that could throw U.S.-sized cars into the sky. "It's an amusement in America to smash up motor cars, isn't it?" he inquires hopefully.

Finally, there's the prospect of flinging a man into space—a living man, that is. This isn't a new idea, Mr. Kennedy points out: Trebuchets were often used to fling ambassadors and prisoners of war back over castle walls, a sure way to demoralize the opposition.

Some English sports parachutists think they can throw a man in the air and bring him down alive. In a series of experiments on Mr. Kennedy's siege machine, they've thrown several man-sized logs and two quarter-ton dead pigs into the air; one of the pigs parachuted gently back to earth, the other landed rather more forcefully.

Trouble is, an accelerometer carried inside the logs recorded a centrifugal force during the launch of as much as 20 Gs (the actual acceleration was zero to 90 miles per hour in 1.5 seconds). Scientists are divided over whether a man can stand that many Gs for more than a second or two before his blood vessels burst.

The parachutists are nonetheless enthusiastic. But Mr. Kennedy thinks the idea may only be pie in the sky.

"It would be splendid to throw a bloke, really splendid," he says wistfully. "He'd float down fine. But he'd float down dead."

—Glynn Mapes, July 1991

54. *Why Tiger Is Glad He's Not Japanese*

TOKYO—Insurance salesman Akira Anzai will never forget the misery he felt on the 173-yard third hole at Japan's Kuju Lakeside Golf Course. There, on a cloudy day in 1983, he watched his tee shot fly straight to the green, bounce once and disappear.

He had hit a hole in one.

"The whole world went black," Mr. Anzai recalls.

Hitting a hole in one can be one of the sweetest pleasures of a golfer's career. But in Japan, it is dreadful. Whoever hits a hole in one here is expected to throw a party and to send presents—to friends, to co-workers and to everyone who witnessed the feat. The cost can run into the thousands of dollars.

Something like ten million Japanese play golf—more than one in every ten adults. The most avid golfers are businessmen, who use the sport to entertain customers. It is part of what the Japanese call "otsukiai," or "relationship-building." One survey found that the average golfer spends more than $100 a month on the pastime—clubs, fees, clothes and such—not counting hole-in-one presents.

Nothing could be more embarrassing than to hit a hole in one in front of a customer, and then fail to pony up with a good present.

But the Japanese, who invented the problem, have also come up with a solution: hole-in-one insurance. For a fee of $5 to $10 a year, the Japanese golfer can buy a policy that will pay off as much as $2,000 should the unthinkable occur.

To collect on a claim, you must send the insurance company receipts proving that you spent money on presents and parties. And you need to send in forms attesting to your lucky shot, signed by the club, your golfing companions and the caddie. (In Japan, almost all caddies are women, known as caddie-san, who wear large bonnets and who pull the clubs around on electrified handcarts.)

Some golfers find out about hole-in-one insurance the hard way.

Shigeji Suzuki, a certified public accountant for the Tokyo suburbs, was playing golf with a group of local notables late last November.

"It was the end of the year, and I was thinking it had been a good year, without any serious mishaps either personal or in business," says Mr. Suzuki. Then he dropped a 147-yard shot with his three-wood on the eighth hole. And he had no insurance.

"At the moment of the hole in one, I was elated and thought, 'I did it!'" says Mr. Suzuki. "Then I thought, 'Oh, no!' I began to worry about the contents of my wallet."

His wife shared his concern. "What a rotten thing to do," she told him when he arrived home. She knew her golf. First, Mr. Suzuki had to tip two caddies $20 each. Then, the Suzukis paid $850 for 15 gold Cross pens, which were engraved and sent to Mr. Suzuki's closest friends and business associates, and to his golf partners. They spent another $400 on 100 golf towels, printed with his name and the details of his feat. The towels went to the B-list of friends and associates. At the end of January, Mr. Suzuki laid out another $850 to rent the Club Fushimi, a hostess bar in one of Tokyo's nightclub districts, where he entertained his friends.

Mr. Suzuki has mended his ways. "I was told that things that happen once may happen twice," he says. "So, although it is a bit late, I signed up for hole-in-one insurance and now am playing golf with peace of mind."

"The Japanese will use any excuse for a party," says Mowa Setsu, an 86-year-old golf historian and consultant who has played the game since 1925. "It isn't just holes in one. They also give out presents and have a big party when they shoot their ages—that is, when someone's golf score for 18 holes adds up to his age."

So far, insurance companies don't offer shoot-your-age insurance. In fact, they are losing money on hole-in-one insurance.

"The trouble with hole-in-one insurance is what we call moral risk," explains one insurance agent. "Especially in the areas south and west of Tokyo—in Osaka, Kobe and Kyushu—where golf courses aren't so crowded, the players can get awfully close to the caddies. They may finish up a round of golf and decide they want to have a party. So they give the caddie $40, and get her to attest that one of them hit a hole in one. Since the maximum amount you can collect is relatively small, it hardly pays to investigate a claim." The agent says he thinks hole-in-one insurance may ultimately be withdrawn.

A spokesman for Tokyo Marine & Fire Insurance Co., one of Japan's largest casualty companies, denies any plans to abandon the coverage. But it is true that the company raised rates by 80 percent a year ago. It may even have to raise them again, says Takashi Icnaka, a Tokyo Marine official, because "the amount going out still is much bigger than the amount coming in." He estimates that golfers hit holes in one on three out of every 10,000 shots, but he says the company seems to be paying out more often than that.

"Of course, we can't say there isn't any cheating," Mr. Ienaka explains. "Only God knows who is cheating and who isn't. But we take the view that we must trust our policyholders."

Golf experts here speculate that the tradition of hole-in-one parties and gifts grows from the widespread notion that good luck should be shared.

"If you keep the luck all for yourself, you will be thrown under a curse," the chairman of Nippon Steel Corp., Japan's largest steel company, told a Japanese golf magazine recently.

The Nippon Steel executive, Eishiro Saito, hit a hole in one while golfing with the chairman of Sumitomo Electric Corp. He thereupon sent 500 golf umbrellas to friends and associates.

Tokyo department stores say the most popular presents are towels. But golfers also buy ball markers, drinking glasses, leather scorecard holders, tie pins, key holders, bag tags and lacquer trays, usually engraved with details of the shot. One Japanese confectioner since 1926 has sold "hole in one" candies made of sweet bean paste and shaped like golf balls.

When the president of Suntory Ltd., Japan's largest brewery and liquor company, hit a hole in one, he had 1,000 golf-ball-shaped whiskey bottles made, filled them with his best liquor and sent them to one and all.

Mr. Anzai, the insurance salesman, had a special problem with his hole in one. When it happened to him he was in the company of other insurance men and customers. And he, of all people, owned just $400 in hole-in-one insurance.

"I was hoping that it wasn't really a hole in one," he recalls. "I looked around on the green, hoping to see the ball, but there wasn't anything white there. Then I noticed there was something white in the hole. My feelings were complex."

After the obligatory spending spree, Mr. Anzai contacted his company and arranged to increase his coverage.

—E. S. BROWNING, August 1985

55. *Not Your Father's Buick*

PORTOLA VALLEY, Calif.—A tank roars from Jacques Littlefield's garage, with Mr. Littlefield's green-helmeted head bobbing from the driver's hatch. Two small lizards leap for cover, but a visiting reporter holds his ground, doing his best to direct Mr. Littlefield out of his garage with minimal destruction.

"There's a fire extinguisher inside in case anything weird happens," shouts Mr. Littlefield when his M24 Chaffee tank has cleared the building. "Now why don't you hop aboard. It's hard to hear, so if you make any loud sound, even if you just go 'woo woo' from excitement, I'll assume it's an emergency and stop."

Suddenly two heads ricochet off the hatch rims; two hearts swell with the hubris that comes from rumbling across the landscape in a thick lozenge of armor. Soon the turret is swiveling, the cannon barrel rising, the scenery tilting at crazy angles.

The usual, here on Mr. Littlefield's ranch.

Take a close look at your neighbor's garage, America. From Birmingham, Ala., to Puyallup, Wash., ordinary Joes—some veterans, some not—are buying and restoring their own personal tanks. A prominent Washington lobbyist owns at least seven, including three Shermans. An Indiana judge owns five. Tom Clancy's wife got him one for his birthday. Where there is one tank owner, there are others, galvanized to purchase theirs by the simple revelation that just about anyone can own such machines, sometimes for the price of a new car. With a federal license, you can arm your tank with live cannons and machine guns. If your tank has rubber tracks, you may even be able to register it with your local motor-vehicle department.

"There's no difference between owning a tank and a Ferrari," explains David W. Uhrig, a private tank broker in Chillicothe, Ohio, "except four inches of armor."

The trade in private armor is surprisingly brisk. Would-be tank commanders scan the sale ads in *Supply Line,* published by the 10,000-member Military Vehicle Preservation Association. If you'd like a Soviet tank, you can order one now through Tanks A Lot Inc., Pennsauken, N.J. Mr. Uhrig, the tank broker, recently ran an ad in *Shotgun News* offering a Nazi tank—to be specific, a Sturmgeschutz Ausfuhrung G mit der Stuk 40 L/48—for $145,000.

He got five serious inquiries, including one offer now pending.

The Pentagon sold lots of tanks to civilians after World War II. In 1960, however, it got stingy and barred the sale of intact tanks to consumers, thus unintentionally ensuring robust prices for vintage armor. Mr. Uhrig, for example, bought a World War II Stuart tank for $500 in 1973 and immediately resold it for $1,200. Subsequent owners restored it. Acting as a broker he sold it twice more, most recently for $52,000.

The demand doesn't surprise him. "Tanks are fun," he says. "You've got to drive one before you die, that's all there is to it."

America's civilian tankers tend to be law-abiding citizens. "The number of instances of tank warfare among street gangs is fortunately zero," says Jack Killorin, spokesman for the federal Bureau of Alcohol, Tobacco & Firearms, to which civilian tankers must apply if they want live guns. Tanks may pose the greatest hazards to their owners. One tanker took a sharp turn only to have a hatch cover fall on its owner's unprotected head, fracturing his skull. Another time, one of his tanks broke loose and crashed through a wall. Tanks are notorious too for causing divorces. "Oh yes," says Jacques Littlefield. "It happens to a lot of guys. It happened to me. You get a tank, you get divorced. You get divorced, you lose the tank to pay the settlement."

Armor can become an obsession. Mr. Littlefield remembers checking out a book on tanks in third grade. While an undergraduate at Stanford University, he built a 180-pound remote-control tank complete with working flame-thrower. He bought his 450-acre ranch expressly to indulge his passion, and now owns 15 tanks, 50 military vehicles in all. The huge 1976 merger of General Electric and Utah International, founded by his grandfather, gave him the buying power.

On a walk through his parts barn (one of seven ranch buildings devoted to his collection), he lovingly points out hard-to-find components: assorted missile racks, air-coolers and tank engines. An armored car transmission remains sealed in its original World War II shipping case. "That's the kind of thing that makes your little heart skip a beat," he says.

The passion to collect old warhorses, left unchecked, can become extreme. Mark Sonday, owner of Sonday's Vans in Kenosha, Wis., owns 16 tanks and more than 100 military vehicles in all. Now he wants a submarine, specifically the decommissioned U.S.S. *Swordfish* last used in the Vietnam era.

"You have to understand," he says. "There is an element of ego involved here."

Tankers put their vehicles to a host of worthy uses. They tool around in parades and stage occasional mock amphibious landings. They lease them to Hollywood for such movies as *Red Dawn* and *The Blues Brothers*. Mostly they like to form convoys.

Thomas Gould, a Grand Island, N.Y., collector and part-owner of a chemical company, once mounted his own 30-vehicle armored column and set out in a line for a Rochester air show.

This was great fun.

The temperature was 105. Plagued by breakdowns, the 60-mile trip took 12 hours, so long that air show officials dispatched a squadron of World War II fighters to look for Mr. Gould and his friends.

When the fighters found the column, they gleefully strafed it with propane machine guns.

Mr. Gould also provides three armored cars for use by regional law-enforcement officials—on the condition that he drives them—for use in battering down the doors of fortified crack houses. "I've got two-inch armor on all sides," he says. "It's probably the safest part of the day for me."

Pat Thelander of Oroville, Calif., put her late husband's collection of armor and other military vehicles to more somber use. In Bob Thelander's last hours, he made a request: He wanted to be hauled to his final resting place in the last vehicle he had restored, a World War II ambulance.

When the sad day arrived, the ambulance had a flat tire and wouldn't start. At last, however, it picked up Mr. Thelander and set out for the crematorium in Paradise, Calif., some 20 miles away, mostly uphill.

Halfway to Paradise, the radiator sprang a leak. The driver fixed it. The procession advanced. The radiator boiled over. "We figured he was just laughing away at us trying to get him there," says Mrs. Thelander.

Now Mrs. Thelander wants to sell two dozen vehicles. She won't sell the ambulance, but she did sell her husband's beloved tank to a friend who had lost his own tank to divorce. She knew the friend planned a loving restoration. Still, it was a dark day when the flatbed truck winched that big old machine aboard.

"Well, I'll tell you," Mrs. Thelander says, her voice wavering. "It really broke my heart to see it going out of the yard. Because that was something Bob always wanted, a tank."

—ERIK LARSON, October 1992

CHAPTER EIGHT

NOTIONS AND CONTROVERSIES

---

56. Naked Assumptions

Are nudes prudes?

Well, most of them don't drink. They don't dance, and some don't even hold hands in public. They avoid erotic or argumentative discussions—even sidestepping talk about religion or politics. Most of the time, they say, they just loll around or play volleyball. That, they swear, is the naked truth.

And that, say a growing number of dissident nudists, is the problem. They don't ask that nudist colonies organize orgies every afternoon, but they do ask that the colonies ease some of their puritanical rules. "The average camp is usually a mudhole where there's nothing to do," complains Wally Rogers.

As a result, Mr. Rogers has set up a new type of nudist park in the Pocono Mountains of eastern Pennsylvania that departs sharply from nudism's long-cherished traditions. Whereas most nudist colonies

231

have little more than some tents, privies, a swimming pool and a volleyball net, Mr. Rogers' Sunny Rest Lodge is more like a Holiday Inn, with carpeted rooms, TV sets and even a theater, pitch-and-putt golf course and private airport.

But most irksome of all to traditional nudists is Sunny Rest's Candle Light Room, a small, dark lounge where nudists can enjoy a drink and listen to a jukebox. The only stipulation is that nudists bring their own liquor.

"We're trying to upgrade the nudist movement," says Mr. Rogers, who usually wears nothing more than a pencil-thin mustache. "We're going after a more sophisticated clientele. Your die-hard nudist wouldn't be happy here." That's the truth. "This could harm the movement," fumes James Hadley, owner of the more conventional Cypress Grove Nudist Park near Kissimmee, Fla.

"Alcohol lowers inhibitions and increases the possibility someone will lose self-control," complains Mr. Hadley. "The cocktail atmosphere isn't conducive to sound family ties, which is what nudism is all about." There has been some talk of kicking Sunny Rest out of the American Sunbathing Association Inc., the oldest and largest of the nation's nudist groups.

A visitor to Sunny Rest, however, finds little to justify all the excitement. Though the conversation is often racy and though a young woman hints to a reporter that the place sometimes "swings," Sunny Rest seems dull on a sunny Saturday afternoon.

The nudists—doctors, teachers, clergymen, executives, electricians and clerks—go out of their way to make a reporter feel at ease. They are quick to sing what they consider the praises of nudism. "The thing about a nudist park is that you just find yourself wanting to play volleyball," enthuses Red N., who, like all nudists, is known to other club members only by his first name.

Near the large filtered pool, several women play a game of hearts. Like most guests, they approve of Sunny Rest's innovations. "When you're a city person you don't want to live like a country person," says Mrs. Sharon A., a pretty blonde whose husband is a chef. Stan B., a

Boston doctor, adds, "It's about time nudist parks caught up with the times."

The nudists at Sunny Rest and other colonies aren't an especially svelte or athletic-looking lot, and few of them cite physical health or physical culture as the basis for their interest in nudism. Some parents insist nudism is great for children, freeing them from the "morbid curiosity" that comes with adolescence. But most nudists say they embrace nudism as simply a way to relax and escape from the daily pressures of life.

"It's almost as though in taking your clothes off you're taking off your anxieties and problems," says Grace T., a 40-year-old Philadelphia clerk. "Your self-importance melts away, and you feel humble and part of nature." The wife of a Baltimore fireman says: "Everybody is on the same level here; there's no social climbing."

Whatever the reasons, nudism is booming these days—and not only at Sunny Rest. Membership in the American Sunbathing Association has climbed to 20,000 from 15,000 five years ago. There now are 134 clubs affiliated with the group, up from 75 five years ago.

"Miniskirts and Hollywood movies have helped liberalize public attitudes towards nudism," says Hal O'Neill, president of the group. Moreover, fewer states now prosecute nudists for violating indecent exposure laws, the means by which states historically have tried to curb nudism.

At the same time, some long-time restraints on personal conduct are being eased. No longer are married couples prohibited—as they once were—from bodily contact in public. No longer are single persons denied membership in most clubs, although their numbers are still limited. And some nudists now are discussing politics; so much so that they have formed a political party and have nominated nudist Robert Clogher for President. He is running, says one wag, on the platform that he has nothing to hide.

—ELLIOT CARLSON, October 1968

57. *Little Feats*

EDENBRIDGE, England—When Vera Squarcialupi first heard that some people in Britain were practicing a sport called dwarf-throwing, she thought it must be a joke. "I just rejected it," says the member of the European Parliament.

Once she was convinced it was true, Ms. Squarcialupi, an Italian Communist, introduced a proposal that condemns competitions where "particularly robust men" prove their strength by "throwing a person of restricted growth, i.e. a dwarf, as far as possible." And she isn't alone in objecting: Members of Britain's Parliament and groups for the handicapped have also protested.

Dwarf-throwing contests are said to have originated in Australia as part of a competition between nightclub bouncers. In Europe, dwarf-throwing has taken place only in England and involves just one willing dwarf. But even if the practice isn't widespread, it is creating considerable controversy. "It's appalling that such a practice would be considered entertainment in this day and age," says John Hannam, a British M.P. Ms. Squarcialupi adds, "This is a new form of exploitation, using a human being as an object."

Dwarf-rights groups say the sport is dangerous and demeaning. "If this were black-people-throwing or paraplegic-throwing, people would be horrified," says Pam Rutt, the acting chairman of the Association for Research into Restricted Growth and herself a dwarf. "It's nothing less than freak-show entertainment."

But to Danny Bamford, the promoter who organizes dwarf-throwing contests in England, it is just good fun. "People say it's degrading," says Mr. Bamford, a wisecracking former welterweight boxer with bleached-blond shoulder-length hair. "But it allows the little fellow to show he can go out and be someone."

The little fellow is Lenny the Giant, a 4-foot-4-inch, 98-pound dwarf. (Lenny, after checking with Mr. Bamford, declines to give his family name. "Just call him Lenny Bamford," says his manager.)

Lenny and Mr. Bamford are part of a four-man comedy act called the Oddballs, whose specialty is a striptease dance done with balloons.

On a recent evening, Lenny is performing with the Oddballs at a cabaret show in a community center in a run-down section of Edenbridge, a town south of London. His attire is a jogging suit and a motorcycle crash helmet. As Mr. Bamford attaches leather belts around Lenny's hips and shoulders, the manager keeps up a lively patter.

"Lenny, have you ever been hurt?"

"No."

"Is it fun?"

"Yes."

Mr. Bamford peers out through the smoke toward the audience. "There's been some controversy about dwarf-throwing," he shouts at the crowd. "But twist Lenny's ear and he'll tell you it's been a lot of fun and he's met a lot of people. All right, who wants to throw the dwarf?"

Each contestant picks Lenny up by his harness and—while the laughing, hard-drinking crowd screams, "one, two, THREE"—swings him underhanded onto a pile of mattresses. Lenny lies motionless while the toss is measured, then bounces up and acknowledges the cheers and laughter with a grin, ready for the next throw.

The Edenbridge contest is won by Jim Clark, a postal clerk from nearby Bexley Heath, with a toss that is well shy of the English record of 12 feet 5 inches. "A lot of people say it's easy," Mr. Bamford says by way of explanation for the mediocre performance, "but when you've got 98 pounds of dead weight . . ."

Ms. Rutt says that this is dangerous, regardless of how far Lenny is thrown. Dwarfism, a hormonal imbalance restricting growth that can be caused by a number of medical conditions, also involves a spinal disorder. Dwarfs like Lenny risk serious injury from jarring or twisting, she says, adding, "He could end up in a wheelchair."

But Lenny doesn't seem worried. Talking after the show in a makeshift dressing room crowded with drunken, middle-aged women seeking autographs, he says his training in karate and judo has prepared him for the sport.

Lenny seems out of place in this seedy milieu. Well dressed and eager to please, he time and again offers to get drinks for a visitor and graciously gives a seat to one of the teetering autograph seekers. The 29-year-old emigrated with his family from India 20 years ago, and still lives with his mother. Before joining the Oddballs, he worked in a factory making circuit boards for personal computers.

He professes to enjoy being thrown and says those who criticize the sport do so out of ignorance. "I don't know how they can say they think it's wrong when they haven't even seen the show," he says. Mr. Bamford pipes in, "It was Lenny's idea, and as soon as he says he doesn't want to do it anymore, we won't do it."

Mr. Clark, who had the winning toss at Edenbridge, wonders what all the fuss is about. "It's just a bit of fun that's not detrimental to anyone," he says. "The little chap is a professional entertainer and if he's happy with the arrangement and is getting paid for it, then it's okay with me. He's not drugged or anything." (Lenny makes an average of about $72 a night for the Oddballs act.)

Another dwarf, a retired acrobat, wrote to a British show-business publication recently saying he saw nothing degrading about being thrown, although he was past the age where he would consider it himself.

Ms. Rutt sees it differently. Even if Lenny is happy with his job, dwarf-tossing "perpetuates the image of dwarfs as nonpeople, as freaks, as something weird," she says. Besides, "if people get the idea that dwarf-throwing is all the rage and just for fun," she says, "thugs and drunks on the street at night will say, 'Let's throw the dwarf!'"

Dwarfs have a long history as entertainers and as objects of ridicule. Household dwarfs were common in ancient Egypt and Rome and also in Renaissance Europe. In the 18th and 19th centuries, Russian noblemen kept innumerable dwarfs, and elaborate dwarf weddings were celebrated at court; in 1710, a dwarf couple spent their wedding night in the czar's bedchamber.

Like Lenny, many dwarfs today still make their living in the entertainment business as circus performers, comedians or actors. But while dwarf entertainers capitalize on their unusual condition, critics point out that they at least use skills—something not necessary for being a human projectile.

Notwithstanding the criticism, the practice could be spreading. A bar in Chicago plans to start holding contests this month. And if Mr. Bamford has his way, dwarf-tossing will spread still further. He wants to stage a world championship next year, after holding national contests in Finland, Italy, Germany and the United States. He also plans to take four dwarfs and the English winner down under to challenge the "Australian champion."

His plans may come to naught, however. For one thing, the manager of the Australian bar where dwarf-tossing is said to have begun says the bar won't hold any more contests, partly because the novelty has worn off. For another, the outcry might be great enough to get the practice stopped in Britain.

Lenny, however, says he hopes to continue being thrown "if the protesters don't stop it. It's fun. And"—he casts a questioning glance at Mr. Bamford as if seeking approval—"it's your job."

—PAUL HEMP, November 1985

58. *China, in Stride*

SHANGHAI, China—Before dawn, Gu Yuling and his wife jog backward down the empty street, narrowly missing a white-haired man walking backward in the opposite direction.

"I have to keep looking over my shoulder," Mr. Gu pants, with mock irritation.

China's economy may be taking great strides, but many Chinese are in reverse, running or walking backward to stave off back pain, improve digestion and heaven knows what else.

The contrariness is just one manifestation of a craze for oddball exercises that makes a walk through many Chinese parks seem like a visit to Monty Python's famous Ministry of Funny Walks. In Shanghai's Xiangyang Park one morning, a young woman repeatedly bangs her upper body into a tree; an elderly man flaps his hands while staring toward the sky; and a dozen women stand in a circle shouting the number 3396815.

"Thank you, nature! Thank you, 3396815!" they cry.

One group of exercisers, moving their hands like a ground crew directing jumbo jets, say they are practicing "fragrant gong," a regimen that is supposed to make practitioners emit a sweet smell. When a passerby sniffs the air, detecting nothing but the aroma of fried dough, an elderly woman says apologetically, "You can't smell it all the time."

The surge in strange exercises is a bit hard to explain. People, particularly those who have lost jobs to economic reform, have more time on their hands. There is a greater willingness to try anything in a society where everything is in flux. But the craze is also rooted in quasimystical traditions that lay dormant through decades of Communist rule. How backward walking, specifically, got its start, no one seems to know. Most retrograde trampers picked it up on the streets or from exercise books and newspaper columns that say it is good for you.

Mad as these exercises seem, they may well work, up to a point: The oldest of the exercisers are well into their 80s, and from all appearances, they are fit, despite a past of poor diets, pollution and political upheaval. They congregate at daybreak, braving the cold in layers of knit clothing, and launch unabashed into their routines. Exercising allows people to "let out their feelings," says Qian Lihua, director of Shanghai's Zabei District Old Age Committee. In Shanghai, life expectancy is edging higher, now 74 for men and 78 for women, up three years for both sexes since 1980.

Tong Hongjia, wearing felt boots and a blue knit skullcap, stands with legs spread as if steadying himself on deck and churns his clasped hands in front of his lower abdomen as if engaged in marathon harakiri. The 88-year-old developed his exercise after fighting off cancer 30 years ago. "You can't see from outside, but inside my belly, everything is moving," he says. People who exercise are "like a running river, not a dead pond," he adds.

Many Chinese believe in the curative powers of these regimens, encouraged by sundry "masters" and their disciples. Lu Guolian, dressed in a white sweat suit, lopes in slow motion along a path in Fuxing Park with the exaggerated gait of an orangutan. "I'm practicing Guo Ling Qigong, named for Master Guo and his mother, Mrs. Ling," he explains, as backward walkers drift past from the opposite direction. Despite its torpid pace, Mr. Lu is convinced the exercise—which he learned from one of Mr. Guo's disciples in another park for $8—will restore his strength, sapped by lung-cancer surgery.

China has hundreds of these would-be gurus. One Tibetan woman teaches yoga on the country's main satellite television station. Sitting on a mountaintop, she demonstrates sucking saltwater up her nostrils and spitting it out—an exercise meant to clear the mind and the septum at the same time.

Many city parks are transformed into ad hoc fitness fairs for a few hours each morning. Lay teachers and professionals lead small flocks in routines based on qigong (pronounced chee-GONG), the ancient practice of concentrating the body's "qi," or energy, to various ends. Long revered in this country, qigong is in fashion today at all levels of society, though it comes in some startling mutations.

In Xiangyang Park, a dozen bundled-up middle-aged women beat their chests as they practice "baby swallow gong." And under a nearby plane tree, a dozen more follow the simple movements of dong yi gong, which roughly translates as "intelligent medicine discipline." Founded by Master Guo Zhichen, who sits on a yellow pillow in a picture hanging on the tree, it is distinguished by the frequent chanting of the magic number 3396815.

The cipher "contains information beneficial to both mind and body," according to Master Guo's zealous disciple Chen Jinghua. Ms. Chen, in a brown velour blazer, says chanting the number will cure gallstones, settle love spats and help flagging businesses. To prove her point, she recounts that a believer smuggling herbal medicine into Taiwan repeated the number under his breath and got through customs undetected.

Other groups practice more traditional exercises, including sword dancing and t'ai chi ch'uan, the Chinese shadow boxing that has had a considerable vogue in the United States for many years. Others march to the beat of an even stranger drummer: A parade of aging men and women swing their arms above their heads as they goosestep around the park.

But nobody seems as serene, as detached from the onward rush of events, as the backward walkers. In Fuxing Park, one lane has become a sort of backward boulevard. It's straight and flat, and all the walkers retreat in the same direction. Gu Xue, 72, strolls backward there twice a day. "It doesn't cost any money," she notes, as a man passes her dreamily. A woman in the bushes stands on one leg.

Mr. Gu and his wife jog backward together, as if facing the wrong way on a tandem bicycle.

"Besides running and walking backward, we also do some other exercises, like rubbing the face and tapping the skull," explains Mr. Gu, as his wife demonstrates vigorously. Those exercises, he explains, "massage the facial and brain nerves and help stimulate the blood vessels and in that way help prevent strokes."

—CRAIG S. SMITH, February 1998

59. *No, This Isn't How They Invented Chicken Tenders*

OTTAWA—The fearsome machine in Jack Noonan's laboratory has all the appearance of the ultimate weapon. Its 70-foot-long steel frame and massive barrel bristle with enough firepower to make the Pentagon salivate.

Several times a day Mr. Noonan sits at the controls of this monstrous contraption, pumps enough compressed air into its 60-cubic-foot reservoir to blow a building sky high, aims the barrel at the target, and fires. For half a mile around the air is broken by the ear-splitting crash of the projectile smashing into its target.

The projectile? A chicken.

Jack Noonan is the keeper of the world's most powerful chicken gun. After a wretched fowl has left the 40-foot-long barrel at 700 miles an hour all that is left are a few feathers floating to the ground. The rest is a red blob.

"When we package an order of chicken to go, it really goes," Mr. Noonan says.

At ease, chicken lovers. Mr. Noonan is not a weirdo who gets his kicks demolishing chickens. The birds he stuffs into and shoots out of his chicken gun are dead. And the cause for which they die is a good one. The purpose of Mr. Noonan's bizarre experiments at a Canadian government laboratory is to find ways of protecting aircraft against mid-air collisions with birds. The theory is that any aircraft part that can withstand the impact of a chicken hurled forth from Mr. Noonan's gun can withstand the impact of hitting a bird in mid-air.

The theory is probably true. Unfortunately, however, to date there isn't any aircraft part that can withstand the impact of Mr. Noonan's chickens at top speed.

The problem is not a trifling one. Over the past few years hundreds of planes around the world have had encounters with birds, from starlings to swans, that have smashed windshields, wrecked tail assemblies and dented wings. In the United States alone, the Federal Aviation Administration received 537 reports of birds smacking into planes last year. About 130 of those collisions caused damage to the aircraft. Typical was the TWA Boeing 747 that was forced to return to the San Francisco airport last December after a flock of large birds flew right into one of its engines and fouled up the works.

Under international air-worthiness codes, a plane cruising at 400 miles an hour must be able to keep going after a four-pound bird has smacked into its windshield or tail. Few planes do more than meet those standards. Mr. Noonan says it is doubtful whether there is one square inch of a plane in flight today that could withstand a 500-mile-an-hour impact with a four-pound bird.

The goal of Jack Noonan, along with various other chicken-gun folks, is to obtain the kind of data that can help aircraft manufacturers come up with stronger materials. In pursuit of that goal, Mr. Noonan has established himself as something of an ace in the chicken-gun field. He has slammed chickens through inches-thick windshields of bonded glass and plastic, has made gaping holes in fuselages and has demolished tail assemblies.

When Mr. Noonan fires one of his chickens the scene resembles the preparation for World War III. Warning sirens shriek. Lights flash. Technicians scurry about yelling commands. The $200,000 gun, which is fired by the sudden release of all that compressed air, is primed. There is a countdown. And another pullet bullets to oblivion.

Messily. Very messily. So messily that for some time there has been an international effort afoot among people in the fowl-firing business to develop a synthetic chicken. Most popular to date is a jellified substance made from seaweed. But Mr. Noonan is skeptical. A jelly bird "just doesn't break up in the same way a real chicken does," he says.

The FAA people who man a rival chicken gun in Atlantic City— and whom Mr. Noonan looks down upon as rank amateurs in the field—don't agree. They use not only phony chickens but even great gobs of hamburger. On occasion, says one man in Atlantic City, "we've bought a turkey at a supermarket and fired that as well."

Last year the FAA complicated Mr. Noonan's life by setting a new air-worthiness standard for U.S. transport planes. Henceforth, they said, tail assemblies would have to stand up to the impact of an eight-pound bird. After crashing a few eight-pounders through tail assemblies, Mr. Noonan came to the conclusion the FAA people have feathers on the brain. "There isn't a chance of developing a tail to withstand that sort of impact," he says. A man at the FAA disagrees, but he does concede the new standard hasn't been enforced yet.

Mr. Noonan considers his own setup more scientific than that of the hamburger shooters down in New Jersey, and it appears to be so. He gets his chickens from a government DDT research farm. The farm electrocutes the birds and freezes them. Mr. Noonan stores them in his lab freezer, 100 at a time, and thaws out each one about 24 hours before the big bang.

Once he agreed to use a fresh-killed chicken when an aircraft manufacturer protested that a frozen chicken would be too stiff, even thawed out, and would thus give inaccurate impact data. Mr. Noonan disputed that, but he did buy some live chickens and set out to slaughter them himself—something he had never done before. He was told the best way to electrocute a chicken was to put one live wire on its crop and the other in its rectum.

The chicken objected to that. "So we spent all afternoon chasing that damn chicken around the gun with a couple of electric wires," he recalls. In the end, he gassed the bird.

Mr. Noonan's firing procedure is also more sophisticated than that of the FAA chicken men, who simply stuff a chicken or whatever in the barrel and shoot it out—at a speed 150 miles an hour slower than the Ottawa gun. Mr. Noonan believes that the speeding birds in Atlantic City begin to break up in the barrel. He puts his chickens in a huge tin can and surrounds them with honeycomb aluminum before loading the gun. On firing, the can moves down the barrel until it is stopped by a device in the muzzle. The chicken then flies out the open end of the can and on to its target.

One day, Mr. Noonan fears, it may go further than that. Canada's Uplands Air Force Base adjoins his lab and the commanding officer's house is right in the chicken flight path. Usually chickens smash into targets in front of a huge earthen embankment. But Mr. Noonan worries that before too long a chicken breaking the sound barrier is going to whiz right over the embankment and land, say, on the CO's dinner plate.

—DAVID BRAND, June 1971

60. Why the Future Isn't Coming Up Roses

"I am concerned that we should take care not to rush into issues which might embitter and divide the American people," said Rep. John Brademas, an Indiana Democrat, a few years ago.

"I must frankly say that this . . . is one of the most difficult choices which has come to me during my legislative career," noted John F. Kennedy in 1959 when he was a senator from Massachusetts.

What piece of legislation could prompt such reflective thoughts from two lawmakers? Repealing the Taft-Hartley act? Broadening civil rights laws? Increasing foreign aid? No, the issue isn't even remotely related to these far-reaching matters that Congressmen are paid $30,000 a year to decide. Rather, it's much more thorny than it is weighty: The selection of a national flower.

A trifling thing when compared to the questions of peace and prosperity, choosing a national flower nevertheless has been argued in Congress since the days of Woodrow Wilson. Advocates of various flowers periodically have stormed Washington to push their favorites, but nothing in the New Deal, Fair Deal, New Frontier or—to date— the Great Society has produced a winner. The debate is still raging, however—this week, it is centered in New York, where the International Flower Show is in progress.

The United States is about the only major nation without a national flower. Canada is so proud of its emblem—the sugar maple leaf—that it recently put it on the new Canadian flag. Other patriotic posies range from the sunflower of Russia to the rose of England, the nopal cactus of Mexico and the leek of Wales.

"Americans have every right to a flower," thunders Clark Kidd, former president of the American Association of Nurserymen. "Big city vandals do not grow flowers. Skid row derelicts do not know flowers. The country could use a symbol so arrestingly beautiful its very view can calm the troubled mind. A boon to the spirit of little children in school . . ."

Everybody has a reason for his own favorite. Says Rep. Lindley Beckworth, a Texas Democrat: "The people of our area are very much interested in seeing the rose designated the national flower. The center of rose production is in Texas and certainly a very major source of rose bushes is Tyler, Texas. Tyler happens to be in the Congressional district I represent." ("I have respect for the rose, but unfortunately it is a tricky flower. If it doesn't get close care, it won't live," says a carnation backer at the International Flower Show.)

Former Iowa Republican Congressman John Kyl: "I am asking that Congress declare the corn tassel the national floral emblem for the same reason that other, older nationals of the world have taken such action—to denote that the story of corn belongs in the history and traditions of this nation. Corn is America."

Joe M. Kilgore, when he was a Democratic House member from Texas: "Designation of the poinsettia as the national flower of the United States would have a particular significance at a time when this nation is striving for closer ties and a warmer relationship with our American neighbors to the south. The poinsettia, known through the Western Hemisphere as the Christmas flower . . . was first brought across the Rio Grande from Mexico. The American Poinsettia Society at Mission, Texas, in my district, is the only floral club in the United States dedicated to the poinsettia alone."

Combatants, too, aren't above taking pot shots at their competitors. David Burpee, president of W. Altee Burpee Co., a major mail order seed company, and a staunch battler for the marigold, says, "The corn tassel has been suggested for our national flower, but the tassel is not a perfect flower. It is merely the male part."

Mr. Burpee also points out that many flowers in the running, such as the rose, already are state flowers, and he says, "The marigold isn't the official flower of any state. As a matter of states rights, it would not seem right to name the official flower of any state as our national floral emblem."

For a flower to be seriously considered it would seem that it must have commercial value. Otherwise, no one would bother to rally behind it, and generally no congressman would take up its cause. Rose raisers are voters, but dandelion growers are just people without a green thumb.

But there is one notable exception. In 1959, a fourth-grade class at Baywood School in San Mateo, Ca., a middle-class suburb of San Francisco, was studying Luther Burbank and the 3,000 plant and flower varieties he created. The teacher, Louise Lytken, explained how the naturalist crossed three different daisies and came up with a Shasta daisy, a hardy breed with slight commercial use. "Is there a national flower?" one youngster asked. "No," Mrs. Lytken replied. "How about the Shasta daisy?" he asked. And the Shasta daisy campaign was born.

Since then, Mrs. Lytken's successive classes have bombarded congressmen, businessmen and entertainers with thousands of letters proclaiming the merits of the Shasta daisy and inveighing, "Let's choose an American flower, propagated by an American." Their efforts have won over a solid cadre of Congressmen as well as support from the California legislature and a host of chambers of commerce,

Rotary clubs, Kiwanis clubs and Lions clubs across the United States.

To further their campaign, the youngsters have a series of arguments, not the least of which is that the Shasta daisy wouldn't benefit any vested interests. Also, they say, the Shasta daisy—a small daisy with slim, white petals ringing a gold center—is easy to grow and can be raised in every state; it is practically free from insect pests and plant diseases, and it needs little care and is a perennial, meaning it doesn't have to be replanted year after year. It has a simple classical beauty, and its petals could signify the 50 states, they claim. And by combining the best qualities of several flowers, the children argue that Luther Burbank's accomplishment was similar to the "melting pot of America," which has "combined the best qualities of many nationalities to produce a stronger and more understanding people."

Battling from nowhere, the youngsters have made themselves heard and, according to Mrs. Lytken, they have been treated to the finest of civics lessons. The Shasta daisy itself has shown signs of growing in popularity. In a "what flower would you like named as the national flower" poll conducted by the Florists' Telegraphy Delivery Association in 1962, the Shasta daisy ranked 17th in popularity, well behind roses (No. 1) and carnations (No. 2), but ahead of the corn tassel and marigold. (Citing the poll, a Newark, N.J., rose grower and rose backer says: "Why force something on the people that they don't want?")

The last Congressional hearings on the question of a national flower were held in 1964, before the subcommittee on library and memorials of the Committee on House Administration. This year, if lawmakers can clear time from Vietnam and other pressing matters, the problem is expected to be studied anew. Insiders doubt whether Congress will be able to settle on a single flower, but they say a compromise may be in the offing: An emblem of several flowers—including the Shasta daisy.

—JAMES E. BYLIN, March 1966

CHAPTER NINE

SCRIBES, DESCRIBING

---

61. *Traveling Cheap, but Not Sleazy*

There's a fine line between cheap and sleazy. I know. Recently I drove right along it. Let me explain.

Some hotels in San Francisco, New York and other places now charge $130 a night for a single. Some people say that's outrageous. My boss says a person could drive across the entire country and lodge for less than that. He told me to do it.

That's where the fine line comes in. *Fleabag* is a relative term. The same dive that you'd be insulted to stay in on the company tab, you might call a great bargain when you're paying for it. A place that you'd never suggest to the boss, he might gladly recommend to you.

So I hit the low road, leaving California for a city where many things are said to be cheap: Las Vegas. I found that within those neon-coated corridors, a person can live awfully well on awfully little—if he just doesn't gamble.

My Sears luggage was dumped in Circus Circus, a quaint 1,610-room hotel billing itself as the "greatest resort saga." A room with two double beds and a carousel horse painted on the wall costs $16. And the hotel has all the humble pleasures you expect of Las Vegas: a monorail shuttle to take guests directly to the roulette wheels, a 125-foot-high electric clown pointing to the building, trapeze artists flying in the casino, and a wedding chapel performing civil or religious ceremonies across from the elevators.

At most casinos, waitresses spilling out of cute apparel provide complimentary drinks. Proprietors probably prefer to liquor up those losing large amounts, but even low rollers can cash in. By plunking coins very slowly in the nickel slots you can stagger back to your room for about a buck.

But scroungers want more than drinks. For only $3.50, the Four Queens casino sells a half-pound slab of prime rib served by a burly waiter who says, "You will enjoy it." One slot-machine haven hawks a foot-long hot dog and a beer for 50 cents. At Foxy's Firehouse casino, those who show an out-of-state driver's license and a little humility get a free hamburger.

Such deals aren't ignored by the local residents. "You can really eat well in this town if you stay away from the slots," Morris Rubin, a Las Vegas grocer, told me. He and his wife often go to a casino cafeteria for its 79-cent ham-and-egg breakfast. When I met them there, he was pulling out a crumpled coupon entitling them to two breakfasts for 79 cents. "It doesn't pay to cook," Mr. Rubin said.

Later, I got a free key ring from the Golden Goose casino, had my picture taken free in front of a million dollars and got a free personalized gambling horoscope. I was on a roll.

Still feeling lucky, I spent a night at the Sahara. Not the big place on the Vegas strip, where rooms can run to $60, but a slightly less glamorous version in Gallup, N.M. For $14.95, I got a room with droopy drapes, postcards of the place when it used to be a Ramada

Inn and free cable movies. (Remembering that fine line, I watched only respectable films.)

But most budgets don't offer such frills. Wesley Jackson Sr., who runs the newly built Motel One in Albuquerque, N.M., says, "We don't spend much and we don't charge much." His $14.50 rooms are sparse. He claims to have spent $38 on advertising since opening in November 1981.

Mr. Jackson, who resembles a streamlined W.C. Fields, says that the place is respectable. "We don't get any more drunks or flakes than anywhere else," he says, "and if we suspect some ole gal's a hooker, we won't rent to her the next morning."

That policy has been strictly enforced since an incident involving a clogged commode that cost $40 in repairs. The clog was caused by two snapshots of a smiling woman wearing little more than one cowboy boot and a look of accomplishment. "Everybody here's seen these," says Mr. Jackson, pulling the photos out of an office desk. "You can bet we won't rent to her again."

The inspiration for Mr. Jackson, and other cut-rates, is Motel Six, a budget chain whose rooms offer the charm and warmth of a hospital, at far less cost. In any city, all Motel Six rooms are $15.95, year-round.

I stayed in a brand-new Motel Six in Texas and an eight-year-old one in Atlanta. It seemed as if I stayed in the same room both nights. Both were all white, and neither had a phone. If you wanted to watch the black-and-white TV, you had to pay 75 cents extra for a key to turn it on.

"If you want luxury, go someplace else," advises Ruth Ann Shaffer, who made a few Motel Six stops with her husband en route from Akron to Arizona. But the Shaffers say they're usually satisfied with the clean, if spartan, rooms. "It all depends on how tired you are when you get there," says Mr. Shaffer.

There is a cost advantage to traveling during a recession. Helen Edwards, the manager of the Clinton, Okla., Stuckey's store, vows to keep her 99-cent breakfasts and 10-cent cups of coffee to lure customers. Taking a puff on her supermarket-brand cigaret, she says: "The economy is so bad now, people don't have much money to travel. You better believe I'm keeping those specials. I'm not in this business for my health."

Under its blazing aqua roof, her Stuckey's offers pickled okra, creamers topped with plastic cows' heads and a dozen rattlesnake eggs for $1.19. I just bought coffee.

Wired by several doses of cheap caffeine, I drove late that night, into the heart of Arkansas. When I realized I was concentrating on the broadcast of a local junior-high basketball game, I knew it was time to stop. Suddenly, it seemed, hotels had vanished. I found nothing in Beulah, Plumerville or Cotton Plant. Panic struck.

Desperately, I exited into another small town. After passing a school, a mortuary and a 24-hour place serving White River catfish, I spied a dimly lit motel. I was thrilled, if not surprised, to see its vacancy sign.

My $18 room smelled older than it looked. The pillows seemed stuffed with Cream of Wheat, and the manager reminded me vaguely of Norman Bates, who ran the motel in Alfred Hitchcock's movie "Psycho." But the place had one big advantage: I got a real early start on the next day's driving.

Even someone with the stingiest intentions may succumb to distractions. Seeing a big sign for fireworks, I stopped at a roadside tent in Byhalia, Miss. T. P. St. John, a friendly man in a wheelchair, gave me such a super price on some Roman candles that I couldn't resist.

I got detoured again after seeing a road sign proclaiming that U.S. Route 78 in Mississippi was officially the "Elvis Aron Presley Memorial Highway" and that a quick exit would bring me straight to "the king's" birthplace. Visitors have to put a dollar in a fishbowl upon entering the two-room home, but you can visit the Elvis gift shop and information center in the back and the Elvis Memorial Chapel next door, free of charge.

Despite such lapses, I easily attained my low goal. When I ended my discount trek in Charleston, S.C., the tab for six nights' lodging, including two in Las Vegas, was $98.

A couple of stops made my food bill impressively low, too. In Hamilton, Ala., a herd of trucks was parked around Kat's Kafe, where big breakfasts go for $2, big dinners go for $3, and all the coffee you want is 15 cents. The owners, Forbus Cooper and his wife, Vester, say they haven't raised prices in five years and don't plan to. Mr. Cooper, a former trucker, says, "If you make more money, you just pay more taxes. Why should I feed the government when I can feed my customers instead?"

Trucker Johnny Jones of Hickory Flat, Miss., chewing on a toothpick and wearing a hat that reads "I Can Still Chase Girls Downhill," says Kat's Kafe is "the best place in the whole world; you can't find a place that gives you more food for less money."

But I can think of at least one. In Amarillo, I stopped at the Big Texan Steak Ranch, which makes an unusual offer to the truly cost-conscious. The restaurant will give you a 4½-pound steak free—if you can eat it in an hour.

Intrigued by the challenge, and prodded on by two tables of boisterous Texans, I told the waitress I'd give it a try. I had to pay $26 up front, refundable on presentation of a clean plate, and fill out a small card, recording among other things my pre-dinner weight of 110 pounds.

I learned that of the 20,000 people who had attempted this feat since 1963, some 16,822 had failed. I flinched. But I was assured that it had been accomplished by a 63-year-old grandmother and by a wrestler named Klondike Bill who ate two 4½-pound steaks in an hour. I was encouraged.

Then the plate arrived. Suddenly I realized that a 4½-pound steak is roughly the size of one small cow. It is equivalent to 23 Big Macs. Besides, the contestants also have to eat a shrimp cocktail, a roll, salad and a baked potato in the allotted hour. And if you get sick, the deal is off.

A pair of huge men attempting the feat threw in their napkins and left in disgrace. After that, a cigar chomping Texas lawyer bet his buddy $100 that I'd fail, too. He lost his bet.

To the amazement of the lawyer, the busboys, the other customers and myself, I ate the entire dinner, in an impressive 49 minutes. Swelling with pride, I accepted congratulations and the return of my 26 bucks. A fellow patron walked up to me and drawled, "Little lady, don't you ever tell anyone what you just did or you'll never get married."

But actually, I don't think it damaged my reputation too much. I know that fine line between sleazy and cheap.

—CARRIE DOLAN, April 1983

62. *In Praise of Small Words*

May I have a small word with you?

I want to tell the tale of a group of folks, some here and some there, who like to talk in one-pulse words. There are no more than a few folks so far—a cult, in a way—but you will want to play their game once you hear more. I shall tell this tale in words of one pulse, if I can. So, please bear with me—it will, of course, be short and sweet.

The head of the group (called the Club for One-Pulse Words) is, as luck would have it, named Jim Grant. He lives in an East Coast town best known for its stone stoops, its Colts, and its soft crabs—the name of the town is more than one pulse, but you know of where I speak. Two more folks who speak in one pulse live there, too; a fourth lives in the Town of Wind, to the west, and the fifth lives in New York.

"It has changed my life," says Jim Grant, who writes tunes to earn his keep. "First, I had to change my brand of booze to Jim Beam (on the rocks). Then I switched beers, to Beck's or Bass Ale. Now I eat beans, rice, and some pork and duck. In truth, though, the best one-pulse meal is a Big Mac, french fries and Coke."

The books he reads have changed, too, since the club formed in March. "Now I read the likes of *Jaws* and *Lord of the Flies*," he says.

Like all groups, this one has a set of rules that all who join must live by. They are:

1) No words of more than one pulse.
2) Words that make use of a small mark (such as *don't*) are fine but should be used with care.
3) Folks' names that have more than one pulse should be changed to code words, or else in court.
4) Don't be a pest.

"We will keep it up as long as it takes for folks to see the point of our cause," Jim Grant says. Their point, in brief, is that words don't have to be long to be good.

With the rules in hand, friends send mail, make phone calls and speak in one-pulse words as much as three hours a day. "Hi there!" is what they say when they pick up the phone. They say "So long!" when they hang up.

If you think that this is a game that just a fool would want to play, you are wrong. Hear the one-pulse words of a star scribe for *The New York Times,* who once toiled for the man in the White House who quit, and who now writes a piece for his sheet on the use of words.

"It sounds like a hell of a lot of fun to me," says the scribe, right off the bat. (His first name is Bill, and his last name is a gem.) Then he thinks on it some more and adds, "Where will it all end?"

Bill thinks that it would have been strange for that great man with the beard, named Abe, to have stood by that grave while the war 'twixt the Blues and the Grays was fought long in the past. What would he have said, the scribe asks, if he had had to talk in one-pulse words?

"Piece of cake," says Jim Grant. "Four score and six-plus-one years back."

One of the one-pulse guys has the top job at St. Paul's Church in the same town as Jim. Asked if he will one day speak to his flock in one-pulse words, he says: "It's not past the realm of chance."

Like his pals, he finds the club a good way to rest his bones; he is five-times-ten-plus-three years old. "It's fun and a dare," says the man, whose first name is Bill and whose last name is the merged form of work and man. And he is sure that the game helps him in his job, too: It's more than dumb luck, he says, that God is a one-pulse word.

To be sure, there are lots of bad things you can do in one-pulse words—like fall off a cliff. And most of the bad words in our tongue come in the one-pulse size, but I can't print those here.

Still, the club likes to point out that some of the great truths in our world use words of just one pulse: "Where there's a will, there's a way." "To thine own self be true." "A stitch in time saves nine." "A bird in the hand is worth two in the bush." "I am not a crook."

But one one-pulse phrase gets used more by the club than all else—or gets asked, at least: "Your place or mine?"

At times, a thought they may like comes in a two-pulse size, so they change it to fit.

In the long run, though, the folks in the club get tired of the game—just like you right now. No more one-pulse words, they say. We must stop right now. Quick.

"When I want to stop," says Jim Grant, "I pause, and then I say 'goodness.' I wait a bit, to see how it feels. Then I say 'happily.' Then I pause some more, shake, and clear my throat. 'Chrysanthemum!' I shout, and it's over. I'm free again."

—DAVE BLUM, *Some Month,*
One Nine Eight Two

63. *Z-less in Zanzibar*

I cover the countries at the end of the alphabet.

Those remote, struggling places that are only an aside in the atlas and slumber undisturbed in the final chapters of the encyclopedia—those are my beat.

Upper Volta is my beat. Uganda is my beat. The issue hasn't arisen, but since they are remote and struggling, it is possible that the two Yemens are my beat.

The back-of-the-book nature of this job has its ha*ards—as, for example, my last trip to *imbabwe, *ambia, Tan*ania and *an*ibar. That's when the * on my typewriter sat fro*en in its socket. Now, consider the enormousness of the problem:

*imbabwe has two political parties, *anu and *apu, and the remnants of two guerrilla armies, *anla and *ipra. Robert Mugabe is the prime minister—no problems there—but his leading lieutenants are Simon Mu*enda, Bernard Chid*ero and Eddison *vobgo.

They eat mai*e in *imbabwe. They revere the spirit *i*i, which is an eagle, and if they are superstitious, they carry a mu*e*e nut as a *ango, a charm.

*imbabwe is bordered on the south by the Limpopo River, which, Rudyard Kipling notwithstanding, is neither great, gray-green nor greasy, and on the north by the *ambe*i, which is. *ambia lies across the *ambe*i. *ambia produces much of the world's copper and cobalt and some of its *inc.

*ambia is linked to Tan*ania by the Ta*ara Railroad, which the Chinese built, and the Tan*am Highway, which the Americans built when the Chinese beat them to building the railroad. Tan*ania used to be called Tanganyika, but in 1964 it forged a lopsided union with *an*ibar and changed its name.

*an*ibar is a 950-square-mile island that once was called the Sultanate of *an*ibar. It provided the United States with slaves until abolition and with cloves until the great clove blight of 1981. Now there isn't much commerce in *an*ibar City, on the northern tip of the island, and none at all in Ki*imka*i City in the south.

Although *an*ibar is a 24-mile hop across the *an*ibar Channel from Dar es Salaam, the capital of the Tan*anian republic, it retains a prideful distance. You need a passport to enter *an*ibar, even if you're a Tan*anian.

*an*ibar keeps its own bank accounts and has its own president (from those bank accounts it recently bought that president a jet so that he can make the 24-mile hop in seven minutes flat). *an*ibar also lays this claim to modernity: It alone in the republic has television.

*aire, which is just West of Tan*ania, also has an enterprising president who has risen from army officer to multibillionaire in a whi*. His name is Mobutu Sese Seko Kuku Ngbendu Wa *a Banga.

*aire used to be called the Congo when the Belgians claimed it. Now when you speak of the Congo, you mean that little country to the north whose capital is Bra**aville. A river separates the Congos. Wherever else it flows in Africa, the river is called the Congo. When it flows through *aire, it is called *aire.

Mo*ambique hugs the Indian Ocean south of Tan*ania. Its problems for the end-of-the-alphabet reporter are compounded by the provinces of Ga*a and *ambe*ia and the coal fields in Maoti*e, which Mo*ambique is counting upon for its economic awakening.

Namibia—thousands of miles of deserts, dunes and salt pans— isn't so much the end of the alphabet as the end of the world. A businessman named Luderit* persuaded the Germans to coloni*e Namibia and they, in turn, named a town for him. Luderit* the man disappeared in the desert and so did Luderit* the town, which is deserted and largely buried under the shifting sands of the great Namib.

End-of-the-alphabet problems aren't peculiar to Africa. I travel to India, whose president is *ial Singh, and to Pakistan, where President Mohammad *ia ul-Haq grabbed power from Prime Minister *ulfikar Ali Bhutto. The founder of Pakistan was Muhammad Ali Jinnah, whom Pakistanis called *Quaid-i-A*am*, the great leader.

The people who sold me this typewriter assured me that one just like it survived a fall down Mount Kilimanjaro, which is in Tan*ania. A competitor's model, they said, once melted in Sudan, which is north of *aire. There was talk too of floods and tramplings and airline baggage handlers. I don't remember, however, any mention of fro*en *s.

Once before this typewriter malfunctioned. That was in 1979. *imbabwe then was Rhodesia. On that trip, it was the R that refused to budge.

—JUNE KRONHOL*, January 1983

64. *Being Hip in Cairo*

CAIRO, Egypt—When Ashgan the belly dancer thrusts her ample hips, a tidal wave of flesh undulates across her midriff. As she shifts her weight in a little leap from left to right, the thud registers on the Richter scale.

Turbaned Egyptians bang the tables in delight. Ashgan's figure is beyond Rubenesque. She is, to be blunt about it, a whale. Pausing in mid-shimmy, she reaches for a Kleenex from a box on a front-row table, blows her nose noisily and stuffs the used tissue into the cavernous cleavage of her spangled bra.

Ashgan doesn't exactly look like a hard act to follow. Except for one small problem: I am the next act.

Trying to recall every jiggle from my brief stint at belly-dance school, I untangle my bangles and climb on the stage in Ashgan's considerable wake.

A few decades ago, a woman of my modest talents appearing at a Cairo nightclub would have been as unthinkable as a camel in the Kentucky Derby. But the art of belly dancing has fallen on hard times in Egypt. "The rise of fundamentalist Islam has made it a very unrespectable thing to do," says Roberta Dougherty, an Egyptologist and sometime belly dancer from Philadelphia.

The fundamentalists fired their opening salvo in a navel battle of sorts: Dancers were ordered to cover their belly buttons. Now, dancers need a license to perform, and anyone deemed too provocative risks being hustled off to jail by a special squad known as the "politeness police." In 1987, the government stopped issuing new licenses; thus, along with regular scarcities of sugar and cooking oil, Egypt is now short of belly dancers.

To me that looked like an opportunity. So I went to see Mahmoud Ramadan, an official with the Department of Artistic Inspection. Before the licensing ban, Mr. Ramadan was responsible for inspecting would-be dancers, to ensure that their costumes had the required navel-concealing layer of gauze that links bra and low-slung skirt, and to check that their choreography wasn't too risque.

"I had a wonderful job in those days," the bureaucrat sighs. Today, he has to fend off irate hotel owners who can't find enough dancers to hire.

Mr. Ramadan, who considers himself a belly-dance connoisseur, has seen performances by all of Cairo's leading artists. Most of those women got their start in the 1950s, when belly dancers had star status in Egypt. Now in their late 40s, they won't be performing much longer. "The next generation, it isn't as good, and after them, well . . ." His voice trails off sadly as he gestures at an empty desktop that once was covered with license applications.

This isn't the first time Egyptian officials have delivered a blow to the belly dancer. In 1850, when the French writer Gustave Flaubert visited Cairo, he discovered that all the dancers had been banished from the city by order of its ruler, who believed they encouraged prostitution. Traveling up the Nile, Flaubert found dancers so erotic that accompanying musicians covered their eyes with folds of their turbans so they wouldn't be too distracted to play.

There's little chance of that happening these days, thanks to all the government regulations. Belly-dance schools, which once flourished on a street of lute stringers and drum makers in Cairo, now scarcely exist. The school in which I enrolled caters mostly to curious foreigners and a few Egyptian pre-teens who take the class as an after-school activity rather than as preparation for a future career.

Visions of Flaubert's sirens soon recede as I struggle to balance a three-foot cane on my head—an exercise in isolating each body movement. In belly dance, as the hips shudder, the upper body must remain languorously relaxed. My Egyptian classmates' canes stay put, as if stapled to their scalp; mine keeps skidding off.

After two months, however, the cane is spending more time on my head than on the floor, and it seems time to try a performance. Mr. Ramadan had warned me that the only way I could get a license was to take my case to the Minister of Culture. But Egyptian officialdom moves so slowly that, if I went the interminable bureaucratic route, a geriatric nurse would have had to wheel me on stage for my first performance. I decide, instead, to risk an unlicensed one-night stand.

All I need is a stage. Seeking advice, I visit Khalid Sarsaa, a drummer in a belly-dance back-up band. He immediately rules out fancy hotels and the clubs that line the road out to the Pyramids. "They range from first-class to fifth-class," he explains. "What you need is something really tenth class."

The New Arizona Nightclub fits the bill. Admission to this downtown dive costs 90 cents, an affordable sum for small-town Egyptians in the capital for a big night out, or for the odd Saudi tourist hard-hit by the oil slump.

Inside, the decor includes peeling gold wallpaper and Christmas decorations that may have been in place since the original Christmas. A seven-piece band lines up along the back of the stage and the first belly dancer of the night makes her entrance. She wears red silk, silver spangles and an Ace bandage on her wrist. She may have sustained the injury fending off members of the audience, one of whom this night runs up to the stage trying to push banknotes into her belt.

New worries suddenly supersede anxiety about the adequacy of my hip-thrusts. What if someone tries to give me a tip? What if no one does?

As I watch the evening's performers, the latter possibility seems increasingly likely. But suddenly the music breaks off. The police are raiding the club. I can see the headlines: "Busted for Belly Dancing." Lucky for me, the police are after hashish, not unlicensed dancers. Frisking a dozen members of the audience, they turn out pockets and inspect Chiclets packs, then depart, taking a couple of customers with them.

The band strikes up again and a few moments later I get my cue. Shaking out my costume—a black and gold outfit with enough beading to buy a small Pacific atoll—I gyrate onto the stage.

Soon, I'm too busy keeping up with the musicians to dwell on other anxieties. Belly dance is improvisational, and goes where the music takes it: frantic shimmying to match fast drum beats, slow undulations to elaborate the wailing notes of the violin. I remember my teacher's admonition that good belly dance shouldn't have any crass, bump-and-grind movements, but should be a subtly erotic, physical illustration of each phrase in the complex Arabic music.

My ten-minute performance seems like a thousand and one nights, and I'm relieved when I hear the shift in the music that allows the dancer to bring the dance to an end with a graceful salaam. As I make my bow, a Saudi leaps up, waving an Egyptian 10-pound note, and demands that I dance again. To my astonishment, the rest of the audience also begins hooting for more.

As an encore, I go belly to belly with Ashgan, the whale. She keeps inspecting my narrow hips and shaking her head disbelievingly at my 106-pound figure. Then, leaning over, she peers down the front of my costume. "Mafish!" she yells to the audience in Arabic. "Nothing there!"

Later, the club's manager, Samy Sallam, gives my performance a hard-nosed review: "Your dancing, it is technically quite good. But you don't have enough feeling. You must learn the emotion as well as the steps." To soften the blow, he hands me his card and says, rather ambiguously, "Give me a call."

I didn't think I'd bother. Reporting debt rollovers suddenly seemed a lot easier than performing hip rolls. But on the way out, I take a last bit of advice from an Egyptian in the audience, just in case.

"Eat more *basbousa*," he says, referring to a sugary Arabic dessert. "In a few months, a year maybe, you could have a very nice figure for belly dance."

—GERALDINE BROOKS, May 1989

65. Check Out That New Model—
Uh, I Don't Mean the Car

DETROIT—I have two blisters on each foot. My shoulders are bare and the drafty hall is freezing, yet I'm sweating with anxiety. Once again, I've forgotten my memorized lines. At my side, a man making disgusting kissing sounds is trying to attract my attention.

Welcome to the exciting, glamorous world of auto-show modeling.

Girls sell cars. Detroit still clings to that age-old notion. So this winter, at auto shows all over the country, millions of people will ogle two-legged female models draped seductively over the four-wheeled automotive ones. To some, the alluring women are a better reason to visit the auto show than the cars themselves. To others, the scantily clad models are one of the most obvious bastions of an offensively sexist sexual sell.

But the fact is that both the glamour and the sexism are in the eyes of the beholder. Being an auto-show model is a job—and a hard one.

To see the show through the eyes of an auto-show model, I memorized a three-page spiel, zipped myself into a slinky outfit and draped myself, as lankily as a 5-foot-2-inch frame would permit, over a Chevrolet Monte Carlo turning dizzily on a platform over a sea of faces.

After two days I was exhausted and ready to quit. Spending six hours in spike heels takes a stamina I don't possess. (Some models work 12-hour shifts.) Fending off harassment and bad jokes takes tact, and some restraint after a while. Delivering an inane three-minute sales pitch—with a smile—takes a little acting skill. Besides, while it may be exciting for the crowds to look at the models, looking back hour after hour gets, frankly, a little boring. "It isn't fun," says June Swaim, my partner and a seven-year show veteran. "It's work."

I got the job with the cooperation of General Motors Corp. Otherwise, I'd never have succeeded. Each car company screens hundreds of full-time models—and part-timers including actresses, nurses and homemakers—to match the woman's looks and bearings with the firm's image. Ford Motor Co. seeks "smiley types." Chrysler Corp. wants sleek high-fashion models: "We don't want to look like we're going out of business," says Thomas Andre, who managed Chrysler's show here.

I came closest to matching Chevrolet's requirements: "Absolutely wholesome—baseball, hot dogs and apple pie," says C. A. Rice of Gail & Rice Productions Inc., an agency handling the Chevy exhibit. It was touch and go at that. "Too short," was Mr. Rice's initial assessment. "A Jeep, definitely a Jeep," was another agency's conclusion, apparently summing up my stocky build.

Although the car companies insist they stress "personality" and "communications skills" in choosing their models, it's clear that looks are of prime importance. "I interviewed 30 women and turned down 29," says Mr. Andre. "They were barking."

The impression that looks count most is compounded by the costumes. Companies have spent up to $800 to outfit a single model in a designer gown. Budget cuts brought on by poor car sales prohibited such extravagance this year. But even with the $150-per model ceiling some companies imposed, the dresses were pretty lush.

Ford outfitted its model from a collection designed by Charlotte Ford, daughter of Henry Ford II, Ford's former chairman. Chrysler's high-fashion look included pencil-thin pants and rakish beanies. GM's Pontiac division was the raciest, with bright-colored silk dresses slashed nearly to the waist. My costume was fairly modest: a black-crepe jump suit with spaghetti straps. My mother helped pick it out.

The bright lights and show-biz atmosphere demand lots of makeup and colorful jewelry. "You just want to wash your face for hours afterwards," complains Wendy Martin, a Chrysler model. Being a non-makeup-wearer, I spend $35 on bright rouge, lipstick and eye shadow, and then submit myself to the others' professional advice. Ms. Swaim makes me up and is impressed with the result of her half-hour's work: "We should do a before-and-after picture," she says. I feel like Bozo the Clown.

Despite the fleshy overtones, the models themselves bitterly resent suggestions that the job is demeaning. Money is one big reason. "It's sexist all the way to the bank," snaps Susan Stark, a nurse who augments her part-time income with auto-show work. Most models earn from $100 to $150 a day working a show. A tour of ten cities could employ a model for three months in an otherwise slow winter season and earn her $10,000.

It's also safer than some other lines of work. "At least no one will throw beer bottles at me here," says Mary Polus, who dances at this year's Chevy exhibit and has worked as a singer in bars. The costumes "aren't so revealing" compared with other things women model, says Dianna Tolley, who has posed in lingerie for department-store ads.

Some hope to be discovered. "I have enough business cards to fill a suitcase," says Ms. Polus, an aspiring songwriter. There's precedent for discovery: One of TV-star Farrah Fawcett's early jobs was modeling sprawled across Ford's Lincoln-Mercury logo.

On the afternoon of opening night, we report to the floor of the show for practice and instructions: Be on time. Don't sit in the car. Don't wave to friends. Be careful with the clothes, especially when taking a break to eat. "I don't want to see my outfits in the hot dog line," says Barbara McIntosh, who costumed the Chrysler models.

As we rehearse our scripts, we get more informal coaching. "Smile at the car—it's your friend," one woman exhorts a dour Pontiac model. I must look nervous. "Don't look so frightened," one woman advises me. Another is more direct. "Stand up straight," she says. "Show your stuff."

The prospect of showing my stuff before a horde unnerves me. It gets worse when I mount the stage to practice. Chevrolet has one of the biggest displays in the auto show, two high revolving platforms under yellow and white flashing lights. From that vantage point I can see the Lincoln-Mercury display where they are handling a live cougar and the Chrysler exhibit, where a robot will soon be thrilling the crowd. And, I figure, they will all be able to see me.

My job: in lilting tones to deliver a three-minute speech about the car. It's black "with contrasting accent pin striping . . . a *full cubic foot* more trunk space than last year . . . and a fully padded vinyl top completely surrounding the opera window." In between times, I am to smile and stroll the length of the car, which is revolving all the while.

On a companion platform, my partner, Ms. Swaim, dark and slender in a red gown, practices her act at a Malibu sedan. Once an hour, we are to leave the platform to make room for a crowd-drawing act: two singing carburetors accompanied by a step-dancing cowboy.

By the time the doors open, I think I have my act down pat. I don't. As dozens gape, I start my speech. "Chevrolet is proud to present the 1981 Monte Carlo—" I begin. Startled at the sound of my voice over the loudspeaker, I freeze. The silence is deafening.

Then comes the surprise: They all walk by. No one pays the least bit of attention. "You feel really stupid talking to nobody," says Anne Marie Regal, another model. I don't. It makes me feel confident.

Midway through the day, I am feeling fine, grinning and waltzing and pointing out the car's features. Then come the mashers. One man makes kissing sounds. Another stands before me licking his lips. Some ask questions: "Hey, sweetie, do you come with the car?" leers a man wearing a combat jacket and a complexion to match. And a balding old man with an accent. And an eight-year-old. And even a woman in a fur jacket and knee socks. The same question.

"They were asking that question back when I was doing auto shows 20 years ago," laughs Ms. McIntosh. Seventeen people in all ask me that question in 12 hours. After hundreds of such encounters, "You really just want to say, 'You can't afford me,'" says a veteran model. But retorts are frowned on. The approved response: "Aren't you sweet to ask"—delivered with a smile. I pretend I don't hear.

One man approaches my partner. "Do you fool around with single men?" he asks. "No," Ms. Swaim answers sweetly. "Do you fool around with married women?" "Yes," the man sighs, and walks away. Dozens of strange men take our pictures. A scout troop listens to my speech in rapt silence, asks for my autograph and wanders away.

There are serious questions, like how much the car costs. "Just tell them about $10,000," a Chevrolet salesman advises me. "That'll shut them up real fast." At the Chrysler exhibit, models are asked about the firm's survival chances. "We're told to say we're very positive," says Ms. Martin. At the Honda exhibit, laid-off auto workers accost Amy Anderson. "Don't you feel guilty working for an importer?" they ask. She doesn't.

Some companies make the models learn technical information. For fear of error, Chevrolet doesn't do that. Once, so the story goes, a model got the cubic-inch size of an engine wrong and promised a customer a 747 engine. The crafty customer supposedly sued, demanding the jet plane engine. For legal reasons, all Ford's scripts "are passed through our legal department," says Bobbie Sharrar, who writes them.

Rules against socializing are strict, and most models say that at the end of the day, they're too tired anyway. "Eight hours feels like eight days," sighs Meg Lemmer. Backstage the glamour evaporates. Smart old timers travel with foot-soaking basins. Lynda Paisley pulls off her sexy shoes to reveal 16 flaming blisters. Most models get a 15-minute break every two hours. That's barely time for a quick trip to the restroom and a touch-up of makeup. An hour for dinner isn't enough time to leave the hall and find a restaurant, so "goodbye to hot meals," says Ms. Stark. We bring carrots, candy, sandwiches and thermoses of iced tea. Several women smoke. Some work on afghans and tapestries.

The dresses themselves are job hazards. When the hall is cold, we freeze. At other times the hot lights soon make the dresses more pleasing to the observer than to the wearer, a problem compounded by ten days of continuous wearing. Also, I quickly learn not to bend from the waist to answer questions from down at the floor level.

It's mainly a woman's world, although there are a few men. Mostly they are cast in sober mien, as engineers mainly, discussing the more technical side of a car's engineering. Dressed in a navy flannel blazer and gray slacks at a Chrysler K-car display, 34-year-old Ed Oldan makes a less convenient target for harassment. No one has asked him whether he comes with the car. "A little old lady did say I was cute," he says.

Feminists should be consoled to learn that woman narrators for the cars are a relatively new addition. In times past, the men did the talking and the women just smiled and pointed and opened the car doors. "They didn't think the women could handle it." says Ms. McIntosh.

—AMANDA BENNETT, January 1981

66. *Puzzlements*

NEW YORK—What on earth is a four-letter word for "Quarterback Brian"?

I need to know in a hurry. I have just the first three letters, S-I-P.

On a muggy summer afternoon, I have left the pace of daily journalism for some real deadline pressure. This is the fifth annual U.S. Open Crossword Championship, where a roomful of fiendish puzzlers squared off the other week in the Grand Prix of American word games.

For many people, solving crossword puzzles is a relaxing activity, something to do on a lazy afternoon in a comfortable armchair. Not at the U.S. Open. We are huddled tensely over a bank of long tables in a university auditorium, with a giant Seiko clock in one corner loudly counting off the seconds. In a few minutes a referee will yell, "Time's up!" and snatch all our puzzles away.

I glance to my left. A young woman is gliding through her puzzle using a black felt-tip pen. I glance to my right. A middle-aged man, already finished, is ostentatiously leafing through a morning newspaper. I glance back down at my puzzle. "Kin of the Potawatamis," it says. "Olive genus." "Ottoman chief." "Trypanosome carrier" . . .

This is the last of five puzzles in the tournament, with time limits ranging from 15 to 45 minutes. We get points for every correct word we fill in, with bonuses for finishing a puzzle before the clock stops. At the end of the day, the top three finishers will step onto the auditorium stage for a sudden-death final crossword, working with erasable markers on giant grids before a crowd of spectators. The champ will win $1,500, a dictionary and the U.S. Open's coveted trophy, a six-foot pencil.

My 249 rivals range in age from 18 to 82. They are from all over the country and work in all manner of jobs: a sociologist, a quilter, a nuclear-reactor operator, several accountants and many computer programmers. One contestant listed her occupation as "boat bum," another as "itinerant peddler" and a third as "diaskeuast," a crossword-puzzle word for editor.

All of us weathered a round of five preliminary puzzles, prepared by the monthly magazine Games, to qualify for this tournament. We all came here believing that we had a certain knack for filling in blank squares with obscure words.

But I have quickly learned that mere knacks count for little here. "A lot of people are really humbled," cautioned Will Shortz, the tournament's director and a Games senior editor, before the event began. "For most people, crosswords are a very solitary sport. They do them with their family and their friends, and they can be a star in their own small circles. Then they come to a tournament and they find they're not champions."

Several battle-scarred contestants echo this warning. "My first year here, I thought I was good," recalls Raymond Cotter, a Corning, N.Y., transportation executive vying in his fourth U.S. Open. "I thought I'd come out here and get in the top ten. I came to one word and the clue was 'mating game,' and I must have looked at that one word for five minutes." The answer turned out to be "chess." Mr. Cotter finished 176th.

"The top solvers here fill in the spaces as fast as my hand can write," laments Carolyn Bartlebaugh, a Camp Hill, Pa., high-school French teacher who has competed in all five U.S. Opens. "If I had the answer in front of me and I could just transfer all the letters into my puzzle, they still would win."

This tourney, in fact, has attracted some of the crossword circuit's most bruising competitors.

They include David Rosen, 33, and Ellen Ripstein, 34, a pair of New York insurance workers who regularly grab top spots at the U.S. Open and leading regional contests. Like many athletes who wear lucky charms when they compete, Mr. Rosen wears his lucky two-piece gray suit. "It goes with my type-A personality," he explains.

Four years ago, Mr. Rosen and Ms. Ripstein met at the first U.S. Open. He finished seventh and she finished tenth, and they have been dating ever since. "We're the Chris Evert and Jimmy Connors of crosswords," Ms. Ripstein says.

Towering over the field is Rebecca Kornbluh, a 35-year-old weaver from Mundelein, Ill., who basically owns the sport of competitive crosswords today. A tense, animated woman with a long braid down her back and a little enamel pig (her lucky charm) pinned to her dress, Ms. Kornbluh swept the last two U.S. Opens and has vowed to retire after this match.

Talking with Ms. Kornbluh, I begin to see what separates the giants from the duffers in this sport. My preparation for the tournament consisted of doing a few crossword puzzles on the airplane to New York and having a lot to eat and drink at a reception for entrants the night before the contest. Rebecca Kornbluh tells me she has been doing 15 timed crosswords a day for the last week, and she skipped the reception.

"I felt I needed a quiet evening, not a party," she says. "I stayed home, did some puzzles, and went to bed early."

The day begins with three unusually devious puzzles. Foxy word-play lurks everywhere. One crossword is filled with puns on detergent brand names. (The answer to "supply the detergent" is GIVE

ONE'S ALL; "print on a detergent box" is BOLD LETTERING.)
Another features movie star names turned into birds. (Answers in-
clude GEORGE SEAGULL, STARLING HAYDEN and DONALD
O'CONDOR.)

Every corner brings agonies of self-doubt. At 7 Down—"fake
golds"—the intersecting across-words leave me with OROIDAS,
which looks extremely dubious. Could "a little more than a bushel"
really be EPHAH? Worst of all, for "site of Cybele's temple," I'm
left with total gobbledygook: MTIDA.

My eyes glaze over. My mind begins to wander. Mtida . . .
Mtida . . . "O Cybele, I have journeyed here to Mtida, bearing ephahs
and ephahs of tribute, to pray for victory for quarterback Brian Sipo
(Sipi? . . . Siph? . . . Sipu? . . .)."

At the lunch break, the auditorium breaks into a din of post-
mortems. "Dominique Sanda? Who ever heard of these people?"
"Narwal? A narwal doesn't have tusks!" All around me, people are
buzzing about the location of Cybele's shrine; it turns out to be
Mt. Ida.

I compare notes with Martha Browne, a contestant who caught my
eye by finishing all three puzzles early and then whiling away the remaining time with an Italian crossword magazine. Ms. Browne, a
free-lance editor from New York, says, "I had a private smirk of
pleasure at the detergent theme. For decades women have had to
learn a lot of sports terminology to do puzzles. This morning I was
pleased to hear a lot of men grumbling."

The afternoon features a puzzle with a twist: About a third of the
words are defined with audio clues played on a loudspeaker, asking
questions such as "Whose voice is this?" or "What work is this song
from?"

Here my '70s upbringing slows me down. I have trouble identifying the singer of "Dream a Little Dream of Me" (MAMA CASS) and
the theme song being played (from "LILI"). On the other hand, I
quickly recognize the ten-letter deep voice hissing, "There will be a
substantial reward for the one that finds the Millennium Falcon"

(DARTH VADER) and the six-letter high, throaty voice warbling, "It's not that easy bein' green" (KERMIT; another hapless solver came up with VERMIN for this one).

The end of the day finds Ms. Kornbluh, the defending title-holder, pitted in the finals against a New York pianist and a Virginia labor lawyer (a pair of dark horses who upset the Chris and Jimmy duo to claim the other two top spots). Ms. Kornbluh eats them alive. Pausing only once, to step back and double-check her spelling of "inimical," she sprints to a perfect finish more than a minute before her opponents, each of whom makes a couple of mistakes.

After her victory, Ms. Kornbluh puffs on a cigaret and reflects on what it takes to be a crossword champion. Is her secret a spectacular vocabulary? "I have a pretty good vocabulary," she admits cheerfully, "but it's passive. I don't know what half the words mean."

As for me, I wind up in 22nd place, an exciting finish as far as I'm concerned but a long way from the six-foot pencil.

Looking over my corrected puzzles, I see that "fake golds" turns out to be oroides, not oroidas. Amazingly, an ephah is indeed a little more than a bushel (it equals one-tenth of a homer, to be exact). And the quarterback's name is Brian Sipe, not Sipo, my eventual guess.

I should have suspected something was wrong there when the crossing word, "sunny vacation spot," came out as OSLO. The correct answer: ISLE.

—MICHAEL W. MILLER, September 1986

67. Play It Again, Ma'am

NEW YORK—I'm playing Bach on my viola, striving to be heard above the passing wail of an ambulance siren. It's Saturday afternoon on Times Square, and about 25 people are gathered on the sidewalk in front of me. After I finish the Bach, a few appreciative listeners pitch loose change, dollar bills and subway tokens into the open viola case at my feet.

The triumphant mood is broken when an usher from the movie theater next door strolls over. "You're blocking our marquee," he bellows in my ear, making it clear that I should move on—hastily.

Carnegie Hall it isn't, but for an amateur musician, a bustling sidewalk can be as good a place as any to begin. With 12 years of classical viola training, and numerous recitals and concerts, behind me, I decided to sample the musical street life.

In this and other big cities, the sidewalks teem with struggling musicians who sing, or play, for their supper. These "street musicians" play anywhere and anything, from classical lute sonatas to punk rock. Money motivates many, for musicians with sufficient talent and hustle can earn up to $20 an hour. There are other inducements as well: "Exposure," offers Sean Grissom, 22, who plays bluegrass fiddle music on an electric cello on Manhattan street corners while dreaming of the Grand Ole Opry in Nashville.

Trading a reporter's business suit for a more Bohemian gauze skirt and dangling earrings, I teamed up with Michael Grossman, a 22-year-old unemployed violinist. The deal: I would play second fiddle to him in duets, and he would keep the contributions.

Three days, several encounters with the law and two job offers later, I was thoroughly exhausted, and my partner was $135.83 richer. For performing a total of about 6½ hours in nine spots around town, we pulled in an average of nearly $21 an hour. Based on a 40-hour work week, that comes to about $44,000 a year, far more than my annual salary as a beginning reporter. For many street musicians, such income is treated as tax-free. Few report their earnings to the Internal Revenue Service.

But it is hard-won pay. Playing to usually apathetic—and sometimes hostile—audiences takes a thick skin. Chronic backaches and jostling by pedestrians are occupational hazards. Simply being heard is a struggle. The clatter of traffic and the jarring rhythms of the ubiquitous "boom box" portable stereo easily drown out the sweet strains of live Mozart.

Even veterans say the life of a street musician takes some getting used to. "I was very embarrassed the first few times I did it," recalls street player John Cheek, a 26-year-old with a master's degree in music who performs Bach on an electric keyboard. "I thought I was too good for it." The problem, confides Rubin Levine, a 66-year-old violinist who has performed on the streets for 12 years, is that "the mere fact that you're on the street immediately stamps you as no good."

It isn't the stigma of incompetence that bothers me as I contemplate my debut on Fifth Avenue. It's the thought of making a public spectacle of myself. With fashionable department stores as a backdrop and throngs of well-heeled shoppers as our audience, we set up. My hands shake as I strategically position the viola case on the sidewalk.

As we begin performing, however, the jitters vanish. Most people hurry by without noticing. Those who stop usually smile and offer compliments. In less than three hours, we earn $41 and attract several devoted groupies.

Emboldened, we move on to more fertile territory. The Radio City Music Hall crowd tends to give $1 donations instead of the usual 50 cents. And Lincoln Center is such a hot spot that four other street acts compete within a one-block stretch. Among them are Mr. Grissom, fiddling away at "Stone's Rag" on his electric cello, and a grinning old man who repeatedly plays "Happy Birthday" on his amplified mandolin.

As we proceed around town, the rules of making street music become apparent. Faster and louder is always better. Never mention money (the subtle open viola case is apt to get better results than open solicitation, which is illegal anyway), and never let too much cash accumulate in the case (heaps of dollar bills discourage further contributions). Theatergoers are the most generous listeners; financial executives the stingiest.

Indeed Wall Street may be the nation's financial capital, but the wealth doesn't trickle down to itinerant musicians. "The vibrations aren't good here," Michael says as we plant ourselves on the corner of Wall and Broad Streets, opposite the New York Stock Exchange. His instincts are right: Pinstripe-clad men and women rush past without so much as a sideways glance.

A few days earlier, an hour-long stint on Times Square drew a crowd and earned us $47.31. But an hour's work on Wall Street at lunchtime brings a paltry $15.36—and that includes a $5 bill donated by a bewildered investment banker whom I had once interviewed.

We ran into other difficulties: namely, the law. Playing on the streets of New York and most other major cities isn't illegal—but private property is another matter. Thus, an attempt to serenade commuters in a concourse at the World Trade Center was cut short by a policeman who threatened us with a warrant for disturbing the peace. We were also ejected from a mall at Rockefeller Center—twice. In one instance, the offer of a $10 bribe initially seemed to weaken the security guard's resolve. But in the end, he remained adamant.

Veteran street performers are inured to such inconveniences. "The cops throw us all out all the time," says a member of one street band. "Maybe because they aren't afraid of us." Musicians also commonly flout a local ordinance forbidding the use of amplifiers without a permit. They use portable three-watt amplifiers and are rarely prosecuted.

Along with a certain insouciance toward authority, street musicians quickly acquire a keen sense of their market. Our strictly classical repertoire, for example, proved too limited. The veterans cater to any audience. Mr. Levine, the violinist, insists he knows 30,000 tunes, ranging from Tchaikovsky to cowboy songs. Guitarist Waldemar Muniz, a 26-year-old aficionado of jazz and classical music, is more likely to render a Broadway show tune or a Frank Sinatra standard when he plays Central Park. "You have to play these things," he counsels. "The tourists—they love it." Another favored gimmick, perfected by the Lincoln Center mandolin player, is to break into

"Happy Birthday" at frequent intervals. If a passerby happens to be celebrating a birthday, musicians maintain, a big tip is virtually assured.

Not that all street musicians are in it strictly for the money. Earnings are highly unpredictable, often depending more on the crowd than on the polish of a musician's performance. Moreover, for every hour of profitable music-making, at least an equal amount of time is spent combing the streets for another promising spot to work.

For many street musicians, exposure and feedback from a live audience are the real rewards. "If you play in your room all day, nobody's ever going to see you except your mother and your grandmother," explains Mr. Grissom, whose modernistic, rectangular electric cello has a raccoon tail dangling from its scroll. As he launches into rousing renditions of "The Irish Washerwoman" and "The Arkansas Traveler," he taps his feet and kicks up his heels. "I like playing commercially vulgar music," he says gleefully. "I like catching all the highbrow people as they leave Lincoln Center."

Like Mr. Grissom, whose goal is one day to play in Nashville, many musicians on the street have big dreams. Mr. Cheek, the electric keyboard player, hopes to enter the prestigious Van Cliburn International Piano Competition and become a concert pianist. And William Garrison, a guitar and harmonica player in a Dixieland street band, aspires "to be the best jazz harmonica [player] around." He thinks he has a shot: "There isn't much competition," he concedes.

For inspiration, street musicians have only to look to pop stars Patti Smith, Greg Kihn and Steve Forbert, all of whom started out with street acts. Moreover, several albums of New York street music have been produced over the years. Memorable tracks include performances by a classical lutist and a 60-year-old percussionist who plays on newspaper vending machines.

Even during my three days as a street musician, opportunity knocked. In the financial district, a police officer suggested that we audition with a friend of his, who he said owns a trendy new restaurant in town. And on Times Square, an aspiring producer asked us to

play in an operetta he is staging. He would even pay us for our trouble. We declined.

The money, my partner explained, is better on the street. He plans
to try it again sometime. I don't

—JOANNE LIPMAN, October 1983

Acknowledgments

Collecting the best stories from the *Journal*'s fabled "middle column" has been a labor of love, despite the challenging and unavoidably subjective task of winnowing a pool of more than 15,000 stories down to the 67 chosen here. This book is a celebration of the feature's popularity for the past 60 years. And if the A-hed's resiliency has relied upon a tradition of staff collaboration, this project is no different. Thus, the following thanks are in order: to the *Journal* reporters and editors, too numerous to name, who helped quicken the selection process by taking time to nominate memorable stories; to various former *Journal* editors, notably Mike Gartner, Fred Taylor, Glynn Mapes and Don Moffitt, who shared invaluable A-hed lore; to Steve Adler, head of *Wall Street Journal* Books, for entrusting me with the honor of handling this project, and to Fred Hills at Simon & Schuster for his patience and sage input; to Paul Steiger, the *Journal*'s managing editor, and Mike Miller, its Page One editor, whose support keeps the flame of the A-hed burning bright; and last but not least, to my friend and colleague Carrie Dolan who lent her keen eye in helping to choose the final selections.

Index of Contributors

Ken Wells is a twenty-year veteran of *The Wall Street Journal,* having served stints as a reporter in the paper's San Francisco and London bureaus, and as an editor on the Page One staff in New York. He has written and polished numerous A-heds and is the author of three novels, *Meely LaBauve, Junior's Leg* and *Logan's Storm.* When he isn't busy with journalism or pecking away at novels, he plunks away at garage-level blues and jazz on his guitars. He lives with his family in the greater New York area.